MW00783266

Communicative Psychoanalysis
with Children

To my family

Communicative Psychoanalysis with Children

V. A. Bonač, MA, Cert PCCE

With contributions from:
INGE BERNS, ULRICH BERNS, PETINA BOWERS,
JUTTA KAHL-POPP AND M. MARK MCKEE

W

WHURR PUBLISHERS

LONDON

© 2000 Whurr Publishers
First published 2000 by
Whurr Publishers Ltd
19b Compton Terrace, London N1 2UN, England, and
325 Chestnut Street, Philadelphia PA 19106, USA

All rights reserved. No part of this publication may be
reproduced, stored in a retrieval system, or transmitted
in any form or by any means, electronic, mechanical,
photocopying, recording or otherwise, without the prior
permission of Whurr Publishers Limited.

This publication is sold subject to the conditions that it
shall not, by way of trade or otherwise, be lent, resold,
hired out, or otherwise circulated without the Publisher's
prior consent, in any form of binding or cover other than
that in which it is published, and without a similar condition including this condition being imposed upon any
subsequent purchaser.

British Library Cataloguing in Publication Data
A catalogue record for this book is available from the
British Library.

ISBN 1 86156 142 3

Printed and bound in the UK by Athenaeum Press Ltd,
Gateshead, Tyne & Wear

Contents

About the author and contributors

Vesna A Bonač, MA, Cert PCCE, is a communicative psychoanalyst in private practice with adults and children in Vancouver, Canada. She has degrees in physics and biology, in counselling psychology, and a Certificate in Communicative Psychoanalysis. She studied privately and received clinical training from Robert Langs, MD. She is the Founder and Editor of the *Electronic Journal of Communicative Psychoanalysis on Internet*, an Associate Editor of the *International Journal for Communicative Psychoanalysis and Psychotherapy*, and Founding President of the Western Canada Psychoanalytic Psychotherapy Association. She has written and lectured on the therapeutic process, the anxiety generated by the securing of the therapeutic frame and on child development. She is currently engaged in treatment, clinical supervision and teaching of communicative self-analysis.

Inge Berns, Dipl Paed, is a child and youth psychoanalytical psychotherapist, a guest lecturer at the Institute for Psychoanalytical Child and Youth Psychotherapy in Hannover, Germany, and a former high school teacher. She has been strongly influenced by the works of Robert Langs.

Ulrich Berns, MD, is a psychiatrist and training psychoanalyst at the Deutsche Psychoanalytische Gesellschaft in Hannover, Germany. He is in private practice of psychoanalytic psychotherapy with children, youth and adults. He has published professional articles in German and English on the theory of affect, on psychoanalytic Ego-Psychology, the theory and practice of psychosomatic therapy, the theory of psychoanalytic interpretations, object relation theory and the psychotherapeutic frame. He has lectured in Germany and the USA.

Petina Bowers is a psychotherapist working with students in an institutional setting in England. She completed a Master of Arts programme in psychotherapy and counselling and is a member of the European Society for Communicative Psychotherapy.

Jutta Kahl-Popp, Dipl Paed, is a psychoanalytical psychotherapist who works with children and their parents in private practice in Kiel, Germany. She is a lecturer and supervisor at the John-Rittmeister Institute in Kiel and the founder and first president of the German Society for the Advancement of Scientific Research in Psycho-Analytical Psychotherapy of Children and Adolescents. She is a member of the European Society for Communicative Psychotherapy and of the International Society for Communicative Psychoanalysis and Psychotherapy. She has written articles on the theory and practice of psychoanalytic treatment and does research of the therapeutic process, published in German and English professional journals.

M Mark McKee, Psy D, is a clinical child psychologist in private practice with children and young adolescents. He also works in the areas of gifted children and infant health. He is a senior associate core faculty member at the Illinois School of Professional Psychology in Chicago and has been teaching in the area of child development, child psychotherapy and psychoanalysis for the past 15 years. He was in private supervision with Robert Langs, MD, and is the first to apply communicative principles in working with young children in the USA. He has lectured in the USA and England.

Preface

*...the aim of a life can only be to increase the sum of freedom and responsi-
bility to be found in every person in the world. It cannot, under any circumstances, be to reduce or suppress that freedom, even temporarily.*
Albert Camus, 'The Wager of Our Generation' (translated from French)

*The poet: . . . but not so dangerous as those who trade in words, principles,
theories . . . to be worked out in the blood and sweat of other men.*
John Galsworthy, 'A Modern Comedy' (1924)

This book has three parts: methodology and technique, clinical material
with discussion, and conclusions. Throughout the book an effort was
made to clearly separate the data from their interpretations.

The detailed discussions of the moment-to-moment events in sessions
with children presented in this book may be used by the psychotherapist as
an example of what they can expect to hear in their own sessions when they
begin to listen in a communicative manner. When one is able to hear what
the patients are desperately trying to tell, albeit unconsciously, one discovers
the existence of two parallel 'worlds': the everyday world, which we experience and understand with our conscious minds; and a second one, an
alarmingly different world of human relationships. To reach this other world
it is first necessary to mentally organize the patients' material with the
immediate environment in mind. Both, the method for understanding of
the unconscious world and the communicative theory of clinical technique
for the psychotherapy of adults, were empirically derived directly from adult
patients' material by the American psychoanalyst Robert Langs in the 1970s.

This book is psychoanalytic. According to Freud's definition, psychoanalysis is recognized by its primary concern for seeking the sources of
mental anguish in the realm of the unconscious. Since the unconscious
cannot be discovered by considering the manifest meaning alone, the
method that enables us to reach the truly unconscious meaning of the
patients' material is quintessentially psychoanalytic - even though such
meaning may be different from what Freud believed to have found. The
communicative method of listening makes unconscious meaning acces-

sible, understandable and intelligible. It enables the therapist to formulate interventions that form a specific response to a currently active need in the patient.

Not only are each patient and each therapist different, but so is every moment in the session with the same patient uniquely unlike the one before. This book is not a collection of recipes for therapy – it does not tell you what to say when a patient says this or does that. This is not possible. All that can be taught is a method of listening to unconscious messages - everything else is construction and elaboration, perchance true, but more often distorted by the unknown bias of the therapist's unconscious needs. The communicative method is successful because it follows the same path which nature has taken when making a conscious experience unconscious.

Some clinical examples in Part II will reveal how therapy can go seriously wrong when the therapist does not follow the patient's communications or when the conditions for treatment are not healthy. The sessions presented here are a true sample of what happened in the course of therapy. Imaginary examples and invented sessions are not used, as such attempts at faking reality can only confuse. The effort to present genuine material created the inevitable problem of protecting confidentiality. Thus, the concern for the patients' privacy and confidentiality determined what kind of sessions are published here. Nonetheless, the material is genuine and detailed and can serve as excellent data for learning and for discussion. Clarification of the therapist's errors as well as the proposals for correct interventions are given in detail. This book is, above all, empirical – based on complete, real data.

The conclusions in Part III might be quite different from what most texts on child therapy advocate. For instance, in communicative psychoanalysis children are treated in the same way as adults. Conclusions about a fundamental equality of all human beings are based on the evidence drawn from diverse material of many years of sessions with adults and children. The reader is invited to seek out, in the material from sessions, that which is fundamentally human. Even the small sample of data in this book might be sufficiently compelling that the commonly used criteria for determining what are the essential elements of human nature are re-examined. The book proposes that our unconscious psychological functioning is the primeval shared component of what makes us human. We all perceive unconsciously in a truthful, undistorted manner. We are all driven by reality. We only fail in correctly expecting the future when we have been damaged in our past within the same type of inter-personal frame in which the prediction is being made. Contrary to the theories of Sigmund Freud and Melanie Klein, the effect of sex on human functioning is found to be secondary, and thus minor, compared with the effects of the impact of the world outside. Thus, the unconscious experiencing of the world is common to all. Since we all function unconsciously in the same manner we are all 'created' equal in a most fundamental way – and are worthy of the same treatment.

Although a rudimentary knowledge of the psychoanalytic concepts is required to fully understand and profit from this book, the reader is asked little more than to keep an open mind and a keen eye for detail. The complexity of psychological phenomena obliges that the conclusions and the theoretical propositions presented here are best understood when taken within the specific context of the clinical data from which they were derived.

V. A. Bonač
Vancouver, Canada
April 1999

Acknowledgements

I wish to thank the five contributors – Inge Berns, Ulrich Berns, Petina Bowers, Jutta Kahl-Popp and M. Mark McKee – for opening the private doors of their consultation rooms and for discussing their work so candidly. I am grateful to Dr Thomas Szasz for his attentive and forthright discussion of my ideas. My deepest gratitude is to Dr Robert Langs for six years of private teaching – in spite of my headstrong ways and needs to find out for myself, it was his insistence on the naked truth, his natural respect for scientific endeavour and his expectation of excellence that formed my professional being. If this book expresses not only praise for his monumental opus and my devotion to his ideals – but also critical arguments and propositions for new directions in communicative psycho-analysis – it is an affirmation of his teaching.

I am grateful to the editor of the *International Journal of Communicative Psychoanalysis and Psychotherapy* for permission to reprint and rewrite the article in Vol. 9 (1994) as Chapter 20 in Part III of this book.

Part I
The communicative theory and technique of psychoanalysis

V A Bonač and U Berns

Chapter 1
Communication

Freud answered the question 'What is psycho-analysis?' as follows, 'A talk between two persons' (1940, p147), 'They just talk with each other, nothing else happens between them' (1926, p213). These remarks show that the founder of psychoanalysis considered that the healing of mental illness is the result of a process involving mutual communications between the patients and their psychoanalysts.

Thus, research of the communicative process in psychoanalysis, contained in the thousands of volumes that comprise all literature, has been going on for a hundred years. The authors of this book thus start from the supposition that the very fundaments of the process of healing, whether of adults or of children, are described and explicated by the communicative theory of psychoanalysis. For a thorough understanding of what goes on during psychological therapy, consciously and unconsciously, the close-to-verbatim transcription of therapeutic sessions in sequence are presented and discussed in accordance with this theory.

Let us start with listing the central tasks the therapist has in the course of the therapeutic process. ('Therapist' is used throughout this book to denote a psychoanalyst or a psychoanalytical psychotherapist engaged in the psychological treatment of a patient – to be distinguished from their other functions as psychiatrists, assessors, consultants, etc.)

1. The therapist gives the patient the opportunity for *free association* of thoughts – this is the ground rule established by Freud.
2. The therapist then engages in *communicative listening* to the verbal utterances of the patient as they are produced in their manifest meaning, guided by the communicative theory of unconscious processes which explains how human beings take in, process and express information.
3. The therapist also endeavours to understand his or her own responses to the patient as they become manifest in feelings, fantasies and actions. Such responses may be realistic or they might be what is generally termed '*counter-transference*'. This represents an additional

opportunity to the therapist to understand the patient's unconscious. It also offers the possibility to improve the therapeutic quality of the therapist's interventions.
4. Eventually, the therapist offers the patient interventions, especially in the form of interpretations, which include the prospect for beneficial corrections of the therapeutic frame – the conditions for treatment.

Free association by the patient continues to be the ground rule and the very condition for psychoanalytic treatment. Psychoanalysis is the 'talking cure' for mental illness. Thus, the patient's free verbal expression of whatever comes to mind is considered the starting point for the therapist's listening by all schools of psychoanalysis. It relates to the important discoveries by Freud of the primary process of thinking and of the formation of derivatives. Freud first mentioned his discovery in the *Interpretation of Dreams* (1900). He described two fundamentally different modes of cognitive and emotional processes: secondary and primary. Freud found the manifestations of primary process cognition in the formation of dreams, in affective and symptomatic reactions, in slips of tongue as well as in spontaneously told jokes, in play and in human creativity in general. By paying strict attention to the patient's comments, Freud (1895a) created the method of free association and discovered that this method of verbal expression produced communications, which included those shaped by primary processing. Ever since this discovery, he listened to his patients in a specific way. When hearing his patients tell a dream or make a slip of the tongue, or when he observed a symptom, Freud invariably tried to understand all of these phenomena as derivatives (end products) of an emotionally loaded mental process which is under the influence of the primary process of thinking.

Since Freud believed that the free association of thoughts (in German *freie Einfälle* – spontaneously occurring ideas) was determined by unconscious wishes or drives arising intrapsychically, within the patient, he listened to his patients within the limitations of his specific model: a one-person-psychology. Conceptually, this meant tracing the expressed derivatives back to those hypothesized inner psychic processes within the patient which were supposed to reveal the vicissitudes of drives in relation to the biography of the patient. For this process Freud coined the term 'transference'.

In *The Interpretation of Dreams* Freud (1900, p532) said that the patient, while following the ground rule of free association, unconsciously aims at the therapist in person. As he gave no clinical examples he did not make it clear what he meant by this. In 1925, he further developed this idea. When discussing free association in his *Self-portrait*, he wrote, 'Nothing will come to the patient's mind unless it is in some way related to the analytic situation' (1925a, p113; translated from German by UB). Again he gave no clinical example of this most important finding regarding this side of the therapeutic process. Thus it is not clear whether this relation to the therapist is one-way only: do the drives originate in the patient and are they aimed at the therapist or is it also possible that the patient's 'drives' were activated by the therapist and thus come as a response to an outside stimulus? It is quite possible that this omission by Freud to clarify and elaborate what he wrote might be partly responsible for the fact that this most momentous insight with far-reaching consequences was not transferred into the practice for long decades.

Chapter 2
The unconscious

When patients produce free associations, while talking freely in sessions, they unknowingly express the elements of complex unconscious mental activity. Thus, the patients ascribe a meaning to, and analyse the meaning of, the implications of the therapist's communications and actions in so far as these communications/interventions are of any emotional relevance to them. The discovery of this highly sophisticated mental activity on the unconscious level was made empirically by Robert Langs in his exhaustive clinical research (Langs 1976b, 1978a,c, 1979, 1980, 1981). Langs gave numerous accounts of detailed clinical examples in his extensive writings. His usage of the term '*derivative*' is more precise and more restricted than Freud's. Thus, in communicative psychoanalysis, the term 'free association' is now limited to verbal narratives and, as regards to children, it extends also to forms of creative play which directly express stories. Narratives and play have been found time and again to be the most immediate and the clearest expressions of unconscious mental processes with which the patients ascribe and analyse meaning.

Thus, Langs did not see it as useful to classify symptoms of all kinds together with narratives, even though symptoms are also generated by, and thus derived from, unconscious processes. Instead, Langs introduced the term '*indicators*' to encompass the patients' symptoms as well as their resistances, for the important reason that the symptoms and resistances were found to be the outcome of, not parallel to, the unconscious processing of information. Langs found that the formation of symptoms came secondary to the unconscious analysis of meaning. The communicative theory of psychoanalysis thus takes the *decoding* of derivatives to be the '*via regia*' to an in-depth understanding of indicators.

It is apparent that communicative theory starts from the premise that the primary process comes into being exclusively in a state of at least partially suspended reflective self-representations (Schafer 1968), and that only in this state of uncensored expression can the derivatives of unconscious psychic input and the unconscious processing of information find expression. This finding is the reason why therapists trained in the communicative theory of psychoanalysis intervene right from the very beginning of treatment, in order to help the patient associate freely – rather than with an interview or assessment or meeting with the patient's spouse, friends, parents, guardians and the like. Freedom of expression, the essence of all psychoanalysis, is severely hindered in many institutional settings and is made all but impossible in situations of forced hospitalization and forced treatment. Psychoanalyst and author Thomas Szasz devoted his professional life to calling attention to the violations of personal freedoms and the corruption of treatment by institutionalized psychiatry (e.g. Szasz 1965, 1970).

Thus, a basic prerequisite for psychological therapy at all times, even in the very first session, is that the patient associates freely. Lacking free-flowing material from the patient, the therapist cannot proceed without the risk of putting his or her own needs and expectations ahead of the patient's. Even the occasional prolonged silence from the patient can only be resolved if the therapist has some recent verbal material available in which to seek evidence for a reason, most likely unconscious, for the silence. Generally, silence may be the analyst's principal intervention or, if any intervention is deemed necessary at any point, it should be such that it does not hinder the patient from 'entering' a psychic state which is open to the expression of the primary process thinking. The communicative analyst endeavours to avoid any such intervention which would lead the patient to engage in a secondary process dialogue and thus to suppress free-association.

Listening to the communications from the patient directs the therapist to take in the patient's utterances in their manifest meaning and, most importantly, to strive for a deeper understanding of the meaning of which the patient is not conscious. The guiding principle of such listening is the communicative theory of the unconscious processes involved in taking in, processing and expressing of information. The therapist is trying to be open to all cognitive information and to all interactional pressures from the patient, verbal and non-verbal. Included are the therapist's efforts to understand (a) verbal narratives and narratives imbedded in play, (b) verbal or play images and (c) efforts to metabolize the patient's *projective identification*.

Communicative psychoanalysts have dedicated their most intense efforts to a systematic research for unconscious meaning by way of decoding of derivatives as they are evoked by *triggers*. Although the patient reacts emotionally to the therapist's manifest communications as well as to the implications of the therapist's interventions, one can observe that the patient processes most extensively the implications of the therapist's interventions. Clinically, it can be shown that the patient's unconscious responses fit the implications of the therapist's interventions. This means that for an in-depth understanding of the patient's unconscious analysing of meaning as well as of the psychic structures which ascribe the meaning, it is essential to first decode the verbal response of the patient. The method of decoding leads to the hidden meaning which was unconsciously communicated by the patient as an unconscious response to the implications of his or her own interventions. The reason for the pivotal emotional significance of the implications of interventions might be that they are not at all conspicuous, cannot be clearly grasped and hence can be easily brushed aside as irrelevant on the conscious level. Although the specific reason for the enormous emotional significance of the implications of interventions demands further research, clinical evidence is irrefutable: the implications of interventions are of vital emotional significance for the patient and he perceives and processes them unconsciously.

Numerous clinical examples of this communicative method of unveiling unconscious meaning are found in this book. Extensive clinical material from sessions of adult patients (found in communicative psycho-analytic literature) and the clinical examples with children in this book reveal astonishing sequence of events and processes:

• The patient first grasps, unconsciously, truthfully and without distortion, the meaning of an emotionally relevant implication of the therapist's intervention in the form of unconscious perceptions. The patient then processes these perceptions, still unconsciously, according to his or her personal experiences and constitutional make-up. The patient then expresses this meaning in the language of the primary process. Thus, the patient tells a narrative which has displaced, condensed and symbolized the original meaning. Only later, secondarily, may the patient react pathologically, i.e. with symptoms and resistances to the unconsciously perceived meaning. The patient may also respond non-pathologically to a trigger with derivative hints, termed 'models of rectification', which show how the therapists might best correct their own initial erroneous intervention. And, astonishingly, if the therapist has made an error, the patient might even offer the therapist, unconsciously, an interpretation about the reasons for the therapist's error (Langs 1982; Searles 1965, 1975).

• It is, above all, those implications of the therapist's interventions which are related to the changes of the analytical frame to which the patient unconsciously responds. Thus, the course of therapy could be described as an interactional spiralling process (e.g. Langs 1976c, 1982): at each and every moment in a session, both participants of the therapeutic process respond consciously and unconsciously to the realities of a given situation and thus contribute to the ever changing process. When the therapist pays attention to the sequence and details of this interactional process the result is a truthful application of the concept of a two-person-psychology in reality, not only in theory and belief. The examples of the sessions and their discussions will illustrate how the communicative theory of technique enables the therapist to carry out in practice what it preaches in words. The readers will be able to judge for themselves its practical clinical value.

Let us explain clinical listening in more detail. When adopting the fundamental stance of listening with silent attentiveness, the therapist is able to distinguish in the patient's material between derivative (carrying unconscious meaning) and non-derivative communications (which do not contain unconscious meaning). The undistorted perceptions of the therapist's interventions, the pathological reactions to these perceptions as well as the wisely given models of rectification are expressed by the patient unconsciously if the patient is left free to exercise the fundamental rule of free association without interruptions and restrictions. Perceptions, reactions to perceptions and models of rectification are all expressed unconsciously in the form of narratives and images.

As will become clearer with the clinical examples, children express their unconscious truthful perceptions in verbal narratives as well as in silent, creative play. Derivatives are always imaginative and their meaning is always specific. Derivative meaning may be carried by a long, complex story, a fragment of a story, or by a single image. Such stories and images may be told verbally by the child or the therapist might be observing the drama on the 'stage' of silent play. Whatever the medium of expression of the derivative meaning, the key to the understanding of any patient's material is the actual, current situation in the session because it is the immediate environmental reality which is always of primary significance to the patient, child or adult.

Chapter 3
The triggering event

Communicative research has shown that it is precisely the matters that are of primary current importance to the patient which are processed not only consciously, but mainly and extensively on the unconscious level. This means that the therapist's search for the adaptive context, i.e. for the event which has triggered the patient's response, is fundamental to a thorough understanding of the unconscious processes within the patient. Most commonly, such an event is a recent intervention by the therapist or it may be a persistent, background situation for which the therapist is responsible.

When the therapist believes that an important trigger for the patient's response has been identified, the trigger must match quite specifically one or more of the patient's derivatives. The therapist waits for the patient to communicate a set of derivatives which portray either perception of the trigger, reactions to these perceptions or an example of how to correct a situation (model of rectification):

i.   Derivatives expressed in the indicative mood of the verbs, i.e. stories told about objective facts, are portrayals of one or more aspects of the therapist's interventions, usually undistorted perceptions.
ii. Derivatives expressed in the functional imperative mood of the verbs, i.e. stories that express a command or a plea, are usually models of correction. They tell in imaginative and specific ways how (and often why) the therapist should correct his or her past interventions.
iii. Reactions to perceptions are expressed by the patient in the indicative mode of the verb (as are perceptions /i/). Reactions to perceptions can also be identified and distinguished from perceptions by the method of exclusion, especially in the case of child's play where the child does not always formulate clear sentences. The first working hypothesis by the therapist would consider all of the patient's narratives and all play as truthful and undistorted perceptions of the therapist's interventions. Then, a systematic comparison may be carried out by taking each derivative and matching it to the reality of the situation for the patient in the session as it is at a given moment, i.e. to the recent intervention or

interventions by the therapist. Only those segments of the patient's material whose derivative meaning cannot be made consonant with a significant intervention can be regarded as non-perceptive. A prime example of a reaction to perceptions is the model of rectification: the therapist has *not* done what the patient is describing (or, has done the very opposite) and the patient is telling the therapist what needs to be done to correct the situation.

Chapter 4
The interpersonal frame of therapy

We shall discuss in more detail the fact that the patient is exceptionally sensitive to the implications of all frame-related interventions as it becomes evident in the abundant and intense material from the patient right after any change in the analytic frame. In turn, the extraordinary abundance and intensity of the patient's material is evidence for the extent of the unconscious processing which goes on in the patient's psyche. At first glance one might wonder how this could come about. However, one is no longer surprised when one takes into account the fact that all interventions which in any way change the analytic frame carry the weight of changing extensively the reality of the social relationship between the patient and the therapist and this is, naturally, of primary emotional significance to the patient.

As this issue is of great importance to the clinical technique of psychotherapy and psychoanalysis, it needs to be elaborated and clarified at some length. Langs discovered empirically that patients generally, and with great consistency, react derivatively to interventions which change the analytic frame (see Langs 1976b, 1978a,b, 1979, 1980, 1981). He found that the patients' derivatives contain complex information about the various implications of interventions which represent detailed unconscious evaluations of the interventions. He also found that certain interventions are unconsciously consistently evaluated as helpful by the patients.

Langs's further research into these phenomena led him to work out a canon of patient–therapist agreements and conditions concerning the analytic frame which he called the '*ideal frame*', and because he found that situations between the therapist and the patient which departed in any way from this canon of the 'ideal' were harmful to the patient he called them '*breaks in the frame*'. These findings have been clinically confirmed in numerous communicative studies of clinical material.

The clinical examples in this book offer new empirical evidence that the conditions of the analytic frame are of pivotal importance to the psychological therapy of child patients. It offers evidence for the claim by

Bonac (1991, 1994) that the same frame conditions are unconsciously experienced and evaluated in the same way by all human beings, regardless of the cultural shaping of the individual.

Usually, only a few elements of the therapeutic frame are explicitly mentioned by either the therapist or the patient at the start of therapy. The most important set of elements comprising the 'ideal' analytic frame is the following list of ground rules of therapy which were derived from his research by Robert Langs, and which do not diverge significantly from traditional psychoanalytic rules:

1 The therapist provides the conditions of total privacy and confidentiality of the patient's therapy which means that the relationship excludes all other people. This also implies that the therapist does not accept referrals from the patient and does not engage in therapy with the patient's family, friends or acquaintances.
2 The therapist provides a fixed location for the therapy to take place. He or she also maintains a fixed weekly time and unchanged duration for all sessions. This is stated to the patient in his or her first session.
3 Also in the first session, the therapist states to the patient a fixed, fair fee which he or she then expects to collect from the patient at the beginning of each month for all the sessions in the previous month, in the form of a personal or bank cheque. The fee remains unchanged for the duration of a therapy. The patient is told that he or she is expected to pay the therapist for each scheduled session whether the patient comes to the session or not.
4 At the time of the first session, the therapist offers the patient an open-ended therapy and will not terminate the therapy unilaterally.
5 When accepting a patient into treatment, therapists accept a type of professional engagement which requires that they subordinate their personal interests to the singular task of understanding and thereby helping the patient. This necessarily implies refraining from all physical contact, refraining from handing out and accepting gifts, and restricting interventions mostly to interpretations. These conditions contain a number of distinctive attitudes and ways of human interaction which determine the roles and the boundaries of the therapeutic interaction and thus determine the analytic frame of therapy.
6 The therapist maintains, as much as possible, his or her anonymity by making an effort to keep private his or her personal information, as well as his or her neutrality, by refraining from deliberate self-revelations in sessions.
7 The therapist will maintain an evenly hovering, free-floating attention by alternating between being open to the influences of the patient's material on the one hand and listening to his or her productions by being guided by communicative technique.

Since the whole of what happens in psychological therapy is determined by its framework, as it is created and recreated by the therapist and the patient while they obey or depart from the 'ground rules', let us now analyse in more depth the elements that comprise the 'ideal' of the analytic frame.

The foremost task of the therapist is to put his or her expert knowledge to the best use to engage in a process of human interaction by communication which is therapeutic to the patient with specific forms of intervening. Evidently, the same fundamental principle of human interaction is valid for all spheres of our social life and can be reduced to a basic need we all have at certain times for the skill and knowledge that others possess. In consequence, it is up to those who know to offer their specific skills to those who are in need of help. Thus, the explicit and implicit content of an agreement between the professional who offers the services and the patient who asks for them puts a heavy emphasis on the responsibility of the professional. All the patient needs to do is ask, come, pay and say what comes to mind.

The first ground rule of privacy and confidentiality is inherent in the very task of treatment: an open and free exchange of the most intimate matters between two human beings is only possible in a space which is secure from all interference by others. This cannot be achieved without providing total confidentiality and total privacy to the patient. The same location, time and duration for the sessions gives the patient (and the therapist) the same kind of a basic sense of stability, safety and reliability as the knowledge that the sun will rise each morning. In essence, the value of human relationships is at stake here. The respective responsibilities of both patient and therapist to come to all scheduled sessions guarantee a fair balance for all parties concerned, thus establishing a guilt-free relation. A parasitic or pathologically symbiotic tendency of a relationship will become clearly visible when one or other partner in the therapeutic process changes the ground rule. Keeping this ground rule shows a sense of responsibility and offers a pillar of stability for both the patient and the therapist. It provides mutuality, respect, equality and fairness.

The observance of the rules 1, 3, 4, 5 and 6 may be highly emotionally demanding on the therapist no matter how strong his or her personal convictions and beliefs. Like a good parent, the therapist will have to make an effort to forego many of his or her own needs in the course of therapy with patients, especially during sessions. Therefore, satisfaction of his or her own needs is required to be limited to taking pleasure in the patient's progress. However, therapists do take pride in success with their patients, they do enjoy some gratifying emotional and intellectual experiences during sessions (especially at times of validated work), and are rewarded financially by collecting payment from their patients for their professional efforts. The rule, also called the 'rule of abstinence', thus limits the satisfaction of the therapist's needs and desires which can be obtained from his or her patients to the above-mentioned opportunities and requires that the therapist abstains from all other gratification.

On a larger scale, the rules that constitute the 'ideal' form of the frame also constitute the fundamentals of intrinsically healthy forms of human interaction, such as taking responsibility, keeping things private and confidential, having a frank and unbiased mind, dealing with people on the basis of fairness, equality and mutuality. An effort to live by such rules therefore reflects, both in the therapeutic situation and in everyday life, a struggle to work towards an 'ideally' structured human relationship. Seen in this light it is hardly surprising that those interventions by the therapist which necessitate changes in the analytic frame are of the utmost significance for the patient in three ways:

1 When the therapist first offers the patient an ideal set of conditions for treatment ('ideal' ground rules, 'ideal' frame), the patient gets an immediate sense of fundamental sanity and security in which his or her therapy will take place, no matter how unconscious this knowledge is for the patient. During therapy sessions the therapist decides to correct his or her own break in the frame. Thus, an element of the frame which has been 'broken' by the therapist will be corrected on the basis of the patient's model of rectification. Such correction is followed by the patient's validation of this correction in the form of derivatives, and usually, also by a reduction of the symptoms from which the patient is suffering. When it is the patient who initiates a 'break' in the frame the therapist follows the patient's derivatives to explain to the patient that he or she is saying unconsciously that it is the patient who needs to correct the frame. Eventually, the patient always benefits from such correction, even though the path leading to correction may be long and winding.

2 Interventions which resulted in the correction of a ground rule, restoring the 'ideal' conditions and 'securing' of the analytic frame surprisingly brought to light intense anxiety in most patients. This phenomenon of 'secured-frame anxiety', in some ways similar to the traditional theoretical concept of the 'negative therapeutic reaction', was discovered by Langs (1981). The phenomenon was further explored by Bonac (1993a,b), who found that much of the so-called 'secured-frame anxiety', i.e. the irrational patient's response to a securing of the frame by the therapist, was actually very easily confused with a realistic response by the patient to the harm done by the therapist's defensive intervening with unilateral, rash changes in the frame even in cases when the frame was secured by the therapist according to the patient's derivatives but lacking the patient's cognitive insight.

3 Those interventions which imply any deviations from the 'ideal' agreement imply that the therapist is offering an unhealthy human environment.

The changes in the analytic frame are thus of paramount importance in psychotherapy. Something that has been neglected for so long is in fact found, in every instance, to be the focal point of every patient's response. Communicative technique thus centres around the observations of what is happening to the frame: the therapist constantly monitors the state of the frame. The way an intervention affects the frame is what makes the therapist's work either beneficial to the patient or not.

Although every communicative therapist agrees that the frame is central to his or her work, there are inconsistencies in what constitutes the therapist's task regarding the frame. The frame is changed by either the therapist or the patient. Even when the therapist works at a place where the therapeutic frame is to a great extent dictated by others, the therapist is the one who can either accept, change or reject such conditions, not the patient. So, even in institutions, it is the therapist who is ultimately held responsible for the state of the frame offered to the patient. Since the frame – the conditions for treatment – affects everything that happens in therapy, what is observed in therapy is determined by the state of the frame.

Chapter 5
Transference response

In therapy, the interpretation of the clinical phenomenon of transference is the primary aim of a therapist. It might not be what the therapist does most of the time; it might even be that a therapist never has the chance to observe transference in his or her sessions. Nevertheless, the patient came to therapy to have his or her own inner puzzle, as it is expressed through transference, explained. How is transference manifested, how do we recognize its appearance and how do we interpret it to the patient with the frame in mind? Bonac believes that the insistence on the therapist's active 'management of the frame' (e.g. Langs 1982, 1984/85) has been responsible for the inconsistency in the communicative theory of technique and for the continuous ambiguity about the concept of fantasy/transference. To be fair, psychoanalysis did not come up with a clear definition of the process of transference in a hundred years (Bonac 1998) even though transference has always been its cardinal focal point. An incisive early criticism of the interpretation of transference was made by Thomas Szasz (1963). He called attention to the dangers of imposing one's own will on the patient when transference is interpreted without the verification that it might in fact be the patient's perception of reality.

This difficulty in determining what is transference and what is reality has plagued the psychoanalytic field since Freud first described the phenomenon. In 1948 Harold Searles punctured the bubble of certainty, with which transference was being interpreted without careful verification with his discovery of the patient's unconscious perceptions of the therapist. Other psychoanalysts who published papers calling for a clearer delineation of the concept of transference in relation to what was real in the treatment process were few. Freud himself made several direct references concerning the effects of reality – to be distinguished from the patient's transference – on the unfolding of the therapeutic relationship (Freud 1912a,b, 1913, 1915, 1920). Later, seminal discussions of similar concerns appeared in the literature: Strachey (1934) pointed out the effects of the actualities on the analytic interaction; Balint and Balint (1939) wrote about the impact of the analytic setting on the patient; and

Ticho (1972) stressed that the personality of the analyst does have an effect on the therapeutic process. Later, in more detail and with greater force, Bird (1972) and Greenson (1978) wrote about the patient's sane and salutary functioning, while Searles (1965) and Langs (1975, 1976a,b,c, 1978a,b, 1979, 1980) discussed the effects of the analyst's errors on the patient and about the dangers to the patient when transference is confused with non-transference.

When the therapist changes the frame from the secure to the unsafe, when the 'ideal' frame is 'broken', when an element in the secure frame is damaged, then the patient always responds with derivatives which predictably depict this act as a violation, harm done, wrong done to the patient. The discovery of this sequence of events has been Langs's great contribution to psychoanalysis. It has changed psychoanalysis and psychotherapy for ever. His theory of the unconscious communication of perceptions is unequalled in the field of human psychology. However, his technique is only applicable in the case when the therapist 'breaks the frame'. When the patient breaks the frame of which an aspect had previously been broken by the therapist, the patient is just repeating the pattern of the therapist, introjecting the therapist's act.

The traditional communicative technique of interpretion no longer applies when an element of the frame is first broken and then secured by the patient (Bonac, 1998). Langs's initial discovery of unconscious communication was based on a specific body of empirical data which all contained such vast departures from the 'ideal' frame that any effects of the securing of the frame got lost in the prevailing damage being done. The theory of clinical technique, which Langs derived from those observations, remained unchanged even when he continued to report the emergence of 'ironic', 'unexpected' and 'paradoxical' anxiety associated with the 'securing of the frame'. This is the reason why his writing becomes vague and lacks clinical specificity when touching on the nature of fantasy, transference and irrational behaviour.

Langs's criticism of the widespread tacit acceptance of a far from 'ideal' framework for therapy was revolutionary, justified and continues to be well supported by evidence. No longer can anyone say that 'breaks' in the frame of therapy do not matter much, that they can be interpreted and thus 'explained away'. Bonac believes, however, that the reason for the lack of clarity in writing about the phenomena associated with the securing of the frame lies in the fact that a whole class of phenomena might have been missing from the pool of data used in research, that is, the securing of one element of the frame by the patient after the same element of the frame had been previously broken by the patient. A distinctly different situation arises in the following sequence of events: (a) the patient first restores an element of the frame to the 'ideal' condition being offered by the therapist; (b) the patient's securing comes as a result of the therapist's continuous interpretations of the patient's own models of rectification; (c) unexpectedly and seemingly without reason, the patient cannot tolerate the new situation and breaks out of it by breaking that very element of the frame which the patient himself or herself had finally secured; (d) now, the very same element of the frame which the patient had just secured is, again, broken.

This precarious sequence of events is the necessary, albeit not sufficient, precondition for transferential phenomena to occur. If a therapist does not permit the development of this specific frame situation then the available material from such sessions lack the very data one would need in order to study transference. If transference has not occurred, it cannot be manifested, and one cannot make its observation. The moment-to-moment conditions of treatment determine the kind of psychological phenomena that arise – and that are observed (Bonac 1998, 1999).

Langs's research data included the consequences of the therapist's securing of the frame which had been broken by the patient and the resulting intense anxiety in both the patient and the therapist. These findings are consonant with Langs's theory of technique which places an obligation on the therapist: to secure the frame as soon as it is broken. Langs emphasized that the therapist has two therapeutic tasks – 'interpreting and management of the frame'. In the article on premature securing of the frame Bonac (1993a,b) discussed the difficulties arising from the therapist's 'management' of the frame. The data show a critical difference in the consequences when the frame is secured by the therapist ('managed') or whether the frame is left to be secured by the patient. In all cases when it was the patient who broke the frame against the background of the permanent offer by the therapist of a secure frame, a different phenomenon was observed. The resulting observations, and the understanding of what happens intrapsychically and interpersonally at moments of the patient's intention to secure his or her own break in the frame, is different from Langs's. When contrasting his approach with Freud's, Langs only briefly alludes to transference when he considers the conscious system: 'Distortion typically is motivated by wishes to protect the therapist and the patient from disturbing conscious realizations of valid unconscious experiences of the therapist's errors – links to past figures, which do exist, are secondary' (Langs 1996, p37).

Bonac's research of the securing of the frame led to the formulation of a new clinical theory of transference and to the proposal for a change in Langs's communicative theory of technique (Bonac 1998, 1999). The therapist's actions are to be limited to making a permanent *offer* to the patient of a secure frame. The therapist must not proceed with any action that would precipitate its 'securing' when the patient breaks it. A 'forced' securing of the frame by the therapist would no longer represent an act of securing but that of coercion and control of the patient. It would represent acting-out by the therapist. When the therapist suddenly secures the analytic frame, such securing is experienced by the patient as persecutory, manipulative and destructive. Typical images in the patient's material are: wrongful imprisonment, forced labour, insane withholding of freedom, sadistic exploitation, pathological symbiosis, etc. These images stand in radical contrast to healthy images patients report in the secure frame: warm home, good school, safe playground, mother's lap, normal pregnancy, breast-feeding, good marriage, etc. Thus, the patients react realistically when they are anxious following their therapist's securing of the frame. The securing of the analytic frame by the therapist is most often initiated to satisfy the immediate emotional needs of the therapist, when the securing neither followed the patient's consciously worked through intent to secure the frame, nor was the patient himself or herself allowed to secure the frame.

Thus, the therapist's interventions which change the analytic frame from 'broken' to 'secure', which Langs calls the 'management of the frame' (e.g. Langs 1982) can only be applied to the corrections of the therapist's own errors in technique – but no further (Bonac 1993b, 1995, 1996a,b, 1998, 1999). If one can create a situation in sessions where there is no coercion from outside of the patient, where the therapist neither demands nor enacts changes in the frame, when the patient is left free to follow the therapist's interpretations at his or her own pace and ability, only then is the patient left autonomous and unrestrained.

Only in such conditions then, when the patient is observed to be breaking something of his or her own creation, can we say that the patient is 'acting out' something which has nothing to do with the therapist but has its source within the patient. When this happens, the patient may be 'transferring' his or her own experience from the past on to the present person of the therapist. When it is clearly the patient who cannot tolerate his or her own securing of the frame we can say that this 'breaking out' of the secure frame is a phobic flight. If the therapist never creates such a situation and such sequence in therapy never occurs then the therapist cannot be observing transference. Without having such data, transference cannot be discovered – it can only be confused with counter-transference. We can now see that Freud discovered counter-transference when he thought he was observing the patient's transference. Since counter-transference is nothing but the transference of the therapist responding to his or her own securing of the frame (effected or intended), the unconscious process is the same. Thus, Freud's basic description of transference was correct in theory but incorrect in the clinical technique of its interpretation.

If it were the therapist's task to 'manage' the frame for the patient, then it begs the question: 'What is there for the patient to do in psychotherapy?' Since human beings express what disturbs them most deeply (their pathology) through the frame (as Langs observed), then it is the patient who is in fact expected to 'break' the frame. Neurotic or psychotic difficulties manifest themselves in the manner in which a patient copes with certain aspects of the secure frame. For each patient there are certain aspects of the analytic frame which are unbearable even when the frame was momentarily secured by the patient himself or herself. 'Holding' the secure frame at all times and 'holding on' to the patient 'in it' does not cure the patient. There is a different, much longer and more gradual process that eventually brings a reduction of the patient's symptoms. Thus in sessions, the therapist can only wait and offer interpretations. And the patient, the other participant in the bipersonal therapeutic frame, will try to repeatedly break it because he or she will not be able to bear some of its elements.

When something 'good' is unbearable, this is 'pathology' of the mind. When the patient spoils what is good, sabotages his or her own success, fears what he or she needs, this is the 'inner' problem. When the patient struggles with other people's problems, like a break in the frame by the therapist, the patient is not driven by inner 'issues' but responds and struggles to adapt to harm being done. In therapy, the patient only gradually reaches a point where he or she is finally able to secure the very element of frame they had themselves broken so many times before, all the while profiting from the therapist's continuing efforts to interpret not only the patient's models of rectification but also the patient's transference (Bonac 1998, 1999).

Chapter 6
Traumata and undistorted perceptions

Unconscious fantasies, the essential ingredients of psychoanalytic theories, have been reported in the literature to have been directly inferred from clinical observations. One is left with the impression that there is little doubt that we are born with irrational fantasies which distort reality. It is therefore daring to say simply that there are in fact no unconscious fantasies in the human mind – only memories of real traumata as valid perceptions, kept 'on record' in memory (Bonac 1998, 1999). This needs to be explained. What is generally 'observed' as unconscious fantasy, has been found to be the patient's past perceptions which unconsciously drive frame-breaks in the immediate present of therapy. What might appear to be the fantasy of the patient, something within the patient which has the function to distort the outside reality, the experience of the reality of what the therapist is doing in the present, is in fact the patient's perception of his or her own intention. It is the reason for the patient's intention to act, which is distorting the current reality with the therapist. What is distorted in the patient is not the perception of the reality of either the present or the past. The only thing that is distorted is the patient's faculty to make correct expectations of the future, which is damaged. Not to be able to draw on the reality of the present situation, when expecting the future, gives rise to a distorted expectation of events outside of the patient. Perceptions of reality are intact but the expectations are fantastical.

Although one cannot form perceptions of something that has not yet happened, the expectations can still be based on the current reality of the situation and thus predicted with precision within the limits of available current data. When such expectations are based on past events rather than on the current events, the expectation is flawed and transference is manifested. Thus, in the session, the patient is suddenly faced with his or her own securing of the frame and not only draws on the data currently available from the existing relationship with the therapist (perceptions gained through therapy) but is also suddenly flooded with a traumatic memory and makes a decision based on that memory.

What we always find at such moments in the material of the patient, are two parallel, yet radically different and opposing themes. The positive theme, which reflects the salutary meaning of the patient's current securing of the frame, is told alongside its opposite, the negative theme. The opposing themes contain opposite meaning. The negative story tells about the meaning of the trauma which, with devastating consequences, broke the promise of a securing of the frame in the patient's past. The simultaneous emergence of two opposing themes in the material of the patient – in the absence of a break in the frame by the therapist – is the hallmark of the manifestation of transference proper (Bonač 1999).

The break of a promise might have been of three types: (a) explicit and intentional – a parent promised to return but sadistically decided to remain away); (b) explicit and unintentional – the parent intended to return but was prevented by higher power or accident; or (c) inherent in the very nature of human health and survival – the sane person, child or adult expects that goodness, not harm, will be the outcome even when dealing with the forces of nature, like starvation or fire. When sane, we all try to avoid explicit harm.

These points of explaining transference are all very difficult to give in theory only and the distinction between this and other theories of technique and their impact on the patient might remain lost or appear insignificant. A clear view of the new theory of transference can only be conveyed by detailed discussions of clinical examples. This can only be achieved in individual supervision where details of uncensored live examples are discussed in great detail.

It is of critical importance to make a clear clinical distinction between the observation of transference and that of a model of rectification (to secure a broken frame) so that the two phenomena are not confused. It is such confusion, so prevalent in most psychoanalytic work, which drives the therapist to interpret transference when it does not exist and which in turn drives the patient crazy. In both instances, that is, in the case of communication of the model of rectification and in the case of transfer-ence, we hear two sets of opposite themes. The model of rectification includes the negative theme illustrating the therapist's actual break in the frame and the positive theme of how this same break ought to be corrected. Not only (a) does the positive theme of rectification include the 'ought to' clause (the patient says that someone should do this or that because of something being wrong) but also (b) the state of the actual frame can be independently determined as being broken. On the other hand, the case of transference shows a different, opposite, picture. (c) The negative theme has the recognizable quality of a memory (even when it is unconsciously communicated as a story) so that it is told as an event that has already happened. In (d) the state of the actual frame can be indepen-dently determined as not being broken – on the contrary, the frame has been maintained as a secure offer by the therapist for some time. The positive theme in the patient's material thus reflects this positive quality of the frame.

Bonac's addition of the interpretation of transference in reality to Langs's theory of technique can in no way be used as a tacit proposal for a return to the view of the therapeutic frame as something of little consequence or as something negligible in the midst of dealing with the difficult, crazy functioning of the patient according to the Freudian or the Kleinian, or whatever theoretical approach to psychoanalysis one relies on. On the contrary, Bonac's theory of transference proper makes it possible to observe with clarity that the patient never experiences the facts of the present reality of a situation in a fantastical manner and out of context. There are no fantasies, only perceptions and expectations of a specific event in the future.

Thus, when a patient does communicate a theme of hurtful, negative meanings, when derivatives do contain destructive images, and when we find that there exists a situation in reality between the therapist and the patient that matches this meaning, only then can we be sure that the situation between the therapist and the patient is in reality also hurtful and destructive, especially when the patient has mentioned this very situation explicitly in the course of the session. We can no longer claim that the therapy frame has negligible effects on the therapy or that the patient is 'only imagining' and has this 'crazy idea' about the reason for the damage done to his or her health. On the contrary, Bonac claims that transference can only be interpreted if one monitors the state of the frame with the utmost precision (Bonac 1998, 1999). Without Langs's theories of unconscious communication and of communicative technique the therapist cannot detect and interpret transference.

Chapter 7
Fantasies and wishes

Thus, whether we are children or have grown to adulthood, we all (a) that perceive the present and the past always validly on the unconscious level and (b) the future is open to unwarranted speculation only when our past includes traumata which had occurred under the same frame conditions, that is, when the 'promise' of a good 'future' was broken. Freud might have sensed something similar when he continued to insist on the ever-present power of the wish in dreams and in transference even when it appeared preposterous that someone should wish that something harmful should come to them (e.g. to dream a nightmare). Freud might not have come to a coherently stated theory of transference, but he sensed that essential to all transferential phenomena is their association with something in the future: a wish denotes something which has not yet happened.

We must remember that Freud changed his mind from the 'seduction' theory (of perception) to the 'transference' theory (of fantasy) because he had evidence of his patients' untruths (imagination, lies) and not because he had evidence that there was no seduction in the current reality of his relationship with his patients. There are several excellent psychoanalytic papers discussing instances of real seduction in Freud's manner of therapy whose authors remain respectful of Freud's achievements and ideas. In effect, these authors found that Freud's patients perceived correctly the seductiveness (and destructiveness) of the situation and that the theory of transference and the theory of sexual drives could not have been derived from those clinical data even though many of Freud's theoretical ideas might have been proven to be correct.

Thus Freud's insistence on the fulfilment of a wish, which has to do with the future, is precisely what my research confirmed to be true, but only in situations when the patient is in actuality dealing with a future event. I believe that my new clinical theory of transference confirms both of Freud's hypotheses, the seduction and the transference theories, but only if they are applied in the proper time-relation with the event in question. The fundamental question we face in the immediacy of the session and in researching clinical data is this: 'Is the patient dealing with something that has already happened or is happening right now or, with something in the future?' Thus, Bonac has found that there is no misperception on the unconscious level, never any distortion of the present, no unconscious fantasy (or fantasy), it is only possible to fantastically expect a future event.

What about the validity of perceptions of past events? Are our memories true? This is, I believe, the wrong question for the purpose of therapy. When this past event was happening the perception of it was valid. It is now stored 'on record' as memory. Does this memory remain intact, a valid representation of the event with time, or does it change in time into a 'fantastical' elaboration on that past event? Does a memory become a distortion of that memory? First of all, let us clear one oxymoron quite commonly found in many texts. Many therapists (and others) are quite preoccupied with the veracity of unconscious memories, most often when dealing with early sexual abuse of now adult patients. Since one cannot tell an unconscious memory because it is unconscious (by definition) this question cannot exist. Regarding the veracity of memories in general, it does not seem that anyone has yet shown conclusive evidence for either explanation. The important thing is that this issue of the state of truth in a memory is irrelevant clinically. Why? Because every communication in the session, whether the report of a dream, a narrative or an image, is only a vehicle for the communication of another story or image, because it is this story, which pertains to the therapist, which might be responsible for the patient's symptoms. It does not matter whether the patient reports a 'memory' from his or her own distant or not so distant past or is inventing a 'story' (a distortion of a memory) because the patient is making an effort to communicate to the therapist not about what happened but about what is happening now. The patient is making an effort to get across to us the meaning about the present with the therapist, here, in the consultation room. The veracity of human memory is unquestionably a very important scientific issue in its own right. Nonetheless, the therapist's knowledge about the veracity of a memory told by the patient in session does not in the least change the therapist's understanding of the patient's communication even when it is a blatant and deliberate lie. Which it was in case of some of Freud's women patients.

Discovering a deliberate lie in the patient's material is an important indicator of the patient's current troubled (pathological) functioning. If we knew it was a lie, we would no doubt be interested in knowing why the patient was unable to tell us the truth, why there was the need for invention. Nonetheless, these facts are of no use to us in our understanding of what it is the patient is trying to tell us now. In the case of a 'memory' which was not true to the facts, our knowledge of the true version of the memory would give us information which is useful for the aetiology of the patient's illness, but which is immaterial to the immediate clinical situation because it is the theme that is the message, not 'who's done it'. In the case of a deliberately told lie, it is not the theme which is the lie, but the identity of the 'characters' and of the 'place and time' which were 'displaced' by the patient. When this substitution is done unconsciously by the patient, the 'untruth' is not a lie but a derivative. We are dealing with the communication of facts in the present. Of course, this view has little to say to those psychoanalysts (and therapists of other persuasions) who still interpret the past and disregard the present, whose very aim of therapy is to elucidate and 'reconstruct' the patient's past life.

Lacking detailed clinical material about Freud's women patients it is only possible to formulate the following speculative explanation: when pressed by Freud to remember the identity of their seducers, the patients produced any plausible name from their past just so they could continue to insist on the theme of seduction while obliging their doctor in his quest. In this way the patients were able to continue to work over, and call Freud's attention to, the issue of being seduced and thus harmed. Since the seduction was happening in the present therapy with Freud, the patients' efforts were directed towards getting their message across to Freud by way of derivative communication. Freud was thus under sustained pressure, albeit unconscious, from his patients to recognize that there was something harmful and seductive in his therapy with them. Freud had little chance to alleviate this pressure because his frame with them never changed. His own seduction of the patients (he was treating wives and daughters of personal friends in his private home while pressing on their foreheads with his hands as the patients lay on the couch next to him) was no doubt unacceptable to his own strict sense of propriety and to the demanding Viennese social norms. Freud seems to have unconsciously rationalized his manner of treatment as his dominant 'professional interest' in sexual matters, particularly in the area of seduction of the younger by the older. Thus, Freud's patients felt the unrelenting need to alert and influence their therapist to their suffering because of the unbearable conditions in their therapy, but also these patients' insistence on the theme of seduction fed into the area of Freud's functioning which drove him, unconsciously, to establish and then perpetrate the seductive analytical frame with his patients.

Thus, Freud's unconscious 'drive' became his focused professional interest. In such conditions of perpetuated unconsciousness of the seductive reality of his own situation in therapy, Freud 'discovered' evidence for his theory of sexual trauma and later his theory of sexual seduction. In parallel, his patients 'discovered' their own past injury of seductive trauma and, in Freud's later period, they discovered 'their own' harmful unconscious sexual fantasies as the driving force for their own seductive tendencies towards Freud. Freud's patients continued to struggle with symptoms while Freud continued to struggle with conflicting evidence spoiling coherence and internal logic of his theories. All this at the expense of becoming conscious of the truth about themselves in the present (see also Langs 1981, 1989, 1991). The immediate truth was too unintelligible and too divorced from their fierce personal and social beliefs to be bearable and thus conscious.

Chapter 8
The dangers of immediacy

Fear of knowing the immediacy of any interpersonal situation is a demoniacally powerful force driving us to not see, to not hear, to hide. Thus, we can observe the process of the automatic, innately given, defensive and momentarily liberating (albeit later enslaving) settlement: the supreme compromise of derivative expression. The brilliant achievement of the ability to communicate and to exert powerful pressure on the other while knowing little or nothing at all about it. The innately human ability to hide, yet show; to not tell, yet tell. The inborn capacity of us all, from birth onwards to encode our communications while talking to others and, in case of dreams and creative works of art, even when talking to ourselves (Bonac 1994; Langs 1982).

Searles tried to call attention to the uncanny phenomenon of unconscious perception and unconscious communication of the immediate reality between the patient and the therapist as early as 1948, but was unable to get his seminal paper of this discovery published at the time (Searles 1978/79). Langs discovered the basic laws of unconscious communication in 1976 and proceeded to develop theories of therapeutic technique in the following two decades. His numerous publications met with a strange wall of silence on the part of the mainstream psychoanalytic establishment. Communicative literature contains exhaustive evidence for the complex unconscious functioning of adults in therapy. Thousands of pages of verbatim reports of sessions and their detailed discussions are now extended with detailed examples of the unconscious functioning of the young. To observe the uncanny ability for unconscious perception and for unconscious communication by children, this book provides a sample of evidence that the human capacity for unconscious perceptions exists in all of us from an early age.

In therapy, we are not detectives searching for facts in the patient's life, we are not even lawyers to argue the logic. In the consultation room, the therapist is there to listen to the patient's themes and images. What the patient is saying is always applicable to the current situation between the therapist and the patient. Whenever the therapist's mind strays outside the consultation room and interprets the themes in the light of what is happening to the patient in his or her life outside or in the past, the therapist will not get such understanding validated by the patient. To stray in this way is so easy because the patient's material is not always clear and the triggering event is rarely straightforward.

When we take in the patient's material we do not change the meaning of the theme, because the meaning is the core of the message. We need only to change the persons and perhaps the place and time to 'read' the patient's encoded message. First, we verify the reality of the moment in the session and determine who it is that has done what the theme is telling us. For instance, if the theme is about someone's uncle being late, and if we know that the therapist was late for this session, we are on the right track when we put forward the proposition that the patient was talking about the therapist's lateness in this session. Doing this, we have applied the 'decoding' of the derivatives by going in the opposite direction, which the patient's unconscious mind took when initially 'encoding' his or her perception of the therapist being late and the implications of this lateness for the patient.

Chapter 9
'Counter-transference'

To understand what has been traditionally termed 'counter-transference', the therapist takes his or her own reactions to the patient as they become manifest in feelings, thoughts, daydreams and actions and tries to reach their unconscious meaning. The awareness of such responses offers the therapist another chance to understand the patient's unconscious and to formulate therapeutic interventions. The theory and technique presented here starts from the premise that patient and therapist are equal in the basic design of their psyche, regardless of their emotional health. For this reason, therapists trained in the communicative theory of clinical technique can decipher, at least in retrospect, their responses to the patient with the same methods which are used to understand the patient's derivatives and indicators – irrespective of whether they are unconscious perceptions, reactions to these perceptions or the therapist's transference. This means that the therapist could ascribe the complete 'counter-transference' response to one or more events which had triggered it.

To understand his or her own symptomatic reaction, the therapist would produce derivatives (guided associations to dream elements or free-associations) and decode them. In a further step, the therapist would take those communications and actions of the patient whose meanings are unclear and formulate an interpretation by linking the triggering event (the patient's material) with the themes in the therapist's own derivatives. Langs developed this technique of self-analysis and called it 'self-processing' (Langs 1993; see also Langs 1990). His method is unique in its systematic search for the event that triggered the derivatives (associations to dream elements) and in its constant focus on the state of the interpersonal frame in which the disturbance occurred. The method makes high demands on the therapist's emotional openness and cognitive clarity. It is, however, the one method that brings much-needed understanding and emotional relief to the therapist after difficult sessions.

Chapter 10
Validation of interventions

The communicative therapist offers the patient interventions, mostly in the form of interpretations, which include the possibility of frame corrections on the part of the patient. The therapist strives to formulate interventions in accordance with the knowledge of the unconscious processes as they are explained by the theory of taking in, processing and expressing of information. After an intervention has been made the therapist has yet another task to complete: the validation process.

The unconscious validation of an intervention by the patient is the hallmark of communicative psychoanalysis. This unique psychological phenomenon was discovered by Robert Langs (1976a,b; see also Langs 1984). It is the one task required of the therapist which makes the technique of communicative psychoanalysis distinctly different from all other of psychoanalytic schools. According to the communicative theory of unconscious validation, the therapist cannot proceed with anything else in the session until he or she has waited for the patient to respond to the previous intervention, because there is no way of knowing in advance whether the intervention is helpful or hurtful to the patient. There is no way the therapist can evaluate the intervention, no matter how consonant it might be with this or that psychoanalytic theory and no matter how sensible and logical it may sound, until the patient has been given time to respond fully with derivatives.

Thus, after making an intervention, the therapist will wait for the patient to express a full set of derivatives which reflect two different properties: (a) themes speaking of something positive, nourishing, motherly, helpful, allowing growth; and (b) themes revealing a new, never-before-heard memory or story, which singularly and specifically extends the last interpretation given by the therapist. The part of the validation process in (a) was named 'interpersonal' validation and the part in (b) the 'cognitive' validation of an intervention. Only correct interpretations can evoke a cognitive validation from the patient. The adjective 'cognitive' was chosen by Langs because the patient tells us that something new is suddenly understood on the cognitive level, something that was 'there' all the time in the patient, but hidden. It is now revealed in a new light and within a specific context. Most often, the patient will say something like, yes, the particular situation was obviously dangerous but he or she was not aware of it at the time – now, however, it is clear to the patient that this is what was going on! Or, the patient might say that there was something intensely uncomfortable about a certain past situation, but that he or she was not conscious until now of the full extent of what the other person was doing at the time. In each case, cognitive validation is evidence for a new, fresh insight into a past situation having occurred to the patient immediately after the therapist's interpretation. The therapist's correct interpretation enables the patient to discover more details about a past event and thus understand more of what really happened.

Without the accompanying interpersonal validation in the patient's response to an intervention, what might appear as the cognitive component alone is in fact not part of the validation process. The particular memory or story told in response to a therapist's intervention must thus be something else, most probably an unconscious perception of the therapist's error, that is, non-validation of the intervention. Only when the therapist was correct in understanding the patient's material does validation of that understanding emerge in the patient's material. The validation always consists of a positive theme or story – a sign that the therapist was in some way good to the patient. It is of course inconceivable that the therapist's intervention was incorrect yet the patient felt good about it – by definition of 'correct'. Whenever an intervention is correct, something good has been 'received' by the patient and there follows interpersonal validation.

Since it is possible to be beneficial to the patient yet not to have provided an insight into a particular issue, it is understandable why it is feasible that the patient feels supported, helped in some way, yet totally lacks the conscious understanding of what happened in the session which produced this feeling of having been helped. Such interventions without insight are not only quite common in practice, they may be more numerous than correct interpretations. In such instances, the patient will communicate derivatives of positive themes because something good did happen, yet the patient will not be able to communicate any sign of new understanding as none was provided by the therapist. For example, the therapist might have received a telephone message from the patient's teacher. In the following session the therapist tells the patient about that call and informs him or her that the therapist did not return the teacher's call. At this point, the patient will feel good about the therapist because the therapist did not talk about the patient behind his or her back. Thus, a positive theme will emerge signifying the interpersonal validation. Since there was no cognitive explanation (for whatever reason) from the therapist, there is nothing for the patient to understand further – be it about this telephone call or about any other similar incident in the patient's past.

Thus, cognitive insight was not provided and the cognitive part of the validation process is lacking in the material.

In this way, the particular structure as well as the aims of communicatively formulated interpretations were derived from these discoveries to form the communicative technique. In the course of a session, the structure and the specific aim of an interpretation follow these theoretical conceptions. This is why we claim that the theory of technique of communicative psychoanalysis is empirically derived and sustained in everyday practice.

The clinical application of the requirement for validation of an intervention reveals that only some of the therapist's interventions are helpful to the patient, the rest are not validated and may be confusing or harmful. One important intervention, especially at times of confusion or insufficient material from the patient, is the therapist's silence. The therapist listens and waits for more material from the patient which is needed for the formulation of an interpretation. When validated, in the same way as described above, the silent listening appears to be helpful by virtue of its holding and containing functions as much as it is necessary so that the patient has time in which to provide the complete information the therapist needs for formulating interpretations. When the therapist does not wait long enough and intervenes prematurely on the basis of insufficient information, the patient senses this unconsciously and communicates just such meaning in derivatives to the therapist. This type of error is another good candidate for retrospective self-analysis by the therapist. Again, the communicative therapist is awed by the incisive and sensitive unconscious responding by the patient to every move the therapist makes. As Robert Langs says to his students in supervision, 'the patient will tell you all you need to know for you to intervene correctly'.

Chapter 11
Interpretation of distress

The intervention of the greatest therapeutic value is a communicative interpretation. A correct interpretation brings the patient cognitive insight and relief to the symptoms – nothing else does, there is no substitute. There are two kinds of communicative interpretations: (a) interpretations of the therapist's error by decoding the patient's unconscious perceptions of the change in the frame by the therapist (Langs 1976b, 1978a,b,c, 1979, 1981, 1982); and (b) interpretations of the patient's transference response by decoding the patient's own breaks in the frame (Bonac 1998, 1999). The reactive breaks in the frame by the patient, which come in direct response to the therapist's break in the frame, are not the patient's own, but the therapist's introjected acts and are thus classified under (a). This type of responsive acting out by the patient is very common in children. The process was first described by Harold Searles in 1958. In 'Acting-out as a response to, or vicarious expression of, the therapist's unconscious processes' he explored this important aspect of acting out not previously discussed in psychoanalytic literature, namely, the patient's pathological and visually grotesque behaviour during sessions which was found to be a direct 'acted-out behavioural response to, or expression of, unconscious elements in the therapist' (Searles 1965, p209). Searles termed such behaviour 'introjective acting-out'.

Therapeutically effective and timely interpretations can be formulated only under certain conditions. Only after the patient has expressed the derivatives, the triggering event itself and the indicators, does the therapist have sufficient information to be able to intervene with an interpretation. If the patient has expressed all three of these elements and the therapist is still waiting, the patient then makes it clear to the therapist that the time has come for an interpretation – most often with a clear derivative message. In such cases, the therapist might hear a 'story' about someone who was not attending to the business in hand or to someone who was deaf to what was being said.

A rough outline of the process leading to a communicative interpretation has the following elements and sequence:

- The emotionally relevant aspect of the therapist's intervention (triggering event) is demonstrated to the patient.
- The patient's derivatives are identified as undistorted, unconscious perceptions and as the unconscious analysis of their implied meaning. If any biographical information is currently available then the patient's perceptions and meaning are placed in their historical context. This procedure always involves making use of the patient's own words, which is ego-strengthening as nothing new is introduced by the therapist and thus the interpersonal boundary with the patient is respected. For the therapist this means strengthening the patient while preserving the abstinence, no matter how urgent the need of the therapist to free-associate and tell what comes to mind in relation to what the patient has just said. All additional explanations derived from theoretical concepts, no matter how sophisticated and perhaps even relevant, fall into this category of the therapist's free association of ideas. The only exception is a triggering event which was not mentioned by the patient, but which was witnessed recently by both the therapist and the patient.
- Those of the patient's symptoms which the patient mentions in the session as well as any current resistances are elucidated in a specific manner as natural responses to the specific aspects of the therapist's intervention(s).
- Any further responses of the patient, such as derivative hints for corrections (models of rectification), are interpreted in the light of the patient's manifest mention of the current trigger and incorporated into the interpretation as something that is yet not present in the session but that the patient thinks ought to be implemented.

This conception of interpretation takes seriously the communicative requirement to interpret derivatives in the current context, never in isolation. Nothing, be it a free association, a possible transference response, a prolonged silence or reported dreams, is interpreted in isolation – however fascinating it may seem. Dreams in particular are such a powerful medium of communication, with their primitive directness and unique images, that the therapist might suddenly become aware of a pressing need to talk.

An intervention is a potent thing. A correct interpretation has the power to make the patient a little healthier. A wrong interpretation, especially when it involves an actual change in the frame, might drive the patient a little crazy. There are really no inconsequential interventions – if nothing else, a therapist might be wasting the patient's time and money and prolonging his or her suffering. Much of the speculative intervening, so prevalent in the actual practice of psychotherapy, can be prevented by employing the communicative requirement to maintain professional discipline when formulating interpretations by way of following well-defined steps. By using the same rudiments of methodology in the course of a session as in clinical research, the communicative therapist has the means to verify that there are sufficient data available from the patient before starting to formulate an interpretation.

When offering an interpretation, we are explaining the source of the indicators of the patient's distress. Indicators may include psychological or bodily symptoms, breaking of the frame or prolonged silences. The patient comes for therapy because of troublesome symptoms: either the patient suffers or else those around him or her suffer because of what the patient does (provided, of course, that such complaints are justified!). The reasons for the current emergence of indicators need to be explained, as only indicators can point to that with which the patient needs help. Thus, an interpretation is an explanation of the patient's distress by taking the themes from the narratives or play and placing them within the current context of the change in the therapy frame.

An interpretation elucidates an indicator of distress as the consequence of the patient's unconscious process which has analysed and ascribed meaning to his or her perceptions of something that happened recently. Thus, a correct communicative interpretation is very effective in resolving symptoms. Interpretations which offer an insight into the dynamics of a conflict and into the unconscious processes which ascribe meaning to it do bring clarification of the patient's motivation. Correct communicative interpretations combine these two elements as they clarify motivation for an action and also explain the patient's coping capabilities by describing the path of the formation of an indicator. As such interpretations employ the unconscious resources of the patient they are, by virtue of this aspect, ego strengthening.

With this in mind, the reader is invited to have a look at the interventions made in the sessions and at those proposed in the discussions.

Part II
In the consultation room

Chapter 12
Stories and mysteries

V. A. BONAČ

> . . . Clement of Alexandria is even more precise, indeed brutal: '*The mysteries
> can be summed up in just two words*,' he says, '*killings and burials.*'
> It is not the men who pass through the mysteries who are immortal but the
> mysteries themselves. When, in Smyrna, the public speaker Aelius Aristides
> hears that a raid by Costobocis has devastated Eleusis, he says: '*The battles on
> sea and the battles on land and the laws and the constitutions and the
> arrogance and the tongues and all the rest have melted away: only the
> mysteries remain.*'
> From *The Marriage of Cadmus and Harmony* by Roberto Calasso (1993, p316)

This book is about mysteries. About true events that became mysterious
and about what happens to the person who 'passed through them'.

When a psychotherapist first begins to listen to his or her patients'
communications of the deeply unconscious meaning, whether in sessions
with children or adults, the first experience is always one of being
stunned, alarmed. The exceptional therapist might respond with
immediate wonder and confidence, but this is rare. We all, the seasoned
communicative therapists included, continue to be awed by the extraordinary capacity of human beings to perceive and communicate on the
unconscious level with such amazing clarity, detail and accuracy. We
continue to be taken by surprise, at each turn of each session, by the
wisdom of the unconscious evaluations and by the genuine patience with
which the patient would unconsciously like to treat the therapist. The
unconscious description of an event is never the same as what we, and our
patients, believe consciously. Unconscious meaning always enters by the
side door, unexpectedly. And we are shocked! It is this singular quality of
the unconscious meaning – to rock the foundations of our beliefs, when it
is exposed in such naked state – which might be responsible for the
current reticent attitude of the psychoanalytic circles towards the new
findings of communicative psychoanalysis.

Nonetheless, when given due consideration, the unconscious meaning, as it becomes revealed in the bipersonal field of psychological therapy, can also be unexpectedly rewarding for the therapist and remarkably healing for the patient – particularly when it is employed to correct a harmful situation. Without the knowledge of the communicative method of listening to unconscious meaning, however, a therapist is quite lost and prone to run for cover to one theory or another that comes to mind in the particular situation. Such flight from the patient is not at all uncommon in present clinical practice and the attribute of being 'eccentric' is still being considered a professional compliment. One could call such attempts at coping with the patient's unconscious material 'psychotherapy by free association of psychoanalytic theories'. Rare is the therapist who is able to make a spontaneous discovery in the thick of a session and communicate this to the patient. Harold Searles comes to mind. He was the first to discover the psychological phenomenon of the patients' capacity to unconsciously perceive the truth about their therapists. Just how shocking this discovery must have been to the American psychoanalytic community at the time can be inferred from the fact that his first paper, written in 1946 and submitted in 1948 to two psychoanalytic journals, was not accepted by either and did not appear in print until three decades later (Searles 1978/79).

Yet, the knowledge of the communicative method of listening cannot, by itself, prevent the therapist's errors. That is to say that the method cannot cure the therapist of making mistakes. The method is only a tool, it can only guide. It is, however, the only available key to the understanding of the unconscious meaning, dynamic in the session. What a skilful application of the method can always do for a therapist is make possible the correction of a past error by providing access to the understanding of what was concealed and kept secret. Occasionally, such correction of an error can be achieved in the same session, sometimes it takes months of struggling with confusion before we gain access to understanding. In the end we are always better off if we know how to 'read' the patient's unconscious so that we respond to his or her needs and not to our own (for pertinent examples in child therapy, see Kahl-Popp 1994, 1996, 1998). In the process we always learn a great deal about ourselves – but only when we understand, and thus help, the patient.

This book is not shy about calling a spade a spade. The authors have tried to use generic words that best describe their meaning. We have also not followed the fashion of replacing old words with those currently in vogue. For instance, 'interpersonal' and 'interactional' remain, although these words can be found in the various contemporary psychoanalytic texts under such terms as 'intersubjective', as some authors discuss phenomena first described elsewhere but do not quote their original source and thus give the false impression that something new and different is discovered. Also common in current literature is to make good use of terms like, the therapeutic *interaction*, *mutual* experiences of the patient and the therapist, *interpersonal* phenomena, the '*real*' therapeutic relationship and the analytic *frame*. Ironically, these terms were originally introduced by innovative authors to denote their new discoveries and were then met with irrational opposition or worse, with deadening silence, by most in the analytic world. Although many contemporary psychoanalytic texts may have adopted the terminology, the content of their papers still does not seem to reflect the changes which these original findings imply, and the borrowed terms are *de facto* misused. The deeply unconscious meaning of the therapeutic interaction is rarely considered in contemporary literature and the result is that the critical source of the therapeutic disturbance is often missed. A significant clinical consequence of this shortcoming is that transference is often interpreted without sufficient verification of whether the process might in fact be non-transference, i.e. the patient's correct experience of reality. It is generally assumed and taken for granted by most psychoanalysts that practically all disturbances within the bipersonal field of the therapeutic interaction must be the result of the patient's transference and are interpreted as such.

A year ago, I asked therapists who treat children and who have been trained in the therapeutic technique developed by Robert Langs of New York (now known as communicative psychoanalysis) to send me process notes of three sessions and to write a discussion. My only requirement was that the sessions were in sequence and that the transcripts as verbatim as possible. Six therapists responded. Two of them did not have sufficiently detailed transcripts of sessions to be able to provide evidence for discussions and decided not to proceed.

I requested the four authors to replace the names of the children with the word 'patient' and to replace all personal identification of people and places with a generic description of their role or function. My purpose was to identify with precision, as much as possible, the factors that might exert any influence on the therapeutic process, while at the same time protecting the confidentiality of both the patients and their therapists. I also asked for racial and cultural information about the people involved in therapy in order to provide the reader with a variety of data for a small sample study of child cases. The clinical material presented here could serve as an example of such data as they are available to a communicative therapist for the research of any possible effects of race, culture, gender and age on: (a) the therapeutic interaction; (b) the attitude of the therapist; and most importantly (c) the fundamental functioning and responding of a human being.

This last concern is reflected in the title of Part III of this book, 'Are We Created Equal?' I wanted to find out, from the minute details of conscious and unconscious communications between the therapist and the patient, whether there is any evidence for the existence of a primary and most basic quality of human nature that is common to all people of all races, ages and both genders, and independent of the times and current culture. I sought such evidence in the way patients of different ages respond to the same event. In my extensive studies of sessions with children (ages 2–18 years) and adults I have looked for evidence of the effects of the cultural background, the socioeconomic status of the family, the race and colour of skin and, most importantly perhaps, the effects of the state of emotional instability on the experiencing of, and responding to, the same conditions of treatment. The following question was asked at each moment of the sessions: Does the degree of 'mental illness' (disturbance in affect and behaviour, the officially classified type of 'pathology') from neurosis to psychosis, and, for children, the officially measured intelligence and performance at a school, have any effect on the experiencing of, and the responding to, the conditions of treatment?

This book contains transcripts of sessions and their discussions by five therapists, including the author. The patients were two girls and three boys ranging in age from five to 12 years. The patients and their therapists are of different races and cultural backgrounds, speaking different languages. The sessions took place within the past eight years in four different countries: Canada, England, Germany and the USA. When selecting their sessions, the therapists chose material which had already been made public in some form or another. Since the keeping of written records of sessions and their presentation is a standard requirement in the course of clinical training, three of the sessions presented here occurred under the stressful conditions of the institutional setting. Consequently, the sample sessions show the reader more about what can go wrong in therapy than what is correct. Thus, as mentioned before, the sessions in this book are not samples of excellent and experienced therapeutic work and cannot serve as an example of technique to be followed directly for the purpose of training. Ironically, to try to publish 'good' sessions with private patients is not possible, it is an oxymoron. As soon as the intention to make a faithful written record of the patent's material has been made by the therapist, before the session has even started, the session is no longer private and confidential and thus not an example of sound therapeutic work because the patient and the therapist both know it, albeit unconsciously, and respond to this very new change in the frame. The material of such a session will inevitably reflect the harmful consequences for the patient of this intention and will centre on the therapist's error and not on the patient's inner needs. This is true even when the patient might not allude manifestly to the cause of disturbance. When there are other, even more pressing and more harmful factors at work in a session the patient will always address those first. Only totally private sessions have a chance to be good examples of sound therapeutic work. Thus, it is in the nature of psychotherapy that the very best of a therapist's work will never see the light of day.

The therapists who contributed their sessions had a good knowledge of the communicative method. At the time their discussions were being written they were also receiving clinical training in communicative psycho-analysis. Thus, the sessions presented here are to be taken as sample data for discussion and research, not as an example to follow in practice. Only individual supervision can serve to provide models for future work to a therapist.

To get the most out of this book, and perhaps discover something new in the data presented, these pages are best approached with a certain multiple attitude, or with the spirit in flux, in which the reader can freely vacillate between 'being adult' and 'being a child'. To not be willing to do this is, in a sense, to unwittingly divide the human race into what is 'us', the adults, and 'them', the children. The consequences, and perhaps the origins, of this division are similar to those at work not long ago when we all were still called 'man'. After all, the time we spend being a child is a third of the time we spend being 'adults', and before 'they' start calling us 'the elderly', 'senior', 'geriatric case'. There is the example of the category 'women and children', appearing at times of natural catastrophe or war, which ought to alert us that something is amiss when we make classifica-tion categories spontaneously, under the duress of circumstance, without asking the question of whether there is anything at all to be classified for the task at hand.

I propose that categories such as 'infant', 'child', 'adolescent', 'adult' and 'the elderly', which denote the physical progression through the growing/ageing process, may have no place at all in our quest to know how human beings communicate and function. We would be putting the cart before the horse if we assumed that there exists a 'development', that is, a progressive or regressive change with time, in the human capacity to communicate and function unconsciously. The employment of such categories certainly suggests that we are subscribing to the belief that there is developmental change in the course of a life span. How can we slot human unconscious functioning into compartments or phases when we have not even asked the question: Is there any change observable in our unconscious functioning with time? Are we getting 'better' or 'worse'? We may yet be surprised by the answer. As if the adult individual were so different from the child which he or she once was! Psychoanalysis ought to be the last discipline of knowledge to fall through this crack in the shaky floor of tacit assumptions. If we are to find that the fundamentals of the unconscious functioning of children are no different from those of adults, then we must question the widespread habit of treating children differ-ently from adults in psychotherapy. If so, the words 'with Children' could well be omitted from the title of this book, which is equally useful to the therapist with a patient of any age.

Patients tell us stories. If we are not to turn simple stories into permanent mysteries, if we are not to take the patients' torment in the present and turn it into a dim myth from the past, then we must take these stories, with all their images and their themes, and seek their meaning in the present of the consultation room.

Chapter 13
Horrors in the mirror

V. A. BONAČ

The first three sessions of treatment of an 11-year-old boy will be presented almost verbatim, followed by a detailed discussion.

At the time of treatment, the patient was attending a public elementary school in a metropolis of western Canada. His mother is white Canadian, his father is Chinese from mainland China. He has three younger siblings, all born in Canada. Treatment for him was requested at the local mental health centre by his parents and by his schoolteachers with the following complaints: setting fires; stealing, especially of food; hoarding of food; lying; unusual sensitivity to criticism; being avoided by peers; not helping at home; poor performance at school; nocturnal enuresis and *pavor nocturnus* with screaming in sleep.

The therapist-in-training, a Middle European woman in her forties, conducted individual psychotherapy sessions with children at the Centre. She was assigned to start weekly treatment with this patient. The assigned therapist was familiar with the basic principles of the communicative psychoanalytic technique with adults. The Centre was not run on psychoanalytic principles and the therapist had a difficult time trying to provide minimum privacy and confidentiality for her patients.

Two years prior to this referral (age nine), the patient was tested at the Centre by the staff psychologist and was found to be well above average in creativity and intelligence. The boy was described as cooperative and eager to please. The therapist was given the report to study before starting therapy. The patient's siblings and parents also received services at the centre. The costs of running the Centre were covered by the government health insurance plan. In the area where the patient lives, all psychiatric and mental health centre services are free of charge, in contrast to the services provided by psychologists, psychotherapists, psychoanalysts and counsellors in private practice.

The therapist's first contact with this patient occurred at a family interview called by a staff nurse. The nurse introduced the therapist and recommended to the parents that the patient be treated by her, in individual sessions of 'play therapy', for six months. The therapist was silent during the family interview, responding only to direct questions. She made an effort to limit her contact with everybody to a minimum, striving to preserve both privacy and confidentiality of future treatment with this patient.

The pressure on the therapist to seek opportunities to chat with other therapists, the parents and their children was substantial. She continued to not discuss her cases with other therapists and to not socialize with the parents. The staff of the Centre met regularly for lunch in a room which opened directly into a corridor where patients and therapists passed on their way to sessions. The door was kept open while the staff discussed their cases casually and without any attempt to disguise personal information. This therapist's repeated efforts to keep the door shut were dismissed as 'unnecessary', 'unfriendly' and ultimately as 'paranoid'.

The therapist was assigned a consultation room with a large observation mirror (one-way window), covering the whole length of a wall, with no cover. On the other side of the wall with the mirror was a large observation room with several chairs and a table. Since the door was kept unlocked, and many times wide open, the possibility for secret observation by unseen parties, and thus the likelihood for violation of both privacy and confidentiality of treatment, was real, ever present and unpredictable.

In the consultation room, the observation mirror was complemented by a large microphone on stand in full view, thus providing full audio and video access to the observation room. The therapist had in actuality no control over the use of either the observation mirror or the audio transmission since the controls were in the other room. It was entirely possible that a chance, non-professional passer-by might have entered the observation room and watched the session in progress without permission and without detection. The consultation room contained one chair and two child-size chairs, a table and a sandbox, as well as shelves and boxes with various toys. There was no couch.

Before the first session, the therapist made a mental list of the state of the analytic frame for this patient - a routine preparation she did before all sessions. The therapist was aware that this patient had already experienced many powerful events, related to the analytical frame of his treatment, before his first session:

1 his contact with the staff (including writing forms and storing of this information)
2 the therapist's contact with his family
3 free therapy
4 recording and transfer of the patient's private information for insurance purposes
5 treatment of his family at the same Centre

6 observation mirror
7 microphone
8 the six-month limitation of his treatment
9 the revelation that his therapist was a student
10 change of therapy rooms (from the 'family' interview to the consultation room
11 the likelihood that the therapist will talk to her supervisor about the patient.

(Note: This patient's treatment was terminated several years ago. At the time, there was no intention to publish the material. The process notes, heavily disguised in this text, were kept by the therapist under lock until this publication. Permission to publish the material was obtained from the patient and his parents a year after the end of treatment.)

Session 1

At the appointed time, the therapist entered the common waiting room, used by all therapists to meet the patients and their families. This therapist greeted her patient and escorted him to the consultation room. It was her intention to write down the session from memory in order to study the material on her own as well as to satisfy the general requirements of her clinical supervisor.

The therapist found the patient in the waiting room. He had come on his own. The therapist said 'Hello' and she walked with the patient along a long corridor to the consultation room. There were several doors on both sides of the corridor, some of them open. Right next to the waiting room was the central office with the door wide open. Three people, two typewriters and file cabinets with open drawers were in plain view. While walking in the corridor, the patient started to talk quickly to the therapist, 'Me and my friend found a typewriter in the park and then we went to some other place because people were watching'. Upon entering the consultation room he quickly glanced around and then started to play with train tracks. He was making and remaking the tracks and they always ended up open ended so that the trains repeatedly fell off and overturned. He was talking very fast and looking straight at the therapist. He said, 'My friend can change channels by pressing different numbers on the typewriter'. He then took a toy soldier out of his pocket and showed it to the therapist, 'I found it in the park; he was just lying there and so I took it. (Pause.) Me and my friend are working on a bomb. If you connect two sides, electricity goes into capacitors and then you can make contact and - it is a bomb!' (Pause.)

First intervention: The therapist said, 'What could you use the bomb for?' The patient answered, 'To blow up the school.' (Pause.)

Second intervention: The therapist said, 'What could happen then, if there were no school?' The patient answered quietly, 'I could play.' (Pause.)

Third intervention: The therapist then said, 'Where would you play?' The patient, 'In my fort. Me and my friend made a fort-house. It was really big and there was a soft, thick mattress for two people. The fort was made of huge plywood and all was made of a bin.' (His voice was low and full of admiration and pride.)

Fourth intervention: The therapist, 'It sounds like a wonderful fort-house.' The patient, 'But, the rain made it all soggy and it took a long, long time to dry. We cannot use it until it dries.'

Fifth intervention: The therapist, 'You had made a beautiful fort where you can play with your friend but the rain spoiled it and you cannot use it now.' The patient responded, 'I saw a movie, those guys, they had eight cars, they robbed a bank and the police in one slow car was after them, then the guys, they blew up the car with a bomb, and POOF! They took lots of money, they stacked all bags of money into one big bag. They had lots of money.'

Sixth intervention: The therapist asked, 'I wonder what the robbers would want to use the money for.' The patient answered, 'I don't know... They would buy things.'

Seventh intervention: The therapist, 'I wonder what other things the guys could have done to get money, besides robbing a bank.' The patient, 'They could get a loan. But, that would be a big loan.' (While talking, the patient continues to connect train tracks into open-ended loops so that the train cars repeatedly run off the tracks and overturn.)

Eighth intervention: The therapist, 'I see that the train runs off the tracks again and again. I wonder if the train could use tracks in the shape of a circle, then it could keep on going.' The patient started to connect the tracks into a large circle while the therapist continued with the intervention. 'Today, you told me about your friend and the typewriter, about your fort and about the movie.' (At that point, the patient completed the circle of tracks, but then quickly opened it up into a U-shape. He ran the train slowly on the tracks then suddenly he let it derail and 'flew' it about two feet away and through the window of a doll's house where the train smashed into and overturned the furniture and the dolls. He said, 'Oops' and smiled but did not set the overturned toys straight. The patient then spent several minutes looking at details of the doll's house with an occasional comment, like, 'Oh, a toilet, but no drain', or 'Two sinks'. The patient then gives a baby-doll a milk bottle and places the mother facing away from the baby, looking out the window.

Ninth intervention: The therapist intervened, 'I see that the mother is looking out the window and cannot see the baby.' The patient responded immediately, 'The baby is asleep.' He then got up and declared that he had 'to see everything in the house'. He put away the train tracks, got up and went to the sandbox, 'I want to play in the sand.' He then took out his toy, the soldier he had found in the park, and placed it face down in the sand, saying, 'This is the desert.' He then built a high circular fence all around the soldier. When he found trees in the toy box, he smiled and put many trees inside the fence all around the toy soldier.

Tenth intervention: The therapist, 'I cannot see the soldier, he is hidden by the trees.' The patient, 'It's a sanctuary.' The therapist continued, 'It is a safe place for the soldier, nobody can come in and harm the soldier.' The patient responded very emphatically (as if correcting the therapist), '*And*, nobody can cut down the trees!' The therapist, 'It is a sanctuary for the soldier and for the trees.' The patient, 'The soldier wears camouflage, the people cannot see him.'

The therapist, 'Just like you' (the patient was wearing a military-type fatigue top). He responded in an eager voice and looking straight at the therapist, 'Top is OK, but they can see my pants. I have other pants with blotches and when I wear them people cannot see me in the bushes. It's camouflage. I can hide!'

Eleventh intervention: The therapist intervened, 'You can be safe when people cannot see you.' The patient listened intently, then immediately took lions and placed them encircling the sanctuary. Then he placed a 'family of elephants' in the sand. They were pursued by more lions and a rhinoceros. He moved the legs of the lions and explained that 'they are going to attack the elephants'. He placed a 'polar bear in the water', 'two black panthers were attacking a sheep', and two snakes were 'hidden' in the sand.

Twelfth intervention: The therapist said, 'The jungle animals are ready to attack the elephants. The soldier is safe.' The patient's face became very tense and he moved the toys with more speed. He moved the lions closer to the elephants, then he took the elephants and placed them in the sanctuary and moved the black panthers to 'eat the trees'. The therapist continued, 'Perhaps the lions will not attack the elephants and the sheep now.' The patient stopped to listen, then put a giraffe next to the sanctuary fence and said, 'The giraffe is eating a tree' which was 'growing inside the sanctuary'.

At this point, the therapist said that it was the end of the session and the patient left on his own, on time. After the session, the therapist started to put the toys, used by the patient, back into storage boxes. She found the patient's toy soldier covered by the sand and hidden by the trees. She took the toy with her with the intention of giving it back to the patient in the next session.

Right after the session, the therapist wrote the process notes of the session by hand from memory. She studied the notes and was not asked to report on this case. She stored the notes in her locker.

Session 2

As before all sessions, the therapist took a mental note of the state of the analytic frame. The therapist knew that nothing of consequence had changed for this patient: she was assigned to lead him into the same consultation room. She was now aware not only of her own anxiety related to the observation mirror and microphone but was affected by the patient's communications and experiences in the previous session. The therapist had the patient's toy soldier in her pocket and she mentally added this fact to the original list of the various aspects of the analytic frame.

The patient came to the waiting room five minutes late and told the therapist in the corridor that he 'almost forgot about the session' because he was 'writing something on the computer'. The therapist did not respond. Immediately upon entering the consultation room, the patient went straight to the observation mirror, put his face right next to the glass and said in a loud voice, 'I can see curtains on the other side!' Then, he slowly took off his wrist watch and put it in his pocket.

First intervention: The therapist took the toy soldier out of her pocket and offered it to the patient saying, 'I found it in the sand.' The patient took the soldier with no apparent interest and dropped it, face down, in the sandbox. The patient said, 'Thanks. My friend left his knapsack on the ground at school and his teacher stumbled over it and took it away from my friend and she said that he can walk home without it. So, he walked 15 minutes to X Street, then he turned around and had to walk all the way back to school to get it back.'

Second intervention: The therapist said, 'I wonder if what happened to your friend is like what happened to you when I took your soldier and kept it and brought it back to you today.' The patient did not respond directly but started to play with dolls from the hospital set, which looked like doctors, nurses and patients. His play showed no clear theme. He took the dolls out of the box, one by one, and right away threw them back into the box. He then abandoned the dolls and turned to Lego blocks. He took out a Lego building plan and began to build something slowly and carefully. His facial expression conveyed defiance and he did not look at the therapist.

Third intervention: Twenty minutes into the session, the therapist said, 'It seems that you have trouble talking to me today. I wonder if something happened in here that makes it difficult for you to talk.' The patient answers immediately, '*I* don't know. Nothing that *I* know of.'

Fourth intervention: The therapist, 'Today, the first thing you did was.... You went straight to the observation mirror and you told me that you can see curtains on the other side. Then, you had trouble talking to me. I wonder if you are afraid that someone might be watching you from the other side of the mirror.' The patient lowered his head and smiled. He then started silently to build something out of Lego very quickly and with keen interest. It took a while before the therapist realized that he was making a large, elaborate house with a door and two windows. The windows had glass panes and he placed shutters on both sides of glass: on the inside as well as on the outside. The patient slowly opened and closed the shutters of the two windows several times. As he was carefully completing the roof of the house, the therapist announced the end of the session. The patient stopped playing, put on his wrist watch, took his toy soldier, and left.

After the session, the therapist wrote process notes, studied them and then stored them in her locker. So far, she had not been asked to report on this case.

Session 3

Before the third session, it became clear to the therapist that the patient's increasing withdrawal into silence was related to his discomfort in therapy and that his silent play with the Lego house was a clear message to her to provide him with a cover (shutters, camouflage) for the observation mirror (window) in the consultation room. With much effort, the therapist succeeded in obtaining permission to use another consultation room without an observation mirror. Before the beginning of the third session, the therapist was aware that the analytic frame for this patient had changed again: (1) they will be moving to another room, (2) the observation mirror and the microphone will no longer be there and (3) the therapist had prepared a sign with the word 'Occupied' for the entrance to the new consultation room.

The therapist greeted the patient in the waiting room on time and walked with him towards the new room.

First intervention: On the way, the therapist stopped in front of the previous consultation room door and said, 'We will be in another room today, without the mirror.'

Second intervention: When they reached the door to the new room, she put the 'Occupied' sign on the door.

As soon as they entered, the patient started to walk around the room picking up various toys, one by one, and placing them back in place. He looked animated and exclaimed, 'Holly!' and 'Wow!' several times and looked pleased. The patient then placed several water toys in a basin of water, showed pleasure in watching them float and smiled. He then looked at the therapist, rubbed his thigh and said, 'My leg hurts a little. This girl at school hit me like this (he hits himself lightly on his leg) and it still hurts a little.' He then went back to the toy shelves.

Third intervention: The therapist said, 'We are in a new room today. You looked pleased, but perhaps our moving here also hurts you a little.' The patient looked down, shrugged, then went quickly to the toy box. He then selected certain animal figures from a pile of animals and placed them in the sandbox.

Fourth intervention: As he played in silence, the therapist said, 'You are playing. Can you tell me what is happening.' The patient responded immediately and talked while he played. He placed 'the big elephant and the small elephant inside' a closed round fence 'with a gate'. He placed 'another small elephant with one ear missing' just outside the fence. The patient then placed several fantastical winged creatures on the outside around the fence and several 'adult lions playing with child lions' inside a separate enclosure, 'their own fenced place'.

Fifth intervention: The therapist said, 'I see that in your play today you are using some of the same animals that you used in your previous sessions. The story in your play is very different, though. Today, the elephants are not out in the open any more and are not in danger of being attacked. The elephants are inside their own fenced place and so are the lions. The lions are no longer dangerous to the elephants, they are playing with their children. Can you tell me more about your story.' While the therapist spoke, the patient was nodding.

The patient said, 'These (pointing to the winged creatures) are guardians.' He then placed one guardian inside the elephant place and said, 'This guardian is guarding the door so that the mother elephant does not open the gate with her long trunk so that the baby elephant doesn't go out of the fence.'

Sixth intervention: About five minutes before the end of the session, the therapist said, 'Today, we are in this new room, and I put a sign on the door to keep people from coming in here. It seems to me that your story tells me that you feel well guarded in here and that you feel safe being here just like the baby elephant feels safe with his mother. It seems that you feel that there is no more danger from outside. In your play, even the lions are now playing behind their own fence. Perhaps you feel safe also because there is no mirror in this room.' The patient looked at the therapist for a long time. He then put three large figures into the sandbox, saying, 'And these are the leaders of the guardians. So the elephants are safe.' The therapist announced the end of the session and the patient left the room on his own, on time.

Just before the fourth session, a secretary at the Centre told the therapist that she talked with the patient's parents. They came to tell her that 'for the first time' the patient had spent the week without screaming in his sleep and that he offered his mother help with housework. The parents also said that there were no complaints from his teacher at school which was quite a change from his previous daily detentions, punitive homework and telephone complaints by teachers.

When the patient came for his fourth session, the therapist could see a marked difference in the patient: he talked freely, smiled more, looked the therapist directly in the eye, he stooped less and he put away toys as soon as he stopped using them. There was a marked general improvement in this patient.

A few days later, the therapist was informed that the parents called the office and requested a session with her. In the session that followed this request, the patient silently played with dolls representing a mother and a father and told the therapist that he was ashamed because he had again wet his bed. Unfortunately, the therapist had no power to reject scheduling a session with his parents but she was successful in delaying it for several weeks, in which time the patient showed sharp fluctuations in his functioning: from mature to delinquent and from playful to depressive.

Discussion

Session 1 started in a way that is typical of child therapy in a clinical setting: with a family interview involving written records from the school, testing results from a psychologist and one or more persons on staff at the clinic. Even in private practice, when the therapist might be trying hard to keep the treatment of his or her child patients private and confidential, the parents are almost always involved. There are some treatment centres where children, their parents and their siblings are routinely treated by separate therapists, but even there, the child's treatment is often recorded, monitored and supervised in one way or another by several people.

Such dramatic improvement in the functioning of a troubled and troublesome child, as happened with this patient after only three sessions, is a remarkable therapeutic achievement. I speak from personal experience when I say that such rapid progress is typical of most children, especially young, when treated by communicative psychoanalytic psychotherapy in circumstances where the analytic frame has a chance to be secured.

My very first child patient was a delicate, five-year-old, elective-mute Chinese girl who had never spoken to anyone outside her home and only to her family inside her home. She was 'given' to me as a 'hopeless case' after she had been 'seen' by several psychologists, counsellors and medical doctors since she was three. To my great astonishment, she started to speak with me freely, like any 'normal' child, in our very first individual session. I told this wonderful news to my supervisor and to her mother (when she picked her up after the session) and nobody believed me! After several sessions, her mother brought this child into my consultation room with a tape recorder, hidden in a toy animal, in order to obtain 'proof' of her daughter's 'magical' recovery of speech. In this session, the patient regressed rapidly to long silences and physical immobility but continued to say a few words to me. A few weeks later, her mother received an excited call from the kindergarten teacher to tell her that her daughter had stood up and spoken for the first time in class. The very same day, her mother telephoned and told me the 'great news' in an alarmed, intensely agitated voice. The very next day, the mother requested from the Centre that she and her husband be treated as a couple by the same therapist (me) as her daughter. My request for another therapist for her parents was treated as ridiculous, 'anti-therapeutical' and contrary to the policy of the Centre. Soon after, an appointment was made for me to see her parents in 'couples therapy'. In the session with me, and outside in her life, the not-so-long-ago lively and gentle little girl regressed even further, to almost complete muteness. She was becoming the same as when she had first come to the Centre. One could pronounce her 'fixated' to an earlier psychosexual state. It broke my heart. For a mad moment, I considered saving her by 'adoption'.

This dramatic sequence of events is a strikingly clear example of a typical difficulty facing all therapists who treat children, i.e. parental intrusion into their children's treatment, driven by unconscious, albeit powerful, forces. By insisting that the same therapist who treats their child, also treats them, the parents can all but destroy their child's treatment. Of course, there is little hope for anything good happening in their own therapy. Many a therapist treating adults could tell you that the main reason why they do not want to treat children is the fact that there is too much trouble with the people other than the patient.

My treatment of this 11-year-old boy was of great significance to my professional development, both for the treatment of adults and of children. I came to see, early in my training, what enormous power the therapeutic relationship exerts on the patient - perhaps even greater than on adult patients. However, I also experienced the painful helplessness of the therapist when faced with the ferocious intensity of unconscious needs in parents to keep their children unchanged. The parents bring their children to treatment out of love and heartfelt concern for their children's suffering. Yet, those very same parents become intolerably anxious when their children show improvement, that is, when their children really start to change. A changed child upsets the precarious balance of the family system which is maintained by the complex status quo in the family. When one part is changed, the whole system is suddenly disturbed and the balance is lost. The system is threatened with inner chaos and the parents' unconscious needs take over. The usual result is blind action: the parents demand that the therapist enact their requests for immediate changes in the analytic frame.

The three sessions with the 11-year-old boy were presented very nearly verbatim, along with the information about the realities of the physical setting which the patient and the therapist witnessed and experienced. When available, the therapist's thoughts pertaining to the therapy were mentioned as they occurred. The reader was thus guided through the therapeutic process of the three sessions with the complete knowledge of data as they became available for observation to the therapist. What follows is my discussion of these data.

Reading the introductory remarks of Session 1, the reader may have already noticed a remarkable parallel between the fact that the patient started to *talk* to his therapist in the corridor *before* they entered the consultation room, and the fact that this therapist had *talked* with his parents (at the family interview) *before* this patient's first session. The patient talked about finding a recording device in one place and then going to another place to avoid being watched. This communication can be explained as displaced and symbolized communication of the patient's perception, unconsciously conveyed, containing many layers of meaning. The fact that the patient starts talking before the session begins alerts us to the detail in the reality of his treatment: that the therapist had met the patient (and others) before his treatment began and that this contact was made outside the treatment room. The patient's communication is a good representation (a close derivative) of the move from one place, where people watched him (i.e. the family interview in the previous session) to a more private place (a play room, alone with the therapist). The same communication also serves as a representation of another event, related to the issue of confidentiality, namely the recording of personal information. At the family meeting, the interviewing nurse, while holding the patient's file open in her lap, requested that the patient's school records be sent to her. The same patient's communication also represents the office of the Centre, as experienced by the patient, with its many implications: its open door with a clear view of the secretary who is busy typing and storing the patients' files. The initial communication from the patient relates also to the disguised general theme of needing to change something for the better.

When I said that there is a 'parallel' between the overt meaning of the patient's verbal material and the realities of his therapy, I was describing the functioning of the human capacity for *unconscious perception* of events and for *unconscious communication* of such perceptions, as discussed in more detail in Part I of this book. Since the patient communicated the themes *after* these events happened, the following working hypothesis (pending validation) can be formulated. The patient's themes conveyed his perceptions of events at the Centre prior to his first session, held by the patient unconsciously in his memory and communicated, again unconsciously, to the therapist at the time of their first session. We might further hypothesize that the aim of his unconscious communication was to somehow influence the therapist so that she would, in some way, be helpful to the patient in his emotionally troubled state. Such sophisticated unconscious communicative efforts by the patient to 'quietly', without undue interpersonal pressures, guide the therapist into the troubled area in need of 'repair', were independently discovered and most eloquently described by two American psychoanalysts, Harold Searles (1965) and Robert Langs (1976a,b).

Upon entering the consultation room, the patient first silently shows the therapist toy train tracks which do not work. He is telling his therapist, silently but eloquently, that the trains are derailing because of faulty design, and that there is something critical that needs to be corrected before there can be safe movement (of trains). This message, unconsciously communicated by the 11-year-old delinquent, lazy, bed-wetting, dishonest, dangerous boy who wants to blow up his school, is sophisticated and powerful. He is speaking, in the symbolic, displaced and condensed manner (discovered by Freud in 1905 as primary process thinking). Before there can be therapy (safe travel by train), there must be repair to the design of therapy (repair of train tracks) so that safety is assured and a therapeutic relationship (train connection between cities) is made possible. Unconsciously, in this session, this boy is *not* perversely attracted to hazardous conditions (he is not doing anything to his therapy or therapist that is in any way inappropriate or destructive). At least, not yet! What he would like to achieve with his therapist is a change in the basic design of his therapy. He is hoping that perhaps this therapist can make some positive changes (if his friend is able to change channels, maybe this adult woman, who is in charge of his treatment, can make changes, too).

The patient used his brief play with toy trains the way poets use words: to create a multi-layered message which is conveyed directly, succinctly, eloquently and with stunning clarity in order to make the therapist herself experience a wide range of implications and possibilities. Unconsciously, this child is neither destructive nor ignorant. He is attentive, prudent, wise and focused. Unconsciously, he is capable of a fast, automatic, sophisticated and valid assessment of the reality of the conditions in which he finds himself. Unconsciously, he 'knows' that something is fundamentally wrong with his therapy and he 'knows' that it can be corrected by changing its fundamental design. We must not forget that he was placed in this situation by his parents, by his school and by the Centre for Mental Health in order to 'help him become a better person'. Looking at the situation rationally and honestly, we are struck by the devastating truth about his present therapy: this child is at risk and his mental health (his normalcy) is in danger of being damaged in a psychological way, albeit with concrete actions.

After the patient shows the therapist the toy soldier, he communicates a story about taking someone else's property, i.e. of stealing ('it was just lying there and so I took it'). This *negative theme* is a remote derivative of what was happening to the patient's property, i.e. private information about him contained in the school records, in the psychologist's report and in his file at the Centre. It was a true fact that this information was accessible to many people, 'just lying there'. The patient was never asked if he had permitted anyone to read his files. His personal property, the private information about his very soul, was made public property, available to anyone who wandered into the secretaries' room.

His communication also implies the aspect of illegality, another negative theme. Then comes his story about working on a bomb: this is a serious message. He appears to be saying that there is something going on in his therapy which is heading towards an explosive destruction of something. No doubt many people would point a finger at this patient and say that he has the inclinations of a terrorist, that he is a 'born' terrorist. It would be easy to suggest that he might have the potential to grow into a dangerous adult capable of subversive and terroristic actions. However, let us suspend our judgement for a while, and continue to follow the material in this session with special attention to the patient's unconsciously communicated meaning. We may yet be surprised to find that the patient's communications in the session do not pertain only to his past play event, i.e. the play bomb he built with his friend. We might be surprised to find something more immediate, much more real, and much more dangerous.

The first two interventions of the therapist are not *communicative interpretations*, however, they seem to follow the patient's line of thought and to advance verbal material needed for understanding. The fact that the patient pauses after each sentence is indicative of his resistance to communicate with his therapist, which we can understand in the light of his difficult situation. The fact that he does continue with his narrative after the therapist asks questions shows that he does appreciate the therapist's interest.

The patient's statement that he would be able to play if the school were blown up, is a strikingly direct message. He is saying that there is an obstacle to his *free association* in therapy ('play therapy') which is contributing to his resistance. Only after the obstacle is removed ('blown up'), he says, is he free to talk ('play'). The obstacle that needs to be eliminated is a structure imposed by authority ('school'). The patient is offering his therapist a *model of rectification*: he is saying that his therapy can begin after the present structure, as currently dictated by the school, the Centre, the psychologist and his parents, has been destroyed. He is talking about personal freedom gained by the elimination of an oppressive 'regime'. I used political terminology to emphasize a rarely discussed issue in psychotherapy: what exactly are the breeding grounds for terrorist and violent inclinations in a person? Of course, one can ask this question in this way only if one has allowed the following proposition: that we are born equally innocent, free of any inborn destructive predisposition. This assumption stands in contrast with direct implications of many psychoanalytical theories which presuppose inborn and/or inevitable destructive traits, phantasies, drives, instincts. Perhaps we need to study interpersonal processes in much greater detail to fully understand *what* is the cause of violence and *who* is doing the violence to *whom* in the course of our development. Is it two children at play, making a toy bomb? Or is it the oppressive structure of some institutions, such as families and schools, in which children are not permitted to play freely? What is play and how much privacy does play require? Can play be playful if it is not free? Is play fundamental to human nature? What is play to adults? Where is respect for another person if our play is not respected?

Studying the moment-to-moment progression of the therapeutic inter-action in sessions, we are able to gain a novel, clearer view of cause and effect, of the context in which events happen, and of the psychoanalytic frame to which our patients respond. Perhaps we can gain a fresh under-standing of what makes a human being, when he or she is young, think thoughts of destruction (making a toy bomb to blow up the school). Perhaps we can find out what we can do, and must do, to not cause such thoughts. Ultimately and inevitably, it becomes a question of public safety and of national security. If adults can provide us, when we are children, with safe structures within which we are free to 'play' at building (rather than tearing down), free to communicate (rather than retreat into silence) and to grow to maturity (rather than remain fixed in the body of an adult, yet waiting for an opportunity to be free to 'play'), then perhaps we shall have less need to search for the 'destructive' gene, innate tendency, trait, drive, the human 'wish' to die and to kill.

The third and fourth interventions are again not interpretative and the therapist does not follow the patient's model of rectification of getting rid of the structure of his therapy as it stands. Since the therapist again shows interest in hearing more, in knowing the patient better, she is rewarded with a more detailed, less violent and more instructive model of rectifica-tion. The patient appears to be perceiving the therapist's genuine interest in providing him with a good structure for his therapy. His response shows that the images of violent destruction are giving way to constructive themes. The patient talks of building a strong structure for protection ('fort-house') which would contain gentleness and comfort ('soft mattress') for two friends. He tells the therapist that the softness was ruined because the protection against outside elements was not good enough ('rain made it all soggy'). He seems to be saying that therapy cannot proceed until there is repair ('we cannot use it until it dries'). This model is a clear derivative appeal to the therapist to not only get rid of the present structure: it also offers instructions for making the sessions private and confidential. The patient needs a protective, enclosed and gentle space for two people ('mattress for two people' in the 'fort-house').

The fifth intervention is again non-interpretative and the patient responds to it by changing the topic. He turns away from constructive themes and instead, remembering the film he saw, the patient seems to be giving up on the therapist because he sees no evidence of improvement. What follows is a negative theme, a clear narrative of destruction and violence ('blew up the car with a bomb'). Interestingly, this theme is also about an illegal act ('robbed a bank'). Again, how easy it would be to label this child as someone with habitual 'ideation of violence, stealing and immorality'. Perhaps we know of therapists who would write such an assessment of him and send it to his school to be included in his official school record where it would serve as a permanent warning - thus 'confirming' the original complaints about the boy's stealing and setting fires. Such therapists would not be thought of as inefficient or incompetent in the treatment of this child, it would be the child who would be labelled as incorrigible in his wickedness. Perhaps his genes are not 'right' - the possibilities for speculation are endless.

To conduct a proper investigation of this mysterious bank robbery and violence against the law we must employ methods fundamental to any sound investigation: a systematic and detailed analysis of facts in sequence. Psychotherapy offers the opportunity to gather sufficiently comprehensive data to which the scientific method of research can be fruitfully applied. Psychotherapists are in a better position than teachers and parents to understand in depth what is going on in the mind and soul of this child because therapists have available the *derivative* material of this child, which constitutes an essentially different type of evidence. We need to pay attention to the sequence of events as well as to the complexity of the circumstances in which the adults have placed this child.

The topic of taking someone else's property, and deposited in an institution for safe keeping (robbing of a bank) shares the same theme with an event that actually happened. This patient's personal records were removed from the file cabinet at his school, because the teacher, the Centre and the therapist did not properly store, nor effectively prevent the removal of, his documents (robbers could get away with their plunder because they were able to eliminate the police car since they were eight in number and the police was only one). This is not a model of rectification as there is nothing constructive about the story that 'crimes pays'. The patient is now directing his unconscious efforts away from showing the therapist *what she can do* to correct the situation, to explaining just how serious the crime is and how ineffective the therapist is in preventing it. This patient has been robbed and he is finding himself among the robbers! This knowledge is unconscious to the patient and so are his comments. This narrative is a symbolized version of the patient's unconscious perception of the reality of events in his therapy up to the present moment: the prevailing of crime over law because the law is outnumbered. This depressing theme shows that the patient is currently giving up on the therapist's ability to rectify the *break in the frame* of his therapy: the police are there but they are outnumbered. Nonetheless, he is not giving up on her entirely; unconsciously, with derivative meaning, he is helping her understand what is going on.

This same *negative image* of stealing and getting away with the theft might also be a representation of insurance coverage of the patient's treatment. The patient, or rather his parents, as well as the Centre, are, in effect, 'stealing' money from the therapist and getting away with it (the student-therapist is not paid for her services but money is being paid to the Centre for the treatment by the Insurance).

The sixth and seventh interventions are both non-interpretative which, not surprisingly, discourages the patient in his efforts to continue to communicate meaningfully with the therapist. His answer is, '*I* don't know', the derivative meaning being that the therapist does not know. From then on, the patient stops talking, gives up his verbal efforts and shows signs of communicative resistance. The patient is no longer communicating spontaneously and richly, but is trying to answer his therapist's irrelevant questions. In his play, the patient is trying to 'show' the therapist his frustration with her by repeatedly disconnecting the train tracks: 'Look', he is 'saying', 'you are not connected with what I am telling you'. He is repeatedly running the train off the tracks: 'Look', he says, 'your "train of thought" is constantly *derailing*.' This non-verbal evidence may be considered scientifically non-conclusive, yet the message is quite clear. It shows that the patient has stopped free associating because he has introjected his therapist's inability to establish a meaningful connection with him, as she is not *connecting* his themes to the real events that have triggered them.

The eighth intervention is again non-interpretative. It instructs the patient to follow the therapist's lesson in geometry (how to make a circle). The therapist's intervention derails yet again and breaks the connection with the meaning of the patient's derivatives. The patient responds by showing her a violent act of crashing into people and property through the window. There are no models of rectification. There are only *themes* of non-connection, accidents, destruction and violent intrusion. Here, the issue with the mirror is less disguised and quite explicit. The patient is saying that the threat is coming from the outside of the consulting room (of the doll's house) and that the consequences are that of violence and destruction. The *communicative resistance* is in evidence as the patient no longer *verbally* communicates in rich stories containing themes. In the end, the patient's narrative does include one tentatively *positive image* of the mother giving the baby a bottle. Nonetheless, even this good image comes with a twist as the mother turns away from her baby and looks out of the window. It seems that the therapist was helpful to the patient on some essential level (the most basic survival requirement for a baby is nourishment). Nonetheless, the therapist is seen as someone who has turned away from the patient. This is a negative image representing a valid perception of the therapist who was not able to make use of the patient's unconscious communications (the circle proved useless: the train can run but it gets nowhere). In reality, this therapist *was* preoccupied by the observation mirror throughout the session, not knowing who might be watching and listening at any time. The patient seems to be saying that the therapist was thinking about the mirror more than she was thinking about the patient (the mother faced the window) - and, he was right!

The reference to the window occurs twice in this session, which tells us that this issue is just not going away from the patient's unconscious mind, just as it is not going away in reality during the session. The mention of the toilet without a drain is a clear image of something that cannot possibly work because something essential is missing. Since it is not clear exactly what the patient is referring to, it seems that his resistance is affecting the clarity of his communications. This might be a sign that the patient is losing hope that any improvement is forthcoming. There is another brief mention of 'seeing and then turning away from it' (following the ninth intervention) after the patient announces that he 'wants to play' - with a clear implication that he was unable to play before. While playing in the sandbox, the patient communicates a negative image of a soldier lying on his face in the desert, turning away from seeing. This image represents the patient's valid perception of his current relationship with his therapist, namely that neither of them are communicating about what truly matters. The therapist might be talking but she does not appear to be connected with the patient's unconscious meaning as she is not responding to what the patient has been trying to convey. To the patient, the emptiness in his therapy has reached the point of a barren desert.

What happens next is, I think, a manifestation of the singular human capacity for 'eternal' hope which appears to be particularly vigorous when we are young. In spite of yet another disappointment, following the ninth intervention, the patient begins to carefully design and construct an enclosure surrounding an oasis in the middle of the desert. The attributes of this enclosure are the same as those the therapist needs to provide: a safe place which shall make his therapy possible.

Although the tenth intervention is not a complete communicative interpretation, its function is constructive and the patient responds immediately with rich verbal derivatives. He offers his therapist a clear model of rectification in the form of a compelling theme of a sanctuary, where the observers cannot destroy the visual and the audio barrier ('nobody can cut down the trees') and where one is safe from being watched ('the people cannot see him'). This is his third explicit reference to the urgent need for effective protection against the horrors of being watched by people who behave like animals of prey.

Our current hypothesis about what the patient is trying to achieve with his unconscious communication is this: he needs to have the mirror and the microphone removed. If the hypothesis is correct, the removal of the mirror and the microphone from his sessions must result in a radical change in the patient's communications and in his functioning. His themes would have to change to their very opposites to reflect a new situation. If they do not change, then we must consider our hypothesis wrong. As long as we have the means of refutation, we can rely on our reasoning.

At this moment in the session, we can in fact observe the immediate healing effects on the patient by the therapist's *linking of his play image to the current and immediate reality of his therapy*. Finally, the therapist has made a correct connection between his themes and the patient himself. The patient eagerly accepts this understanding with yet another, much more immediate and encouraging *model of rectification*. He is 'saying': 'Look, it *can* be done, if *I* know what to do in order to protect myself from watchers, then you, an adult, can also succeed.' After his therapist made conscious what before was unconscious, the patient becomes aware that it is *he* who is in desperate need of protection, not only sheep and elephants in the desert. The verbal lesson about protection by camouflage is yet another appeal by the patient to his therapist to provide a proper sanctuary for therapy. It seems that the patient has correctly perceived the therapist's efforts to understand him because the patient is now communicating again with rich images and his communicative resistance is diminishing.

The eleventh and twelfth interventions are only a weak attempt at interpretation. They are correct in the sense that the patient's need for privacy and confidentiality in therapy are finally explicitly addressed - and, this is important. Nonetheless, the interventions remain general and, this is critical, the essential part is missing! The therapist has promised *no actual rectification* of the situation! Even though the therapist is aware of what needs to be done, she is not doing it. It is not surprising that the patient, again, changes the topic and renews his efforts to point to the urgency of the situation. He presents intensely negative themes of powerful predators ready to attack the weaker animals (lions and a rhinoceros ready to attack a family of elephants; panthers attacking a sheep; lions encircling the sanctuary). The nature of these themes is *persecutory*. The images convey *imminent threat of violent death* for those exposed (the sheep), as well as for those within the sanctuary (the family of elephants and the soldier). For this patient, his therapy in a room with the mirror and the microphone, is a jungle where he is alone (the therapist is not helping in his efforts to have the mirror covered). His *unconscious* feelings of horror are the consequence of his unconscious experience of a situation which resembles this scene of imminent carnage: powerful predators (unseen observers) are closing in on him, some have already pounced on him and are tearing him apart alive and devouring him limb by limb (taking into them his live words and images of his body).

The present terror, emanating from the observation mirror, begins to shed light on this child's own long-standing unconscious terror during sleep (*pavor nocturnus*) as he continues to re-experience, in his dreams, the 'crashing' of the privacy and safety of his play (Freud's 'day residue' of his dream theory) which he seeks to find, during the day, in his fort-house.

I think it is unfortunate that so many patients, both children and adults, are so quickly declared 'phobic' or 'paranoid' by mental health practitioners, without a thorough investigation of the actual data, i.e. without a thorough search for a possible existence of a source of persecution in reality. It would indeed be quite easy to label this young boy as paranoid. After all, his parents and his teachers have found his unusual sensitivity and his preference for solitude reasons enough for serious complaint. One might be tempted to ask, 'Why would he want to blow up the school if he were not indeed paranoid?' I think that this material shows quite clearly that, at the moment, the source of fear comes not from something fantastical within the patient, but from the observation mirror. Our knowledge of the arrangement of the walls, windows and the audio equipment tells us that his fears are justified. We know enough facts about the reality of this therapy to be able to formulate the conjecture that his fear of persecution is, at this moment in therapy, not intrapsychically generated. It is not imagined by a damaged mind in the grips of *transference*. This patient's paranoia is, more likely than not, iatrogenic, that is, generated in the session. In other words, his fear is realistic because the danger is there. We are learning empirically that we require the most private and confidential of conditions, from an early age, as a prerequisite for much of what we do and certainly for the most intimate of human relationships - the psychological therapy of one mind by another.

What follows in the session, is another model of rectification conveyed by the theme of the black panther turning away from threatening to attack the sheep and eating the trees instead. Since the mirror is still there and since the therapist has made no promises for correction, this theme is not a perception. The patient is describing to his therapist what life could be like for everyone involved if secret watching stopped. The patient is saying that the staff of the Centre ought to leave the two of them (the patient and the therapist) alone, that the staff ought to be satisfied with such forms of gratification for their work that do not harm their patients (sheep); the staff ought to turn away and stop making use of the observation mirror. He is also implying quite clearly that eating sheep constitutes non-reversible damage (killing), while eating trees is reversible since trees can grow new branches. He is talking about the humanity of 'vegetarianism' and about the cruelty of 'cannibalism' of the human soul.

The patient offers another model of rectification with the image of elephants being placed in the sanctuary (where one cannot be seen). He then follows the same repetitive theme: stop watching and provide a private and confidential treatment within a sanctuary instead. This theme has emerged so many times in this session that it takes centre stage. It is not difficult to see that the patient is so preoccupied with the privacy and confidentiality of his session that other concerns do not even emerge as dominant topics in his communications.

The therapist's very last intervention 'Perhaps the lions will not attack the elephants and the sheep now') is not only non-interpretative and speculative, it goes against the patient's every effort to appeal, albeit unconsciously, to his therapist to correct the situation. The intervention contains a devastating aspect: it functions as an implied *refutation of the validity* of the patient's unconscious perceptions that there is a real, not imagined, threat to therapy. The patient's response is, understandably, non-validating. The therapist's intervention does not extend his understanding of the issue. Instead, it evokes in the patient an eloquent negative image: something that could be used for protection (the trees inside the sanctuary can hide the soldier from being seen from outside) is being destroyed *from the outside* (a giraffe is eating the trees from the outside of the fence).

The overall understanding of this session agrees with Robert Langs's findings about the unconscious functioning of adults in therapy sessions and follows closely his theories of human unconscious verbal communication. The amazing finding with child patients is that their play can convey such clear and sophisticated messages if we take into consideration all of the facts that comprise the therapeutic interactions, that is, the frame. The linking of themes to the frame-related events which triggered their formation yields meaning.

As a most general overview of this session, we can say that the patient communicated images and themes of destructiveness, danger, violence, lawlessness, stealing and malfunction - in the presence of his therapy frame that bears a striking similarity. The vicissitudes of the patient's communicative resistances faithfully followed the vicissitudes of the moment-to-moment interaction in reality between the patient and the therapist. Resistances diminished when the therapist understood his unconscious communications and they intensified when the interventions revealed her failure to understand.

Session 2 starts with the patient arriving late since he 'almost forgot about the session'. Before the session begins, we already know that the patient would rather be somewhere else and that he would rather communicate with a machine than with a human. He is demonstrating *behavioural resistance*, which is very likely interactional in its origin, since it comes right after the last session in which the therapist failed to act upon the patient's repeated pleas for privacy. The patient was punctual for his first session and he came to both sessions on his own.

Upon entering, the patient goes straight to the point. He continues where he left off at the end of the last session - which is typical of children (and adults) in therapy. The observation mirror is represented manifestly ('I can see the curtains on the other side'). When he takes off his watch he may be communicating a disregard for the realities that are illusive, e.g. time. Another reality, illusive to this therapist's understanding, has been the observation mirror. Yet another hypothesis for the meaning of his removing his watch might be: if the therapist is wasting time by not responding to the patient's urgent messages, then the patient, too, will waste therapy time with idle activities.

Since the therapist makes her first intervention (hands him his toy soldier) right after the patient's first communication in the session, his derivative response appears to apply to this intervention. The patient is commenting on the therapist's taking, keeping and returning of his toy, in a symbolic manner. The negative theme, contained in his story about the schoolfriend and his knapsack, is that of unreasonable punishment (by the teacher) for a minor mistake made by a child. This theme is also about the confusion that such punishment brings (his friend walked for 15 minutes to a street and then turned around and walked back to school). Dropping the toy soldier into the sandbox, the patient might be saying that the therapist should have left his toy right where he had left it: in the sandbox. The theme is not fully developed and there are signs of increasing communicative resistance as the patient stops talking and shows no clear theme in his play. He might be 'saying': 'This is leading nowhere. I cannot talk as long as this therapist is not covering the mirror!'

The second intervention is an attempt at interpretation. Nonetheless, there is no clear admission by the therapist that her having taken the toy was inappropriate and that she was responsible for the patient's confusion, which might have contributed to his late arrival to this session. The patient's indicator (his late arrival to session) is not explained in the light of the therapist's actions in the previous session. It is not surprising that the intervention is not validated. I would like to propose that the patient feels more deeply about the fact that the therapist did not acknowledge her responsibility and did not take the blame *because he is a 'mere' child and she an adult*.

My clinical experience shows that children's sense of justice is strong and that they suffer greatly when justice is not done in therapy. I think it is reasonable to expect that the effects of unethical actions by the therapists towards their child patients, who have been referred for unethical behaviour, will sustain and encourage their symptomatic behaviour. We touch upon morality again and again when analysing sessions with children. Working with children, I have observed consistently that the rules of morality they unconsciously reveal appear to be based on a firm, inborn sense of justice and that the rules exist, perhaps solely unconsciously, even in the most immoral of children. Moral rules appear to be part and parcel of the therapeutic process. Thus, morality needs to be made part of the interpretations as well as to guide the therapist's actions.

A vague negative theme can be identified in the non-verbal play that follows the last intervention. Playing, the patient (as the doll patient) finds the interaction with the helping professionals (dolls of doctors and nurses) useless, abandons all efforts to communicate a story (drops the dolls back into the box) and regresses into silence. His unorganized play with the dolls who represent the 'helping' professionals might also be a reflection of the patient's own current confusion, which is, I believe, a consequence of his prior introjection of the confusing and destructive nature of the therapist's speculation in the previous session ('Perhaps the lions will not attack the elephants and the sheep now'). His abandoned play appears to convey non-verbal valid perception of the vagueness and confusion in the therapist.

The patient's communications display the delicate nature of the unconscious messages, exquisitely sensitive to the context in which they occurred and to which they were a response. Humans of all ages reveal this astonishing capacity. The products of this capacity manifest their existence in a relationship and thus become available for observation whenever we are allowed the freedom to 'play'. Then, we spontaneously create symbolic representation of meaning by using all and any memories in our conscious and pre-conscious repository which will carry the relevant meaning. We can be understood, and we ourselves can gain the understanding on the conscious level if only the context of the relationship with the listener is considered. The single drop of a toy into the toy box and a child's simple tale of the knapsack conveys: (a) a perception of a state of confusion, (b) a perception of what happened and (c) an implied moral lesson of what would have been right.

The third intervention is an attempt at connecting the patient's current resistance with events in therapy. Although correct, it is not a sufficient explanation (interpretation) of what the therapist did to cause it. The patient reacts verbally and it seems that his implied message is that it is not *his* but the therapist's responsibility to understand and to explain - as he is the patient and she the therapist.

The fourth intervention can be considered an incomplete communicative interpretation. It is a marked departure from previous, inadequate attempts to understand the patient: the therapist finally connects the major trigger for the patient's communications, symptoms and resistances in both sessions (i.e. the observation mirror) with his current indicator (trouble with communicating, withdrawal into playing 'alone'). The therapist explains one aspect of the unconscious meaning related to the trigger (someone watching behind the mirror), and links it with the patient's symptoms (his fear and his troubled silence). This material might also offer a glimpse into the kind of circumstances that drive the patient into being a 'loner': being misunderstood, confused, blamed, punished and his property unreasonably withheld.

A critical point is being revealed here: even though the interpretation is correct, it does not receive validation from the patient because it is not complete. It does not include a rectification of the situation by the therapist, *in actuality* (see also Langs 1982). The apparent dissonance is not difficult to understand. The therapist did nothing to change the situation. How can the patient's fear be eliminated if the mirror is not eliminated? The patient seems to welcome (he smiles) the interpretative, and therefore healing, part of the intervention, that is, the linking made between his unconscious, intense fear of persecution and the mirror. He now knows *what* it is that he is terrorized by. His fear is no longer 'irrational', no longer displaced into the jungle. If he is driven to blow up something with a bomb, it would be this mirror, not some innocent bystander in the park. However, he might also become suspicious of his therapist's motives: he knows now that his therapist understands the reason for his terror, yet she does nothing to change the situation! His smile shows some measure of *interpersonal validation* (i.e. the introjection of the well-functioning therapist interpreting the mirror). His verbal resistance continues. His non-verbal communication, however, is quite eloquent: he builds the windows and closes the shutters on both sides of the window panes. His current play confirms our previous hypotheses that the patient has indeed been working over, unconsciously, the consequences of the observation mirror for his therapy. His play theme is a straightforward, non-verbal model of rectification. The patient appears to be saying that the observation mirror has to be covered also *from the inside* so that nobody can watch the sessions. Since he played in silence, the implicit message is that he cannot talk before this is rectified.

Upon leaving, the patient does not forget to take either his toy or his wristwatch. I believe this is yet another non-verbal form of interpersonal validation, showing that he is, at the moment, functioning a little better than he was after his last session because of the correct part of the interpretation. There was no *cognitive validation* from the patient, however. The patient did not gain any deeper understanding of his terror of being watched in secrecy because the therapist did not rectify the break in the frame. My research of the therapeutic processes in children shows that we are able to further our understanding of a specific damage done to us (a break in the analytic frame), and to understand more fully the respective original trauma in our past, only *after we have actually experienced the change in the interpersonal frame*, that is, only after the current damaging factors have been eliminated (securing of the frame). Such findings in children are in agreement with Langs's (1982) extensive research of similar processes in the psychotherapy of adults.

In Session 3, the therapist intervened three times before the patient was allowed to talk: she announced the change in rooms and put the sign on the door. The patient's first communication comes very likely as a response to these events as well as to the new consultation room. Since the patient began his session by exploring the new room, looking and sounding pleased (non-verbal communication), I understand this behaviour to be tentative proof of the original hypothesis that the absence of the observation mirror and the microphone in the new room would have a major beneficial effect on the patient and that he would appreciate the therapist's efforts at correction.

The patient's first verbal response is about being 'hurt a little' by someone. This message can be explained to mean that the sudden change of rooms and the therapist's sudden announcement in the corridor was hurtful, but only a little. Her manner was wrong but the principal aim of her actions was right.

The fourth intervention is mostly correct as it does relate the trigger (the change of rooms) to the hurt of the patient. It is, however, not complete as it does not place the responsibility for the abrupt changes on the therapist. The patient responds with a shrug (undecided opinion) and with a negative image of something missing ('the small elephant with one ear missing'), as if there had been damage to his hearing. Verbally, the patient responds with a mixed theme when he puts a couple of animals (big and small elephant) inside their own protected place (fenced place). The negative image of an outside danger is held at bay and rendered harmless by a *positive theme* of protection from this danger (lions in their own fenced place). There is a moving positive image of 'adult lions playing with child lions' which shows that the patient and the therapist are finally in a place which allows them to engage in therapy (play). This last, positive, image is a powerful expression of the patient's feelings of being free to play (lions playing) and of feeling safe (elephants are inside their own fence, apart from the lions). I think this is a beautiful example of the manifestation of derivatives. They explain and extend this child's overtly observable feelings of "looking pleased" and reveal the unconscious depth of feelings in their proper context. The fifth intervention is non-interpretative and does nothing to further the patient's understanding. However, it does seem to further the patient's willingness to tell more stories. There seems to be a *representation of the trigger* of the sign on the door in the derivative form of the image of the 'guardian guarding the door'. The theme of his story is that of the necessity for protection (guardian inside) of the child (baby elephant) from his own caretaker's (mother elephant) careless inclination ('to open the gate with her long trunk') to expose the child to outside danger ('so the baby elephant does not go out').

This might be, and this is a speculation at this point, a manifestation of the patient's transference: his fantasy of what will happen in the future, his expectation that the mother (therapist) will, in the future, expose her child (the patient) to danger. This sense of mistrust in the future, as it comes precisely at the moment when the therapeutic frame is secured, is the hallmark of a transference response as I attempted to define in communicative terms. Transference can only be speculated here, because of the following important considerations: (1) since the therapist was in fact involved in placing the patient in dangerous circumstances in the past, she could do it again, and (2) because this aspect of the frame (mirror and microphone) was neither broken nor corrected by the patient himself, but was entirely the responsibility of the therapist. According to my research of transferential phenomena and following my communicative theory of transference proper, *transference can be observed with clarity, and interpreted with conviction, only when it is the patient who initiates both, the breaking and the consequent securing of the same aspect of the frame* (Bonac 1998, 1999).

Thus, the patient's theme about the necessity for a guardian to be placed inside the enclosure can be understood as the carrier of messages on several levels. On one level, the patient has unconsciously perceived the function of the 'occupied' sign on the door as acting as a guardian to protect the baby (patient) from the outside danger (people in the corridor) as well as from his own mother (therapist), who had exposed the patient to danger before (the observation mirror in the first two sessions) and by talking to him in public in the corridor. On another level, we hear a model of rectification, a plea for an even safer place where the entrance to the consultation room would be fully secured and the danger from the outside eliminated: perhaps the door should have been locked. Both levels of communication involve images of a justified request for protection and safety.

The sixth intervention is partly correct. It does connect the patient's story to the immediate reality of his therapy (the sign on the door and the elimination of the observation mirror). However, it does not explain the patient's unconscious perception of the therapist as dangerous (the dangerous mother elephant). The therapist does not accept, and does not interpret to the patient, her responsibility to provide safety for his therapy. The interpretative part of this intervention did receive unconscious interpersonal validation from the patient ('elephants are safe', 'the leaders of the guardians'). This indicates that the patient has introjected the therapist's positive efforts at securing his space when she took on the 'leadership' for his therapy vis-à-vis the Centre and insisted on the change of rooms. Nonetheless, there is no unconscious cognitive validation by the patient. It is possible that the patient senses that the space is not yet effectively secured, with only the sign, and that the door needs to be locked - a valid unconscious evaluation of the erratic conditions at the Centre. Since the patient cannot experience and respond to something that has not yet happened (the complete securing of the door), neither can he acquire a deeper understanding of what a completely safe physical space might mean to him, consciously and unconsciously.

As my discussion indicates, these sessions are a poor example of properly conducted communicative therapy. They are, however, an eloquent illustration of the singular human capacity for unconscious perception of situations, related to the analytic frame, introduced by either the therapist or the patient. In sound communicative therapy of children, the therapist's input would be restricted to providing the patient with a safe, private, confidential, constant, predictable and reliable analytic frame and the physical setting, as well as with a *constant offer* by the therapist to the patient, of an analytic contract. This contract pertains to the interpersonal aspect of the analytic frame. It includes payment, scheduled holidays, and restriction of the verbal contact with the patient alone and in the therapist's office.

Conclusion

I hope that the detailed description of the presented material has offered the reader an opportunity to examine the minute details of evidence: the complete empirical data (as much as this is possible). This patient started his therapy in such chaotic, dangerous and unpredictable circumstances, that one is not surprised that his material did not show evidence of transference. The great bulk of the patient's communications pertain to his desperate attempts to alert his therapist to his terror. He spent most of his time 'requesting' from his therapist a change in his situation. The functioning of this child reveals that he was doing little else than trying to cope with the chaos and insanity of his environment. Under such conditions, there appears to have been no opportunity for the therapist to observe and to heal the existing intrapsychic damage to this child for which he found himself in her care in the first place. The fact that the patient had been ordered to come to the Centre, that he kept on coming, on his own, and that he never missed a session in the next six months, is a compelling testimony to the genuine interest in therapy which existed in both the child and the therapist.

In spite of the overwhelming evidence that it is the current, immediate environment that determines the current functioning of human beings, I still do not believe that all that was needed for this child was a social worker/therapist team to set his family 'straight'. I believe that this child would *not* have been all right even if his circumstances at home and at school miraculously improved. I believe that the psyche of this child had already undergone a (pathological?) change, with the power to impair his future functioning and to make him suffer *even if no further damage* were done to him. I also believe that this therapist was not able to help this patient with his intrapsychic difficulties because of the insanity in the structure and policy at this Centre. I believe that the healing effect of the third session produced such remarkable and fast improvement in the child because the interventions included partly correct communicative interpretations, meaning that her interventions were just what the patient needed on the deepest, albeit unconscious, level. Most importantly, her interventions provided, for the moment at least, in actuality the essential requirement for treatment by psychological means of any human being: a physical and emotional sanctuary to guarantee personal freedom.

The functioning of this patient did improve dramatically after his third session, although this was only a correction of the damage done to him in the first two sessions. I would not want to underestimate the healing power of such 'prior damage repair'. On the contrary, one can infer that this child rarely experienced people who changed their behaviour for his sake, who did not act at his expense. Nevertheless, the improvement in the therapy room is *not* an improvement in the patient: the difficulties he had 'brought' within him to his first session are still all there, intact. The patient might have gained a rare memory of a good experience. Perhaps his sense of hope and trust in people received a boost, but little else was accomplished in the six months of his treatment.

Only when the essential prerequisites of therapy are in place will transference make an appearance. Only then can real treatment of *the patient's own* difficulties begin, those acting to sabotage his own good intentions.

My discussion focused on the meaning of the perceptions this patient communicated unconsciously. In my clinical practice of communicative psychoanalysis of adults and children, such exquisite sensitivity to the essence and to the nuances of the immediate therapeutic environment has been demonstrated in all sessions with all patients of all ages, in their narratives and in their play. I believe that without a continuous monitoring of the state of the interpersonal frame, I could not have gained access to the most troubled recesses of my patients' minds. Without communicative intervening I would not have been invited to hear more.

Chapter 14
Seeing, touching, destroying
(translated from German)

JUTTA KAHL-POPP

The patient is a twelve and a half-year-old white German boy. His mother, a white, German woman, called me on the telephone and explained that her son had just been dismissed from a three-week stay at the hospital. The doctors responsible for his case had urgently recommended psychotherapy with me. The patient had undergone an operation for dysentery. Intestinal pockets had formed, in which were found excrement of several months. The danger of sepsis and dehydration had made an operation vital. The doctors viewed the patient's abnormal residual excrement as an indication of an overflow-encopresis, i.e. a combination of constipation and encopresis (faecal incontinence not due to physical illness or organic defect). We agreed to an initial session with the parents in my private practice, and both attended. My practice is located on the ground floor of a two-family house. My office does not have immediate contact with the neighbours except for the apartment above my practice. This apartment is separated from my practice by a double-layered, sound-absorbing ceiling and is occupied by a couple who work, have no children and are usually not at home during my office hours.

My patients ring the doorbell at the front entrance of the house. I control the electronic release for the front door from my office. The patients then make their way through the hallway on the ground floor to the entrance of my office. I also control this door by an electronic release. When opening the door to the office, the patients enter into a hallway, which has five closed doors leading to: a room for parental conferences; the child therapy room; the toilets, clearly marked as such; an unused, locked kitchen; and my study, with a telephone, but which is inadmissible for patients. The windows in all rooms block any vision from the outside and are covered with blinds which can be adjusted to allow sunlight. As is customary in Germany, the government Housing Office officially approved my set of rooms as commercially used office space. The hallway of my practice contains a coat rack and serves as a waiting room. On the doors to both consultation rooms a sign is posted, 'Please do not enter until called'. When the time for the appointment comes, I open the door to the appropriate consultation room and let the child or the parents enter. This is the moment of initial contact in person. Neither the patient nor the parents had experienced any previous psychotherapy. A psychologist at the hospital had had a talk with the patient and one with his parents, recommending psychotherapy.

On the telephone the mother, under pressure, was trying to set an appointment solely from the point of view of her own interests. Before the appointment for the parental session she burst into the consultation room, followed by her husband. At the end of the session, she tried to hold me in conversation even after our time had expired.

After we greeted each other, following the obligatory procedure in Germany, the parents gave me the health insurance transfer slip from their family doctor. This slip enabled me to charge the costs of preliminary sessions, prior to a fixed therapy agreement, directly to the parents' legal health insurance company, which also covered the patient as a member of the family. The specific charges are indicated by code numbers without describing the contents of treatment. The patient's presence or absence at each appointment is also recorded.

The parents began by spontaneously expressing their concern for the patient's precarious condition. They said that his symptoms had completely surprised them. They had noted only his diarrhoea, which had prompted them to consult their family physician. The rest of the story was known to me from our telephone conversation. Then they looked at me inquisitively, waiting for my response. I indicated that today was our first parental session, that I would make an appointment for the patient at the end of our session, and that we would arrange for an additional parental session. They nodded with relief. Then I asked them to tell me anything which might occur to them at the moment, which they thought would be important for me to know.

The mother was very talkative, while the father was more reserved, nodding silently or occasionally supplementing some point. As I listed, the following information emerged.

The patient is the second child of an ordinary German family and has a sister 12 years older. The mother became pregnant with the patient totally unexpectedly. The parents felt too old to raise a second child, resulting in the mother's decision to abort the patient. The doctors had consented to this plan. The mother said that at the very last minute she jumped from the operating table, saving the patient from having been aborted. From then on, she said she especially looked forward to his birth, but suffered from permanent guilt feelings. The mother experienced every subsequent misfortune or accident as punishment for her past desire to abort the patient.

The parents told me that during his first two years, the patient's grandmother, an impulsive and harsh old lady addicted to alcohol, looked after him during the day, while the parents were at work. When the patient was four years old, an optometrist diagnosed a severe visual disorder: The patient told me later that he could see in only two dimensions, had a limited field of vision like 'blinders', as he said, and needed spectacles. He compensated by hearing 20% better than average people. The parents told me that the patient suffered a serious car accident when he was eight. He was on his way to visit a friend and was about to cross the street right in front of his house in a quiet residential area when he was hit by a car driven by a woman. Obviously the patient had not noticed the car in time. After the accident he was in a critical condition, suffering from severe damage to his head and face, especially to his teeth and nose. His condition necessitated several operations during the following 18 months. I no longer recall the exact length of each hospital stay. In addition, the parents related that the patient completely forgot the circumstances of the accident shortly after it happened. From that time on, he suffered from recurring nightmares, in which he was persecuted and threatened with death by grey creatures without faces. He woke up from the nightmares crying and told his parents about them.

Session 1

The patient came on time to his first appointment, which I had arranged with the parents. He was a tall, lanky boy with clumsy and awkward movements and hanging shoulders. He wore thick spectacles. He looked at me suspiciously when he greeted me and had a gloomy, closed expression on his face. I said he could choose either of the two consultation rooms, and he chose the child therapy room.

In the left corner of the child therapy room there is a stack of construction cushions and a sitting sack. On the adjoining left-hand wall, there are two low wall units, each framing a case of open shelves with toys, as well as drawers also containing toys. In the back left corner, there is an armchair for patients. A desk with art material is located beside it. My chair is located in the opposite corner. There is a couch by the right-hand wall. The patient's and my chairs are placed slightly asymmetrically to each other, about 2 metres apart. When seated, the patient can use the desk adjoining his chair for artwork or playing without having to stand up. Or, the patient might sit on a stool directly in front of the desk and have a larger area available for play. There are no pictures on the white walls, only a colourful tapestry hangs over the couch. Since the room faces north and is darkened by the blinds on the window, two ceiling floodlights, one in the back left-hand corner and the other in the front right-hand corner, serve to illuminate the room. The floor is covered with a blue carpet.

Upon entering, the patient headed in a determined manner towards the patient's chair and let himself fall into it with a loud groan. After I sat down, he took a short penetrating look at me, then began staring directly ahead. He complained about the long bus trip to my office. The patient sat diagonally across from me to my right; I was seated to his left. We could see each other without having to turn our heads.

I introduced myself with my name and occupation and told the patient that we could spend the next 50 minutes together. I then said, 'I wonder how you feel about coming for this appointment with me, which I did not make with you, but with your parents. Could it be that you groaned and complained about the long bus trip because I ignored you?'

Suddenly, his face brightened, he made visual contact with me again, and his whole body jolted. He began telling me, spontaneously and in detail about his hospitalization because of diarrhoea and intestinal problems. He said that he was lucky again. He spoke openly about his treatment for intestinal pockets and the old excrement. He said that he needed to follow a strict diet. He concluded with the remark, 'I must have swallowed too much'.

I took up this remark and said: 'You are telling me that because you want help so that it will never happen again you swallow so much that your life might be in danger.' I then offered him, in a rather spontaneous manner, psychoanalytical psychotherapy with two sessions per week. The patient consented to my offer just as spontaneously, with obvious pleasure. We quickly found two days a week that suited both of us. I explained to him that I would maintain confidentiality, that the things he would be telling me, I would keep to myself. I said that he would be paying me indirectly by means of his parents' medical insurance. I told him the amount of the hourly fee which I would charge directly to the family's medical insurance. I detailed the stipulations of the insurance company: He would have to have an appointment with a specialized certifying medical doctor. His parents would have to fill in an application form and give it to me, and I would then forward it to the health insurance company along with an anonymous report placed in a sealed envelope. The insurance company would then send this envelope confidentially to an advisory expert, who would read it and advise the insurance company whether they should pay for his psychological treatment or not. The insurance company would then inform his parents about the outcome. The patient listened carefully.

I explained to him further that the insurance would pay only for the therapy sessions he attended and that I thought I would be entitled to receive the same fee from him whenever he did not come for an appointed session. The patient nodded in agreement. I concluded my explanation by letting him know he could tell me anything that might occur to him, including dreams and stories. I said he could play or portray by art the things which came into his mind.

After looking attentively around the room, the patient started telling me spontaneously and in detail about his visual disorder. He demonstrated to me how his restricted field of vision affected the movements of his body, having to turn the whole upper part of his body if he wanted to see to his side. Then he stated with pride that he could hear much better than most people. He located a faint noise in the transformer of one of my lamps, which I heard for the first time only after he had called my attention to it.

Session 2

In my second session with the parents I discussed the formalities of treatment with them. At their request and from my own evaluation of the situation, I arranged psychotherapy with them and we agreed on regular appointments every two weeks. The mother made it very clear to me how difficult it was for her to 'hand her son over to me', to not be present during his sessions and to not hear anything about them from me. From the manner in which the mother controlled the patient's compliance with his diet and his other activities, such as school, homework or visits with friends, I could see that the parents had considerable problems with intimacy with their son and in separating themselves from him. Thus I expected and feared that they would react negatively to his therapy and might even try to disrupt it or provoke termination. I had already experienced similar behaviour with parents of some of my other patients.

The approaching summer vacation for both the patient and for me, as well as the nearly 6-week period required for processing the patient's application for therapy, postponed the next session for 8 weeks following his first session. I was aware of the complex circumstances of the *analytical frame* for the patient which existed prior to his second therapy session:

1 Even though the patient urgently needed therapy and had expressed this fact in the first session, a long time elapsed after our initial contact because of our vacation schedules and the formalities of payment.
2 I had included the patient's parents in therapy even before my first contact with him.
3 I had contact with a certifying medical doctor as required by the health insurance company's regulations.
4 An advisory expert received information about the patient from me.
5 I informed the health insurance company about the patient's therapy appointments.

(Note: The treatment of this patient took place in the past. At that time there was no intention to publish this material. According to the health insurance company regulations I wrote a report after each session with all my patients.)

In the initial stage of the patient's therapy, he was not able to play or to draw. He broke off several attempts to do both. He seemed to be deeply depressed. When we were together, the patient watched all my motions, especially my breathing, movements and sounds of digestion. He did not like to move and appeared constrained, stiff, and controlling of his feelings and impulses.

The patient always sat on the same chair as in our first session. He was either silent or else he overwhelmed me with floods of words. Sometimes he modelled clay into amorphous creatures, resembling cuttlefish with tentacles, which were devouring either themselves or objects on the table. Once the patient commented on his modelling by saying spontaneously, 'Seeing, touching, destroying'.

His first drawing was done quickly and impulsively, picturing six pairs of scratched eyes and a flaming red background. Two pairs were in the middle and four inside or outside the formless red surface. Sometimes the patient talked about his dread of being persecuted by his parents and his schoolfriends, who might attack and beat him up. In fact, he told me that some schoolboys had attacked him verbally and beaten him several times. Only with his dogs did he feel secure.

I felt that the patient projected his anxiety of persecution on to me. It seemed he had to keep me under his total control, which gave me the intense feeling that I was not permitted to move, even to breathe.

In the course of therapy the patient became more relaxed. He developed better orientation, and it seemed to me as if he felt contained. He came to his sessions by bus on his own and rang the office bell, usually on time. Occasionally, he told me that he took an earlier bus so that he could watch the surroundings in front of my office before his session. He rarely did anything that could change the psychoanalytic frame, apart from the fact that he could not associate freely when he was anxious, rigid and controlling. On such occasions he often broke off his emotional contact with me totally and withdrew into a depressive state.

Once the patient asked me to report to him about his parents' session. After I had said that he was trying to test my confidentiality, he validated my intervention by saying, 'Now I am a specialist for bus connections. I found one that got me to my sessions right on time to the second.'

Session 34

At the beginning of the session the patient swamped me with words, reporting on a science fiction film about the attack of creatures from outer space. He spoke so fast and monotonously that I sensed that he was not talking to communicate content or meaning, but rather to hold me in check or to project his persecution anxieties. When he finished, he became quiet and relaxed. He took some toy bricks out of a drawer behind him and put them together on the edge of the desk. From time to time he fixed his eyes on me, building with the bricks while apparently in reverie. He did not build anything specific. He gave no further signs or hints of expecting any interpretation. I kept quiet too, watching him with silent attention. After he completed his building, he stood up and moved a little bit in the therapy room. Then he sat down again and continued his building until the end of the session. It seemed to me that we were feeling comfortable together and that the patient was less controlled and showed more confidence in his own body and in me. I neither asked questions nor intervened.

Session 35

The patient entered the therapy room and sat down. He fixed his eyes on me intently and, as it seemed to me, his ears as well, as if he was trying to control my facial expression, my emotional state and my posture. Then he became more relaxed. He got up and went to the shelf with toys, saying, 'I want to take a look here'. He was now on his knees for several minutes in front of the shelf with his back towards me because I was seated opposite the shelf.

I felt suddenly relieved of a burden and became completely absent-minded and emotionally withdrawn from him for a few moments. I recall that my withdrawal was an intentional act, in thoughts and possibly also made concrete by a slight movement of my body, which served to break the contact with the patient in order to save a part of my inner world, which was mixed with my rather aggressive emotions designed to get rid of him and of his controlling pressure on me.

Suddenly the patient's state of mind changed. He lost his interest in the toys and sank down, whining depressively, 'There is nothing for me'. He then returned to his chair. I felt that he became acutely depressive as conveyed by his sunken posture in his chair. His shoulders hung low as he looked depressively and reproachfully toward me. I asked myself silently why the patient fell into such a sudden, deep depression. I began to understand that he had perceived the interruption of my contact with him unconsciously and had introjected my subliminal aggression which expelled him from my mind and 'threw him' to fall into his chair. I gave the following interpretation while he sat silently and depressively in his chair.

First intervention: 'You felt that I broke off my contact with you behind your back, when you were on your knees looking for toys. That is why you are feeling deeply depressed now.' As soon as I finished talking, his mood changed. Spontaneously he began to paint a picture and explained what it meant: 'A big sand-glass, one part with a good, light world, the other part a dark, bad world. The dark world is above, overflowing into the good world below. The good world is nearly destroyed by the bad world.' He was quite involved in painting and appeared emotionally moved and concentrated. When he was finished with the picture, he slid it over to me, as if he were waiting for an answer.

Second intervention: 'You painted this picture with two worlds inside the clock and gave it to me in order to show me what is going on within you and your feelings. The consequence of my breaking off contact with you within our appointed time, inside the sand-glass, is that your good, inner world would have been almost completely destroyed by me, because you sensed my aggression against you in my breaking off contact. So you took my aggression inside your inner world, and this is the bad world which is flooding your good world and causing your feelings of depression and desperation.' Spontaneously the patient turned the picture upside down and said, 'The good world could be saved'. Then he added, visibly relieved, 'Finally somebody who takes the blame'. Then he became excited and suddenly remembered spontaneously all the circumstances of his car accident for the first time in his life.

He said, 'Just as I wanted to cross the street, I saw a car out of the left corner of my eye. I felt an impact and fell down in front of the car. Blood was running over my head and some down into my face. I stood up and looked through the windshield and saw the lady at the steering wheel. She must have been terrified that I stood bleeding in front of her car. Then she drove forward and hit me a second time'. The patient was breathing heavily and paused a while.

Third intervention: 'You are remembering the circumstances of the accident because of what I just did to you, not noticing you, when I was absent-minded, and throwing you out of my inner world for a few moments. That resembles what the woman in the car did to you years ago.'

The patient went on reporting: 'I flew through the air and landed on the opposite side of the street. I was lying on the ground. The neighbours were standing around me. Then my mother came and later the ambulance. I could not move, but I was aware of everything going on. Then I was taken to the hospital. The doctors had to hurt me often when they were examining me and operating on my teeth and nose.' The patient showed me his denture which he had to wear since the accident and continued, 'The police didn't find out anything. I knew the lady was to blame. She acted as if I had not seen her in time. But I saw her, and she did not brake. And the second time she accelerated instead of braking. She never did apologize to me. She visited me only one time in the hospital and tried to settle the whole matter by giving me a game as a present.' The session came to an end.

Session 36

The patient started to talk spontaneously, 'After the last session I went with my mother to the site of the accident. We stood there a while. Then we sat down at home and I told her all that I remembered. My mother said that she, my father and the police thought that I had not seen the car because of my problems with vision. But I did see and hear the car. I thought that since she saw me she was going to brake. This was a residential street. But she was travelling faster than was allowed. My parents were told by the police that the lady had stated in her accident report that she had confused the gas pedal with the brakes when hitting me the second time. In spite of that the woman never apologized to my parents, but said instead that I had not been alert. Her liability insurance paid nothing because I supposedly did not pay proper attention.' The patient looked very distressed. 'This woman was the cause of all my pain, my terror, my hospitalization, the doctors, my denture and my nightmares. In my dreams, creatures were running after me and trying to murder me. If I could get my hands on her, I would make her suffer for all that she did to me.' The patient was breathing heavily and waving his fists in an agitated manner. I sensed his helpless outrage and his desperation.

Fourth intervention: 'Now it is clear to you what you already knew deep down inside yourself, but couldn't remember: The woman hit you twice with her car, the first time because she didn't watch out, the second time because she was shocked at what she had done to you, yet didn't want to admit it and declared you to be the one at fault. She persecuted you and you feel persecuted and threatened by death because she gave gas instead of braking. You were really almost killed by her. And now it is clear what she did to you, and you would like most of all to take vengeance on her.'

The patient said, 'If she had told me just once that she didn't see me and that she confused the brake with the gas pedal . . .'

Fifth intervention: 'If she had assumed her responsibility, you would have been relieved of your doubts. Because she did not do that and because your parents and the police believed her that you did not notice her in time, you were not sure whether or not you were to blame for the accident. So you forgot the accident and suffered nightmares instead, because you thought that if you were to blame for the first hit, then you were also to blame for the woman's confusion which caused her to run into you again instead of braking.'

A few weeks later the patient reported spontaneously that he no longer had any nightmares.

Discussion

My discussion of the therapy sessions is based on the communicative approach to psychoanalysis and psychotherapy. I shall begin by presenting some psychodynamic considerations to clarify how the patient processed my interpretations. At the beginning of his intrauterine life, the patient was supposed to have been aborted. What happened to the mother's desire to destroy him after she saved him at the last minute? Did this desire disappear, was it completely eliminated from her mental life? I think his mother only repressed the impulse to destroy. It became unconscious.

The depth of her guilt feelings remained unconscious, too. Her ever-present fears and fantasies of punishment suggested that her desire to abort and destroy the patient was still virulent in her psyche. I think his mother developed a defensive reaction in 'especially looking forward' to her son's birth and in her overly protective, close and strict, supervisory relationship (reaction-formation), from which his father, respectively her husband, was excluded. When the parent–therapist sessions had reached an advanced stage, the patient's mother admitted to me, 'I could have killed you at the beginning because you were sharing things from which I was excluded.' On the one hand, the 12-year-old patient was not supposed to be able to live without her; on the other hand, the mother's triangular problem became evident because she could form only 'two-dimensional' relationships. The intruding third person on her two-person relationships, i.e. first the patient, second the father, and third the therapist, all triggered the mother's destructive impulses, which were ultimately based on her deep anxieties at times of separation and loss. The father presented a similar psychic constellation. Shortly after the patient's birth, the parents acted out their desire for abortion totally unconsciously by handing their baby over to his harsh, despotic grandmother during the day.

How did the patient cope with the intended abortion? We know from recent research with infants how quickly and sensitively they are able to perceive and apprehend even deeply repressed affective states of their parents (Dornes 1993, 1994, 1995; Lemche 1995; Lichtenberg 1991; Stern 1985, 1995). The results of the empirical research with infants confirm Bonac's conclusion, inferred from her research, that the capacity for unconscious perception, especially the perception of subliminal, unconscious motives, which determines behaviour of others, is innate (Bonac 1994). I think that the patient did sense, somehow perceive, his parents' desire to abort him. What happened to this perception in his developing psyche? I believe that the patient introjected from his mother and father the repressed desire for destruction and the associated guilt feelings. He, like all children, needed a predominately good inner representation of his parents in order to live and develop. He had to take the 'bad' components of his parents into himself, incorporating them into his own components so that his parents could 'remain good'. This meant that parts of his psyche, certain impulses, affects and notions, were destructive, malicious and dead. The patient represented his 'dead' components by the formation of the hidden intestinal pockets full of old, poisonous excrement. I understand that his concretized introjects (i.e. excrements) are intrapsychically 'coagulated' unconscious perceptions and the results of the processing of the interaction with his parents. During therapy the patient gradually began to symbolize his introjects arousing fear: the amorphous clay creatures without faces and contours, devouring themselves and their environment.

I believe that the patient was not able to integrate psychically his parents components because they were so destructive and directed against his very existence. They were indigestible in the truest sense of the word and thus had to be split off. This splitting off could have influenced the development of the patient's visual disorders: To split off meant 'not allowed to see and feel'. As therapy advanced, the patient laid aside his spectacles more and more and reported that he 'could see very sharply' whenever he was angry with provocative classmates.

Towards the end of his therapy the patient said, 'People who are unable to face death have a grey spot in their field of vision'. As he bade farewell, he said that he could now see me inwardly in three dimensions. The early introjections and splitting off of aggression and guilt probably led the patient into a primarily depressive psychic processing mode. The depressive affect was enhanced by notions that the catastrophe feared had already occurred (Brenner 1982).

The patient's psyche contained, I think, an unconscious image of himself, characterizing himself as an evil persecutor and destroyer bearing guilt and expecting punishment. How must he have experienced and processed the trauma of his automobile accident? Was there not a merging of the roles in his inner world of the offender and the victim in the moments of the life-threatening encounter between him and the woman driving the car? Was not he the 'bad' person and she the 'good'?

What else could the patient do, when after the accident everyone was speaking against him? The woman driver, the police and his parents all believed he was to blame. I think that he introjected again, this time the aggression and guilt of the woman driver, and split off the experience by completely forgetting the sequence of events surrounding the accident. Only in his nightmares did he witness his inner distress of persecution and fear of death. An example of the patient's introjection of aggression presented itself when he reported in therapy that he was unable to defend himself against assaulting schoolmates and that he ran away instead because the idea tortured him that he would definitely kill them whenever he stretched out his hand against them.

At the outset of therapy, the patient appeared to me like someone who has lived through trauma and who feels persecuted. He could not depend on himself or on his environment. His developmental frame had been chronically damaged by his parents' repressed desire to kill. There arose in him a '. . . peculiar situation of knowing and at the same time not knowing . . .' (Freud 1895b, p165). I believe that this splitting, as described by Wurmser (1995) as a rupture of the connection between the world of emotions (affects) and the world of ideas (representations), occurs between the unconscious, valid perceptions, especially of the repressed intentions of his parents and the internalization of parental distorted interpretations of these perceptions. The split hindered the patient's healthy development of his ability to symbolize. The patient's acute trauma of the car accident added to his already present chronic traumatizing by his parents' repressed and psychically virulent desire to destroy him. Again, the patient saw himself confronted with a person (the woman driving the car) who shifted her own aggression and blame to him and hindered his truthful perceiving of himself as the innocent victim of a real persecution and of an attempt to destroy him.

What did the patient expect from this therapy with this therapist? What did he want from the therapist in view of the life-threatening catastrophes already behind him, which he later directed against himself and unconsciously re-enacted within his body to the point of nearly dying of intestinal sepsis?

With this psycho-dynamic background in mind I shall now analyse the patient's section of his therapy from the perspective of communicative psychoanalysis (Langs 1976a,b, 1978b,c, 1988, 1992b, 1995). The following three questions will guide my discussion: (a) How did the patient unconsciously perceive and unconsciously process the analytic frame of therapy, as I managed it, as reflected in my interventions? (b) Did the interventions reappear in his derivative responses as encoded messages? (c) What was my thinking at the time of therapy and what is my thinking about the therapy today?

At the beginning of our first session I experienced the patient as depressively withdrawn and suspicious. I traced this state to the fact that I had made the appointment for his sessions with his parents without having asked him. It was not he who had decided that he should come to me. The decision was made by his parents, doctors and by me. After my interpretation in the first session related to this context, the patient's mood suddenly brightened and he explained spontaneously his own desire for therapy by relating his symptoms and indicating that they involved 'swallowing too much'. With the same message about his past cause of intestinal trouble, he also conveyed the following encoded message: the fact that I and his parents talked behind his back (suspicious) and decided for him without consulting him first, was too much for him to swallow.

While setting up our appointment spontaneously and without further comment, the patient commented on my interventions by listing all who contaminated his frame of therapy, excluding him and me: father, mother, the certifying doctor, the advisory expert, the health insurance company together with the extensive case description of his visual disorder restricting his movements ('blinders') and his proof that he could hear better than I. At the time of the session I viewed the patient's 'response' as further information about his problems, but today I view it as an encoded message shifted to himself, indicating how he unconsciously perceived and processed the breach of confidentiality mentioned at the beginning. If the patient unconsciously equated the *secure frame* with full visual strength and ability, then the deviations are shown to lead to restricted perception and movements and to disorders in social contact. The patient's second message contained a *model of rectification* for me: I was expected to hear as well as he could, then I would better perceive the faint, yet disturbing incidental noises in my therapy room. With these incidental noises the patient made an encoded reference to the presence of other people who were more or less secretly involved in his therapy.

At the beginning of therapy I thought that the genetic and psychodynamic factors formed the basis for the patient's inability to symbolize, for his preference for the projective and projective-identificational *mode of communication* (Dorpat 1993), for his unpleasant effect of controlling my subliminal expressions of life functions (such as respiration, digestion, facial expressions and posture) and for his depressive mood. I did not at the time connect his deep suspicion and his persecution anxiety with my management of our *therapy frame*. In retrospect, I can now see clearly that his connection of his grim comment of his amorphous clay creatures devouring themselves and their environment 'seeing, touching, destroying' was the patient's encoded message to me about how he felt about my involvement of his parents and third parties into his therapy.

The patient's unconscious communication to me means that with me as his therapist, he had experiences similar to his nightmares. With the six pairs of eyes in his first picture and their lack of contour the patient was representing unconsciously the *interaction context* of his therapy. Perhaps these pairs of eyes represented unconsciously also the patient himself, me his therapist, his mother, his father, his doctor and the health insurance company. Concealed persecution (concealed closeness and contact) with the patient is genetically and psychodynamically linked with serious, life-threatening aggression. Because I did not interpret the presence of the advisory expert, the certifying doctor and the medical insurance company, but rather split it off, I held them secret. Thus, I became threatening and confusing to the patient, somebody he had to watch out for. The woman driver had acted just as arbitrarily with the traffic rules as I had with the therapy rules - the frame conditions - failing to perceive some, while observing others and processing them continuously with the patient, such as the inclusion of his parents in his therapy and its consequent effect on him.

It was only clear to me later that the projective pressures, such as the patient's persecution anxiety, which I tried to manage with the most secure containment (in Bion's sense; see also Petersen 1996) possible, must be investigated in light of the possibility that his persecution anxiety might have been his response to my interventions and specifically to those related to the analytical frame.

In the patient's therapy the elements of the *secure analytic frame* predominated, thus helping him to develop confidence and to increase his ability to communicate with derivatives. Even though he sometimes used words as ammunition when making contact with me, as at the beginning of the 34th session, he also showed me by his film report how the threat from outer space can be successfully repelled. Of course, at the time of the session, I attributed his derivatives to the implications of my *modifi- cations of the frame*; nevertheless, we had good contact. He was deeply involved in his building with bricks and in his play; I watched him and my attention wandered back and forth between his activity and my own thoughts. Perhaps this is the kind of playful situation he had anticipated when he stood at the side of the street on the way to visit his friend, just before the accident.

In the 35th session the patient stood up to look at the toys. When doing so, he turned his back toward me. I withdrew my attention from my thera- peutic work for a few moments, just as the woman driver had neglected the task of driving for a short time. The patient did not see me. Presumably, I became aware of my unconscious guilt feelings which I tried to repress, 'throwing him out' of my inner world and acting as if he were not in the room. This situation corresponds to the woman driver who did not see him the first time, but who did see him the second time and, conscious of her own guilt, tried to get rid of the patient and of her own guilt by hitting him the second time.

From the very beginning I had an intuitive feeling that the patient's acute depression was connected with the many frame breaks I allowed in his therapy. I did not believe it was a transference fantasy with the associ- ated affect due to a corresponding spontaneous, genetic memory, possibly triggered by the toys. I had the feeling that something was repeating itself which he was experiencing at that moment of therapy and which had in the past a decisive effect on his formation. He wanted to be alive, to play, but the therapist and the woman driver, and his mother, all wanted to get rid of him because they did not want to assume responsibility for their guilt. It was from this understanding that I formulated my first interpreta- tion, which links my breaking of my contact with his affect. Amazingly, the patient's depressive mood disappeared. With his picture, he communi- cated to me that it was especially my hidden aggression that had affected his inner processing. Artistically encoded, he told me precisely where his depression-based idea of being destroyed and eliminated originated. He shoved the picture over to me, clearly indicating his need for a further interpretation (see Langs 1992b).

In my second intervention I linked his unconscious perception and his processing of it with my triggering, latent (unspoken), but nevertheless aggressive intervention (to get rid of him) in a way that explained to him that my intervention of passive aggression was the trigger for his response. In his picture the patient had portrayed what had just taken place sublimi- nally in our interaction (the sand-glass): my aggression threatened to destroy his good world. He showed me how he was internalizing my aggression, i.e. how he turned it into his own aggression directed against himself in the form of his helpless depression by dropping into his chair.

With this interpretation I made it clear to the patient that I was in agree- ment with his inner reality (see Freud 1944). In his work on 'tally interpretation', Berns (1994) describes how Langs's *concept of validation* provides a valid answer to Freud's open questions about the patient's confirmation of interpretations. This material shows how *unconscious validation* of psychotherapeutic and psychoanalytic interventions by the patient can be used as an intraclinical, empirically elaborated guideline to establish the effectiveness of therapeutic actions. The patient unconsciously validated my interpretation with the image of a positive introject: the good world can be saved (*interpersonal validation*, i.e. model of rectification lies in the theme that bad can be turned into good).Validation was also evident in the sudden end of his depression (*cognitive validation*, i.e. symptom alleviation) and in the removal of his repression. Since in my second intervention I had assumed the responsibility for his injury caused by my aggression, the patient was able to recall spontaneously the sequence of events surrounding his car accident.

In my third intervention I made a causal connection between my behaviour and the patient's inner experience with his memory of the woman driver's behaviour, including the serious health consequences for the patient. At this point the difference between a *communicative psychoanalytic interpretation* and the traditional psychoanalytical transference interpretation becomes especially apparent. The interpretation following Freudian theory of transference would have been something like this: 'Because you suffered such a bad trauma, you are now experiencing me as you experienced the woman driver.' In this way, the therapist would have arbitrarily ascribed to the patient the process of displacement from his past, i.e. from 'there and then', to the 'here and now' of the session, implying that what he was experiencing with the therapist originates in a constellation of the patient's memory and not in the current reality of the session. Communicative psychoanalysis gives us a means to investigate the unconscious reality of the *interactional context* and its implications, as Langs (e.g. 1982) has set forth in his extensive work. The communicative approach to psychotherapy and psychoanalysis

> ...will use trigger-decoding as the primary means of deciphering unconscious meaning and will append genetic connections to that centre point as they emerge in the material from patients. Formulations will move away from a concentration on the mind of the patient either in isolation or as it responds through fantasy to the interaction with the therapist - the intra-psychically centred paradigm. In its place, there will be a largely interactional-adaptional focus in which the mind of the patient is seen as adapting to the specific interventions of the therapist - first and foremost, in terms of unconscious perception (rather than fantasy), with secondary reactions to these perceptions in the form of adaptive suggestions, models of rectification, genetic stirrings, fantasy formations, and the like (Langs 1995, p120).

According to Langs's theories, the patient's memory of the details of the car accident represents a secondary reaction: the current interactional context at the time of therapy formed the basis of my approach to the patient's material. Thus in my view, the intervention that triggered his memory recall was my aggression, having traumatized him at the start of the 35th session, and my ready acceptance of the blame for it, which represented the patient's emotionally corrective experience with me. By recognizing his unconscious perception of me as the source of his trauma as valid, the patient was consequently able to distinguish between his correct perception of the accident as a child and the distorted interpretation forced on him by others so that they could be defended against their own guilt. He was told that he did not see the car and was thus to blame for the accident. In the process of hearing my interpretation he was able to 'dissolve' his introjection of the driver's guilt and aggression. This became apparent when he clarified the facts with his mother and when his nightmares disappeared. The patient was thus cured of his debilitation symptom by a communicative interpretation.

With this understanding I formed my fourth intervention. This intervention was not a communicative one because I did not base it on a frame-related change. I thought at the time that the patient was still processing his accident trauma. At first his response sounded plausible: of course the woman driver would have saved him years of suffering if only she would have confirmed his perception and assumed the responsibility for her perceptual defect (not seeing him and confusing the accelerator with the brake).

Today, I believe that the patient's narrative about his memories of the accident and about the painful consequences might contain his further unconscious perceptions and commentaries on my management of the frame. I am asking myself which perceptual disorders had I not (yet) assumed responsibility for.

Concerning the management and rectification of the analytic frame Langs said,

> 'The most common error in this regard is to miss the representations of the prior adaptive context, thus including neither this contact nor the patient's responsive derivatives in offering the patient interpretive understanding' (Langs 1992b, p478).

The patient talked about the fact that the woman driver still owed him a confession about what she had done. Did I still owe him something? Can a derivative message in his extensive memory offer insight into this question?

When the patient wanted to cross the street, i.e. when he was at the beginning of a new experience – starting therapy – the woman driver had not seen him. I had violated privacy and confidentiality, and the patient reacted immediately, reporting on his visual disorder and the concealed noises in my therapy room. He also said that he had seen and heard the driver and her mistakes – the same way he had seen the gaps in my perception and pointed it out to me – the hidden noise in the lamp. The driver had not accomplished her task properly – I had not accomplished my task properly. We both did not accept our responsibility and we denied the evidence of our deficiencies. Two accidents with the same driver had taken place in rapid succession as in his therapy. The patient could have pointed to the current adaptive context (in the 35th session) and to the background context at the time of initial contact. According to Langs's observations, the therapist's acute deviations from the analytic frame activate in the patient all other frame deviations as well (Langs 1992b).

The patient's account of the painful consequences of the accident contains many infringements on his privacy (the neighbours standing around, the doctors examining and operating, the police investigating, the parents, the insurance company), the loss of credibility by fraudulent means, the isolation and being 'bought' by the woman driver with a game. As the patient's account communicated his encoded derivatives about his unconscious perceptions and their analysis of the meaning of the activated background context, he was thereby commenting on the beginning of his therapy, i.e. the complete lack of my interpretation of my frame breaks concerning the confidentiality and privacy of his therapy. Instead of deciphering his derivative messages in light of my mismanagement of the analytic frame, all I had offered him were playthings ('a game').

The clarification of the facts of the car accident with his mother, which the patient reported at the beginning of the 36th session, could be understood as a model of rectification. He indicated that there was something important that could be clarified between him and me regarding the details of what happened to his therapy.

With hindsight, I would formulate my fifth intervention as follows: 'There might be two accidents which have also taken place between us. At the very beginning of psychotherapy I left you at the mercy of the certifying doctor, the advisory expert and the insurance company, thereby violating the confidentiality and intimacy of this therapy that I had offered to you. When you came here, you were relying on me, as you did on the driver of the car that she would see you and brake in time to make it safe for you and to stop the rolling of the insurance process. Just like the driver, I did not see you, even though you told me immediately that you hear the faint and hidden noises. Because I did not listen to you, as was the case with your parents, the police and the insurance company, you had doubts about me, could not rely on me and had to watch out for me. You felt persecuted by all of us and had the worst images of destructive creatures with many eyes as in your nightmares. Since I continued to say and do nothing about all this, you felt that I was trying to buy you with playthings, as was the case with the driver who did not concern herself with you. You probably became angry and had desires for vengeance because you could not feel safe with me, as I still did not take my responsibility. Consequently, you had doubts about it all and sought the blame first of all in yourself, while I was acting as if you were not there. You became depressed and felt malicious, as you explained to me in your picture. Later, when I accepted my responsibility, you were able to recall the entire accident. When you told me that you told your mother how the accident really happened, you were also telling me that I should recall our entire story from the beginning the way it really was, and I should acknowledge that I had hurt you at the very beginning, all the things which I did not want to admit up to now.'

In conclusion I would like to discuss the frame conditions under which I started the therapy:

1   I did not find the long pause between the first sessions and later represented in the patient's derivatives.
2   The inclusion of the parents with several parallel therapy sessions was initially reflected in the patient's unconscious perceptions and comments as persecution and as lack of containment. As I did not talk to them about his and their therapy, the patient seemed to be able to bear the accompanying psychotherapy of his parents. He believed me that I made a conscientious effort to hold 'tight' the information between him and his parents confidentially. The patient sensed, I believe, that his parents were able to let go of him as a result of their own therapy. They terminated their sessions with me independently of the patient's progress in his therapy.
3, 4 and 5   Inclusion of the certifying doctor, the advisory expert and the health insurance company (in Germany it is the state Krankenkasse), following the guidelines for psychotherapy as is legally binding in Germany. Without entering into a detailed discussion of the state health insurance system of Germany, which requires by law the participation of all psychotherapists, I would like to emphasize that the German system differs considerably from the health insurance systems of other countries. The Krankenkasse evolved as a representation of the solidarity of the whole German community. The premiums paid by members of the state health insurance (in German called 'gesetzliche Krankenkasse') are not employed to maximize profits, but are used exclusively to pay the costs of treatment needed by its members. In his lecture entitled 'Thirty Years of Psychotherapy in the National Health Insurance System: is sound communicative psychotherapy possible under these conditions?' Berns (1996) pointed out that the payment of the therapist by the health insurance of German patients is not falsified. The reasons lie in the solidarity principle of the health insurance and in the need and distress of the patients. In the patient's derivatives I also was unable to find any indication that my payment from the medical insurance should have been modified. The patient clearly represented all other implications of the health insurance arrangement in his psychotherapy, such as the infringement on privacy and confidentiality. This background context was activated at the beginning of the 35th session.

Chapter 15
The ghost of my father

M. MARK McKEE

The following clinical material illustrates the multiple meanings of loss, both conscious and unconscious, as perceived and experienced by a seven-year-old child.

The patient, a seven-year-old white American girl from a lower economic background was referred to a private therapeutic school where she was seen in individual psychoanalytic psychotherapy once to two times a week. Prior to her admission to the private school she had experienced a short inpatient hospitalization for depression, suicidal ideation and physical aggression directed at a sibling and other peers.

The child's mother reported her pregnancy and the child's birth as normal. She had no medical difficulties in her background and she had achieved all her developmental milestones within the normally expected ranges. She had previously been evaluated for placement in the private school by the hospital where she had been hospitalized and by her public school. Her psychological and educational testing revealed average to above average intelligence with no learning disabilities or concerns with attention.

However, the patient's background portrayed a number of issues which clearly placed this child at risk from the very beginning. Her mother was diagnosed as having a severe borderline personality disorder and she had, at times in her past, regressed to a psychotic level of functioning. Her mother thus had a history of psychiatric treatment from early adolescence and, as an adult, had also developed a history of extensive drug and alcohol abuse.

The care-taking of the child from birth onwards followed a chaotic and pathological course which served to disrupt a wide range of opportunities for her healthy attachment and trust in the world. Indeed, the mother informed the patient at age four that her biological father was dead and took the child (between the ages of four and six) to see 'his grave' on a number of occasions. However, six months prior to the session to be reported, the biological father had shown up at the child's home and began demanding custody of his daughter. The argument for custody was continuing in court at the time of the session. Further, at the time of the session, the patient lived with her mother, a stepfather who also had a history of drug and alcohol abuse, and a half sister who was two years younger than the patient.

The patient was seen twice a week in individual psychoanalytic psychotherapy at the private school she attended. There was also extra-therapeutic contact in the halls of the school with her therapist. The therapist had regular contact with the patient's teacher, and the patient knew that the therapist treated other children in the same school. Her therapist, however, had no contact with the patient's parents although they were offered consulting services by another agency as well as consultation by another staff member at the patient's school.

This rather minimal background information serves to provide the reader with a basic understanding of the historical background of the child and her current setting. While all these conditions represent adaptive contexts or stimuli to which the child might well respond, and certainly their implications for this child would need to be interpreted at some point, these process notes will begin by looking at the therapist's actions prior to the session to be presented:

The therapist had cancelled the previous session on the day of the session. The patient had been informed by her teacher that her therapist was sick. The therapist was then absent for two more days and returned to school in the middle of the following week. Given that the patient was aware that her therapist treated other pupils at the school, she was keenly aware that her therapist treated other children during the course of the week that her own session was cancelled. Thus, there are three activated *adaptive contexts* to which the child might respond: the cancelled session, the involvement of a third party (the teacher) and the child's observation of her therapist with other patients.

The following clinical material is presented verbatim from the process notes written after the session and is followed by a detailed discussion. The session occurred early in the second year of therapy.

The therapist went to the classroom, knocked on the door, looked at the patient, nodded, and then waited in the hallway for her to come out. As she walked out of the room the therapist overheard her say, 'I'm going to tell the teacher when I get back'. She entered the hallway, smiled at the therapist, and asked, 'How are you today? I'm okay today.... I brought my aunt's picture album.... She said I could bring it and show my therapist.' The therapist and child then walked down the hallway and entered the therapy room, and the therapist sat down in his usual place. The patient stood close to the therapist and asked, 'You want to see a picture of my aunt?' She began opening her aunt's album in which she had also placed a photograph of herself. 'This is me when I was five.' She turned the pages of the album. 'This is my aunt... See?... She was about 12 when she was in that school... She's about ... oh, 17 or 18 now.' (Pause) (She had been speaking softly and appeared very sad.) She next pulled an easel close to the therapist and wrote either 'hot' or 'not' on the blackboard. (The therapist was unable to decipher which word it was, which was quite different from the patient's usually legible handwriting.) She asked, 'Now, what's that word?', in a very quiet voice. She next moved away to the doll's house and looked back at the therapist and stated, 'I'm going to the bathroom now. Okay?' She began walking towards the door and then turned around and said, 'I know why.... It's because I drink too much water.' She smiled and shrugged as if helpless to do anything about it, turned and walked out of the room.

The patient returned from the bathroom in approximately three minutes, walked over to the doll's house and picked up the little boy doll out of a set of family dolls and set him down. She next picked up the girl doll and said, 'She's been hurt.' She next picked up two white plastic doctor dolls and said, 'This is going to be the hospital.' She brought the dolls within inches of the therapist and said, 'Let's pretend you're one of the people that work at the hospital.' She picked up the little boy doll and said, 'He's been hurt too.' She next got the toy ambulance, put the boy and girl dolls in it and then put the doctor in it as well. She drove it in a circle and stopped it in front of the therapist and said, 'Now they're putting them in here (the hospital). First they work on the girl.' (She made movements with her hands as she was pretending that the doctors were working with the girl.) 'Now they're working on the boy.' (She made the same actions.) She then stated, 'He's okay now; she's okay too. But she can't walk.' She put the girl in a wheelchair and walked over and picked up the mother and father dolls. 'Now they're going to come see them.' She put the mother and father dolls in the ambulance. 'This is their car.' She paused and then said, 'No', and looked around the room. She then took the father doll to another table at a distance from the therapist and said, 'He was working. He was out working on the farm.' (She put him on a tractor and had him fall off.) 'He got hurt.... He died.' She then made the mother doll get hit by the tractor but didn't say anything. 'He's dead now.' She brought the mother and father dolls over near the therapist and laid the father doll inches away from the therapist and said, 'He's dead.' She next picked up the other family dolls and positioned them around the father doll and stated, 'They're all crying.... Now they go home.' She took the mother, boy and girl dolls to the doll's house and pulled the doll's house next to the therapist. She put the boy doll in a bed and the mother and girl doll in another bed. She then stated, 'Now they just stay in bed all day and cry because they're sad.'

She picked up the father doll, paused, and said, 'But he's not really dead, and he comes home.' (The patient brought the father doll inside the doll's house and set him down. She then pulled all the furniture out of the doll's house, set it up on the table away from the doll's house and placed the girl doll on a toy wheelchair in front of the therapist.) 'She's watching TV.' She next picked up the boy doll and said, 'He wants to watch TV with her, and he wants to sit on her lap.' She placed the boy on the girl's lap and picked up the mother doll. 'She's in the kitchen.... No ... in the bathroom taking a bath.' She next placed the father doll into an empty bedroom of the house. 'He's up there all by himself, just getting drunk.... He's drunk.' She paused and then brought the mother doll over to the children and picked up the boy doll and placed him in the mother's arms. 'He wants to be held.' She next picked up the father doll and said, 'He's going to come watch TV with her (the girl).... He sits down to watch TV with her and the boy, and the mother comes over.' (She sets the boy on the girl's lap and the mother on the father's lap.) 'Now, they're all together.' She next picked up the boy doll, placed the mother away from the father, and had the boy doll approach the mother. 'She asked if she can play outside.' She then turned the mother doll to the father doll and said, 'Ask your father.' She then had the father doll reply, 'Ask your mother.' She repeated this message back and forth between the mother and father dolls four times and then had the mother doll reply, 'No.' She then had the boy doll look at the mother doll and say, 'Oh please, can I?' Mother doll, 'Well, okay.' The patient looked at the therapist and said, 'She changes her mind,' and then pointed to the boy doll and said, 'She's happy now.' She then had the boy doll approach the father doll and say, 'Why don't you do some work around here? You're lazy.' She then looked at the therapist and said directly to him, 'She's talking to him!' She then picked up an obvious kitchen sink, held it up to the therapist and asked, 'Is this for the kitchen or the bathroom?' This was approximately 30 minutes into the session.

First intervention: The therapist said, 'You're unsure about something and also seem to feel very sad today. In the hallway you asked how I was, which is a concern since I was sick last week and you missed your session. You also talked about the little girl here who was hurt and injured and then very sad when she thought her father was dead. Then he wasn't dead but was drunk. Then, he was together with the family and then lazy. I think my being gone last week made you feel and think a lot of things like perhaps I was not here because I had died which was very sad or maybe I was drunk which made you mad.'

The patient stated softly, 'No, I didn't think you were drunk.'

The therapist continued, 'And that I was lazy like the father here who wouldn't do his work.' (The patient softly murmured, 'No.') The therapist continued, 'At the same time, what you want for us is to be together like the happy family watching TV, and you brought a picture of your aunt and yourself because you wanted me to know more about you.'

The patient looked at the therapist and then at the toys and began placing the furniture back into the house and stated, 'Now they move back into the house.' She next placed the table and chairs inside the house and said, 'I used to have toys like this when I was five ... but I don't now. This is a good school. It's good for me.' The patient completed placing the furniture in the house and set up the rooms in a very orderly manner. She then looked around and said, 'We need markers (Magic Markers). I know what we'll do.' She then picked up two sheets of paper and stated, 'We're going to make sticker books today. Here's yours.' And she handed the therapist a piece of paper. 'And this one's mine.' She placed hers on the easel. She next said, 'Now, how do you spell your name?' (The patient was much more animated and less depressed at this point.) 'I know.' She spelled the therapist's name and said, 'Right? Right. Am I the only one on Thursday? I mean, am I the only one you see?' (She was moving closer to the therapist.) 'You know, am I on Thursdays?'

The therapist responded with Intervention two: 'You're asking if I only see you on Thursday, and I had earlier said that my being gone had made you feel sad and angry. I think you also want me to know that you want to be very special to me and want me to feel special about you.'

The patient responded, 'Okay. Which markers do you want? I'll take these, and you take these.' She handed the therapist a set of markers and said, 'Now write your name here.' (She showed the therapist where to write his name seven times in seven different colours copying exactly what the patient had done with her own name on her paper.) 'Now you write here.' (Again the therapist followed her and copied on his paper what she had done as she had written her name on her paper six times.) The patient then said as she was working, 'I know that when you're not here that means you're sick.' After a long pause, 'Now, let's count.' She counted the names on her page seven times and looked at the therapist's page and said, 'Now yours.'

The therapist intervened and stated, 'Our time's up for today.' The patient responded, 'Okay.' She began walking to the door and then stated, 'Oops, I forgot.' She then ran back and got her album of pictures.

Discussion

I shall now discuss segments of this session in their sequence

As noted, the therapist went to the patient's classroom, knocked on the door, nodded at the patient and waited for her in the hall. (This was the usual practice since pupils were not allowed alone in the halls.) As the patient walked out of the room the therapist overheard her say, 'I'm going to tell the teacher when I get back.' She entered the hallway, smiled at the therapist and said, 'How are you today? I'm okay today. I brought my aunt's album (high school picture album). She said I could bring it and show my therapist.'

By means of *unconscious encoding*, the patient has already represented two adaptive contexts. First, she mentions telling her teacher something on her way out of the room, thereby alluding to the therapist's having told her teacher to tell the patient that he was sick the week before. She next enquires about how he is and touches upon his illness. She then shows him an album and mentions talking to her aunt about her therapist. The patient is alluding to having a third party involved in her therapy. As will be repeatedly seen throughout the patient's material, children are quite capable of clearly communicating and, indeed, will fully provide therapists with all the information needed to intervene with interpretations.

The patient and therapist entered the therapy room, and the latter sat down. The patient stood close to him and asked, 'Do you want to see a picture of my aunt?' She began opening the album in which she had placed a snapshot of herself and said, 'This is me when I was five. This is my aunt. See? She was about 12 when she was in that school. She's about 17 or 18 now.'

The patient had been speaking softly and appeared to be very sad, which represents an indicator of the symptom related to an affective state of the patient. She paused and next pulled an easel next to the therapist and wrote either 'hot' or 'not' on the blackboard. It was impossible to determine which word it was because of the way she had written it, and it appeared to the therapist that the patient was unaware of the meaning of the word as well. The ambiguity was quite unusual which contributed to a sense of confusion in the therapist. Such a state of confusion with the therapist may well relate to a successful projective identification on the part of the child in which she was able to place a sense of confusion in the therapist which may well have related to her own sense of confusion about why the therapist was seen in the school the week prior to this session and did not have therapy with her. It might well also include a state of confusion related to the patient's own specific perceptions of what an 'absence due to illness' meant when she was told that the therapist was 'sick' the week previously.

The fact that the patient then asked, 'Now what's this word?' indicates that the patient was trying to make the therapist explain 'things' to her. She next moved away to the doll's house and looked back at the therapist and stated, 'I'm going to the bathroom now. Okay?' She began walking toward the door, turned and said, 'I know why. It's because I drink too much water.' She then smiled at the therapist, shrugged her shoulders as if she was helpless to do anything about it, turned and walked out of the room.

In this segment of the session the patient continues with the theme of a third party in her treatment (her aunt's album). Her having a picture of herself added to her aunt's album might also be understood as an unconscious perception of the therapist's involvement with another party. That is, the patient might have been saying that the therapist did not really belong in the classroom talking to her teacher. It is important to note that the picture of 'the aunt' which the patient showed the therapist was selected after skimming over many pictures in an undecided fashion. The name the patient proposed for the picture she selected was not drawn from her known family history or from the page of the picture album and thus was a lie. As such, she may well have unconsciously perceived the therapist cancelling the session and reporting he was sick as a lie also. This was followed by her leaving therapy because she 'drank too much'.

Both the therapist's sense of confusion and feeling abandoned as the patient left the room may be seen as efforts on the patient's part to project on to the therapist her own sense of confusion about his absence and a mutual sense of abandonment along with an unconscious perception of his having been absent because *he* 'drank too much'. This latter perception is especially understandable given the patient's history of relationships to adults who abuse alcohol and drugs. It is likely that for this patient an adult's being 'sick' was and is very much connected to drug and/or alcohol abuse.

When the material is reviewed communicatively we see that the patient has already represented two major stimuli (adaptive contexts), the therapist's absence and his talking to the teacher, and a number of indicators (bringing something to therapy, talking in the hallway, sadness, dishonesty and leaving the session). These indicators can be seen as being in response both to the therapist's absence and his contact with her teacher. However, the patient has not provided, up to this point, sufficient derivatives which would guide the therapist in identifying the specific adaptive context to which she was primarily responding.

After approximately three minutes, the patient returned. She walked to the doll's house and picked up the little boy and the girl doll and stated, 'She's been hurt' (an image of someone having been injured). She next picked up the two white plastic dolls and said, 'This is going to be the hospital', and brought the dolls directly in front of the therapist. 'Let's pretend you're one of the people that work at the hospital', conveying an unconscious suggestion by the patient that the therapist should be helpful with the injured girl. She next picked up the boy doll and noted that he had been hurt too and then placed the children in the hospital. She put the girl in a toy wheelchair and brought the mother and father dolls into her play.

In this part of the session the patient introduces the theme of being injured or 'hurt' which may be readily connected to the therapist's cancelling the prior session. Thus, an emotional pain becomes represented as a derivative image reflected in a bodily injury which is not uncommon in my work with children. She next creates a pretend hospital and tells the therapist manifestly to work there, with the underlying suggestion that he, again, should be helpful. Indeed, as noted elsewhere, a patient's most common derivative reaction to errors on the part of the therapist often centres on *models of correction* or *rectification*. She next represents the boy as having overcome his injury (the therapist is, in fact, back at work) but the girl continues to be hurt.

After picking up the mother and father dolls, the patient stated, 'This (the ambulance) is their car. (Pause) No.' She then took the father doll to another table and said, 'He was working on the farm and ... got hurt ... died... He's dead now.' She brought the father and mother dolls next to the therapist and placed the mother, boy and girl dolls around the father doll and said, 'And they're all crying. (Pause.) Now they go home. Now they just stay in bed all day and cry because they're sad.'

The patient continues to describe a girl who is sad, which clearly supports the other previous indications of sadness and pain. In addition, she also portrays the father as dead (which introduces significant genetic material and perhaps a fantasy perception related to the therapist's absence). Indeed, for this child, given her developmental history and social background, there is clearly an understandable confusion on her part as to the absence of a male figure in her life. (As can be recalled, she was told earlier that her biological father was dead. She, in fact, was taken to his grave and then, at a later date, he showed up at her doorstep wanting to take custody.) Following this, the patient picked up the father and said, 'But he's not really dead, and he comes home' (again portraying, through play and displacement, an actual traumatic episode in her life) and she set the father doll in the doll's house. She next pulled all the furniture out of the dollhouse and set it on the table and placed the girl doll in the wheelchair in front of the therapist informing him that, 'She's watching TV.' She places the mother doll in the bathroom and then places the father doll into an empty room in the house stating, 'He's up there all by himself just getting drunk.... He's drunk.' (This final 'scene' portrays a powerful description of a girl's actual experience of being abandoned, confused, reunited and then abandoned again due to an adult's own self-absorbed pathology which was reawakened and recast in the therapy relationship.)

Again, unconscious encoding is adaptive and, as such, serves a number of self-protective functions. It is automatically brought about by emotionally charged, anxiety-evoking, internal and external situations, disturbing affects and/or threatening perceptions of oneself or others. It serves to ward off and conceal these experiences from consciousness while simultaneously permitting them a measure of representation and working over. Once encoded, these unconscious perceptions, fantasies, etc., do indeed gain expression in disguised forms of manifest communications and thus adaptively remain outside of the awareness of the patient. Moreover, given that the basis of emotional disturbance is composed of critical, unconscious perceptions, introjects, fantasies, conflicts, self-images and memories *which are outside of the patient's awareness*, it is only through unconscious or *derivative* communication that a patient is able to communicate about these issues. In work with young children, it is crucial to understand that their *play often serves as concrete representations of unconscious processes and derivative communication.*

At this point the patient has already represented the three categories needed for an interpretation - an adaptive context or stimulus (a direct allusion to the therapist's absence), indicators (sadness, leaving the room, being hurt) and derivative perceptions of the therapist as also having been hurt or dead. In this last segment, these themes become richer. Her removal of the furniture from the doll's house is representative of things being out of place and messed up, which may well have been how she felt in response to both the therapist's absence and his talking with her teacher. Further, she also portrays the father as 'drunk', which may well have been her fantasy perception of the therapist's absence, as stated earlier, which brings into play additional genetic material. However, rather than being disturbed by the continued silence of the therapist, the patient continues to communicate meaningfully, and her images become richer.

The patient then brought the mother doll over to the children, picked up the boy doll, placed him in the mother's arms and stated, 'He wants to be held.' She picked up the father doll, 'He's going to come watch TV with her (the girl). She doesn't know he's alive. She thinks he's a ghost. No, he's not a ghost.' He sits down to watch TV with her and the boy, and the mother comes over. (Pause.) 'Now, they're all together.' She then picked up the boy doll, placed the mother away from the father and had the boy doll approach the mother and said, 'She asked if she could play outside.' The mother doll says, 'Well, okay.' The patient looked at the therapist directly and said, 'She's talking to him!' She then picked up what was an obvious kitchen sink, held it up and asked, 'Is this for the kitchen or the bathroom?'

In this segment the patient introduces a need for support and nurturing by placing a child in a mother's arms, which is the first clear indication on the patient's part of a wish for intervention. She then describes the father as a ghost. This may well allude to her having seen the therapist in the halls of the school the previous week and also connects to her earlier traumatic experience of having her biological father, who she believed was dead, show up at her door. The child's confusion in her play about asking her parents for permission to play may also be seen as a veiled representation of her confusion about who in the school is, in fact, in charge of her therapy - the teacher or the therapist. Finally, she brings the therapist directly into the session by asking him a direct question. It was at that point, approximately 30 minutes into the session, that the therapist intervened.

The therapist stated, 'You are unsure about something and also seem to feel very sad today. In the hallway you asked how I was, which is a concern since I was sick last week and you missed your session. You've also talked about the little girl here who was hurt and injured and then very sad, and then she thought her father was dead. Then he wasn't dead but was drunk, then together with the family, and then lazy. I think my being gone last week made you feel and think of a lot of things - like perhaps I was not here because I had died which was very sad or that maybe I was drunk which made you mad.'

The patient stated softly, 'No. I didn't think you were drunk.' The therapist continued, 'And that I was lazy like the father here who wouldn't do his work.' The patient stated softly, 'No.' 'At the same time what you want is for us to be together like the happy family watching TV, and you brought a picture of your aunt and of yourself because you wanted me to know more about you.'

The above intervention attended directly to the therapist's cancellation of the previous session as the primary adaptive context or stimulus. It includes the patient's indicators of sadness and confusion as well as her encoded, unconscious perceptions and fantasies (encoded derivatives) in response to the therapist's absence. However, no mention by the therapist was made of the third party issues and the patient's indicators which were a response to these issues (talking in the hallway, bringing in her aunt's album). Although the therapist alluded to her bringing in her aunt's album, he failed at the time to understand the meaning of this which is clearly reflected at the end of the intervention. The intervention also has specific technical difficulties in that the therapist began with the patient's indicators rather than using the adaptive context (stimulus) as a starting point to explain her indicators of sadness and confusion.

It is crucial to understand that interpretations must be explanations, and, although not technically perfect, this interpretation does, in fact, offer a sufficient explanation to the patient of her indicators, unconscious perceptions and fantasies, which were in response to the context (stimulus). If correct, we would expect that the patient's response would portray some level of validation of the intervention. As explained in the introduction to the book, an interpretation is considered valid only when the patient's immediately ensuing associations (including the child's play) convey derivative *cognitive validation*, *interactional validation* and some measure of *conscious insight*.

The patient responded, 'Now, they move back into the house.' (She began placing the furniture back into its original place inside the doll's house.) 'I used to have toys like this when I was five. (Pause.) But I don't now. This is a good school. It's good for me.' (She completed placing the furniture back into the doll's house.)

The patient's first response involves a portrayal of something having been corrected (things being placed back into their correct places). This is followed by the introduction of new material related to another loss in her life. This fresh extension of the theme of loss implies a degree of derivative *cognitive validation* by the patient of the interpretation. The patient goes on to state that, 'This is a good school. It's good for me.' Her response, which alludes to a helpful setting, represents a measure of interactional validation. This is strongly supported by her replacing the furniture in the doll's house, which portrays a corrective action on her part and which can be seen as an introjection of the positive functioning of the therapist. Further, the patient became much more animated and less depressed which signals a *decrease or improvement in her depressive symptomatology* (indicators).

However, the patient then continued, 'We need markers. I know what we'll do.' (She picked up two sheets of paper.) 'We're going to make sticker books today. (Pause.) Here's yours. And this one's mine.' (She placed hers on the easel a distance from the therapist).

The fact that the patient did not continue to expand upon the previous themes or to show any additional measure of cognitive insight might be seen as a direct response to the errors in the interpretation. Indeed, the patient suggests on one level a need for specific boundaries which might be understood as her response to the therapist's misinterpreting her bringing the picture album to the session. She might be saying that there should be specific boundaries which should be maintained to insure a healthy separateness which stands in contrast to the implications of togetherness which the final part of the therapist's interpretation contained. It is also important to note that a patient's most common reactions to the therapist's errors consist of encoded correctives of the errors which we call models of rectification.

Overall, however, the patient's response conveyed a clear validation of the therapist's intervention. It is very clear, through her representation of something being good for her as well as a reduction of her symptoms and the image of things being put back into place, that the patient was eventually able to relax and begin to engage in a new direction which offered to the therapist and the patient a new understanding of her own unconscious processes. This, indeed, is the hallmark of communicative psychotherapy.

The communicative approach recognizes and elaborates the findings that human beings are adaptive organisms. Furthermore, they possess the unique capacity to communicate simultaneously on two distinct levels. There is the manifest or conscious communication which is singular in meaning, logical and reality-oriented. Such communication is governed by laws comparable to secondary process thinking and serves a basically utilitarian purpose. The sender of such messages communicates only that which is consciously intended and essentially nothing more except for implications which relate to the direct message (i.e. there is a relative absence of encoded meaning). The receiver of the communication should be able to directly comprehend the message intended by the sender within the specific surface context in which the exchange took place. While this type of logical, single-meaning communication well serves direct adaptation, it tends to be somewhat deficient as a response to emotionally charged stimuli. Further, as can be seen in the patient's initial presentation in which she brings a picture album and questions the therapist about how he is doing, there is little evidence of such easily understood direct communication.

In contrast, unconscious or derivative (encoded) communication proves to be highly serviceable for adaptation to emotional issues. It is an exciting, provocative means of expression which is rich in texture in creating meaning. This mode reflects the unique human capacity to communicate a surface, conscious or manifest message which simultaneously serves as a disguised vehicle for one or more underlying, unconscious messages. That is, a surface message offered in one context conveys a second, related message whose meaning pertains to a different (latent) context.

This capacity to communicate on two distinct levels at the same time - consciously and unconsciously - proves to be adaptive in that it provides a means of encoding or camouflaging psychologically disturbing perceptions, fantasies, conflicts, etc., and facilitates their working over in a relatively anxiety-free fashion outside of awareness. Such communication is under the influence of rules comparable to primary process thinking which is not governed by reality and logic as is the secondary process thinking described above.

It is, again, extremely important to understand that there is also no such thing as a 'perfect intervention' and that all of our interventions are approximations toward the ideal. Patients are also able to unconsciously perceive our honest efforts in trying to reach the ideal and will show an appreciation for such functioning by the therapist. It is, then, in response to relatively good or 'good enough' interventions on the part of the therapist that the child will, as can be seen in the session above, clearly move towards a reduction in symptoms and toward overall better functioning.

Further, when this communicative-adaptive process fails, the patient is propelled towards other means of coping. This may take the form of action and efforts at discharge in which meaning is, in fact, destroyed. Often there is also the development of an increase in psychopathological symptoms rather than a reduction of such symptoms. Such symptoms can be seen as derivative expressions representative of the encoded perceptions and fantasies including instinctual drive wishes, super-ego response and the ego's defensive reactions. Nonetheless, such symptomatic responses do not reveal their own unconscious meaning and often stem from failures of derivative expression and understanding on the part of the therapist. It must be stressed again that the move from non-derivative to derivative communication takes place automatically in the patient. It is always a response to an adaptation-evoking context or adaptive context emanating from external reality and the patient's object relationships.

The clarity of the above material portrays an adaptive context of the therapist missing a session which consistently, throughout the patient materials, relates to the entirety of the patient's early disturbed object relationships. Thus, it is absolutely essential to begin to decode the patient's derivative communications by clearly recognizing and understanding the specific adaptation-evoking stimulus or adaptive contexts which have summoned up the specific unconscious communicative responses on the part of the patient. Again, when such work is done relatively well, there is clearly a pathway open for unravelling the confused and often terrifying unconscious memories, conflicts and introjects which contribute to a child's current symptoms and difficulties in living.

The above material also portrays the capacity of a child to communicate, in a clear and concise manner, through play and verbal derivative expressions, all of the material needed for a therapist to intervene with interpretations with the communicative approach to psychoanalysis. The material additionally portrays the need for a quiet and containing function on the part of the therapist as well as the need for the therapist to limit his interventions to interpretations as the basic intervention of psychoanalytic work. Finally, this session invites the reader to view the clarity of the child's communication and to experience the excitement which one can experience when attending to a child's unconscious processes.

While the above clinical material may be seen as a 'wonderful fit' with the specific approach presented in this book, it is the author's contention (based on almost 20 years' experience in working with children using this approach) that there is more here than a 'good fit'. Rather, experience with a wide range of ages, races and cultural backgrounds portrays that child patients are extremely sensitive to the conditions of the therapeutic framework which they are invited to participate in. Indeed, the type and quality of the 'invitation' they receive and each subsequent intervention on the part of the therapist in managing the treatment will determine the degree to which the child will feel safe and invest in the ownership of the therapy experience.

Chapter 16
The bell rings

(translated from German)

INGE BERNS

The patient is a five-year-old white German boy who was brought to me for psychotherapy by his parents, both middle-class white Germans, because of his aggression. He was hitting his brother and the children in kindergarten and shouting at his parents. He began treatment with me twice a week while his parents were seen every other week, as is common practice in Germany. His treatment was arranged to be terminated after nine months because the family was planning to move to another city. I shall discuss Sessions 45 and 46 which took place six weeks before the agreed termination. His parents paid my fee directly because they didn't want to take up their medical insurance for this treatment. Although they could have claimed the reimbursement of the costs by the state insurance, his parents didn't want to have a third party involved in their son's treatment.

I, the therapist, am a middle-aged white German woman in private practice with children and youth, working according to the communicative approach of psychoanalysis, founded by Robert Langs. My office is on the ground floor of an apartment house, which is common arrangement in Germany. Patients use a separate entrance and are thus separated from the residents of the building. This same entrance is also used by me and a professional colleague. The two therapy rooms are not absolutely soundproof and there is no waiting room. If patients arrive early for their sessions they are let into their therapy room to wait until the appointed time while their therapist remains in her office. Usually, there is enough time between the sessions so that the patients do not meet each other.

Summary of Session 44

The patient arrives with his mother, who also brought along the patient's younger brother. While the patient was still busy hanging up his coat in the wardrobe, his brother let go of his mother's hand and ran into the therapy room. Since the mother did not catch the patient's brother I asked her to do so. She did, and the two left. The patient started playing a game in a toy city where a robber first wreaked havoc but was eventually driven away out of town. The townsfolk then celebrated their success with a party by asking the sheriff to fulfil increasingly grotesque tasks. In the end, there was absolute chaos. The patient lost interest in this game, left the toys on the floor and walked around the room. He found the toy robber whom he had thrown away earlier. He picked it up, brought it to me and told me a story about the interesting experiences that the robber had while on his own. The patient said that the robber had exciting experiences which made him stronger.

At this point, I intervened. I told him that driving away the robber was like driving his brother out of the therapy room before the session. I said that my unnecessarily harsh demand that his mother caught his brother triggered at first a chaotic reaction involving triumph, arrogance and exaggeration, but then led to his telling me a story about the positive way the robber went away on his own. Just before the end of the session I suggested that we follow his story and do what the characters in his play did. I proposed that the next time he comes to session, he says good-bye to whoever brings him at the gate and that he walks by himself from the gate, along the corridor and into the therapy room. The patient validated unconsciously my proposal by making his own proposal: that both of us tidy up and put away the toys we had used in the play. When his mother came to pick him up after the session we informed her about his decision - and she agreed.

Session 45

The patient walked alone the few steps from the gate to the door of the therapy room. He came a little early. I asked him to wait in the therapy room until it was time for our session. I went into my office and closed the door. After a few minutes I re-entered the therapy room on time for the session.

I found the patient sitting in his chair holding two teddy bears. I sat down in my chair across from him with a table in between, as always. He gave one bear to me. He made his bear growl and make threatening gestures at my bear. I remained still and did not say anything. The patient ordered, 'You must fight! They will fight now, and my bear will win!' So it happened - I let my bear be defeated by his bear without fighting. The patient was not satis-fied and said, 'That's wrong. You really have to fight, otherwise it's no fun.' I continued to hold my bear still while his bear fought my bear. The patient swore at my bear and used several offensive words. The patient looked at me and said, 'He is too slow, he should become a wild beast.' Again, I did not follow his instructions and held my bear still.

When the patient repeatedly tried to overturn my bear I held it firmly and did not let it fall over. 'Give me your bear and watch me!' said the patient, and showed me how to do it. He took my bear and made both bears attack, insult and offend each other. He described the severe wounds they inflicted upon each other while fighting. At last, both bears were lying on the floor, seriously wounded. 'They cannot fight any more,' he said, 'they have to be operated on and bandaged.' He brought a toy doctor's case and gave it to me.

At this point I did engage in his play and I cared for the bears with bandages and dressings. The patient brought more animals which suffered the same fate as the bears. After the fight he brought them over to me for medical care. He repeated the same play with increasing speed several times. While fighting he made one animal shout at another, 'Get out of your hole, get out right now, or I will get really angry!'

As we saw at the beginning of this session, the patient did carry out the decision he made in his previous session to walk the short distance from the gate to the therapy room by himself. Having done so, he corrected the psychotherapy frame on his own accord (Bonac 1998). Then he was left to spend a few minutes in the therapy room alone. When I re-entered the room he was holding the two teddy bears and began to play immediately. The play that followed appears to represent the state of our relationship at the time: his play seems to convey that we were in a situation of repeated fighting and repeated demands and that I, too, was engaged in the fighting. How did this situation arise? Did I do anything the patient might have experienced as an invitation to fight? During the session I tried to find the trigger for the patient's behaviour by recalling the events that preceded this session. During the session I thought that he might have reacted to my having left him waiting alone for the beginning of the session by feeling hurt and turned down. His aggressive play appeared to have been in response to an insult.

I believe that it is possible that, for the patient, the session started at the moment he entered the therapy room even though he was there a little before his set time. It appears that he was not waiting for the beginning of the session, he waited for me. His entering the consultation room might have indicated to him that the session had begun. Although waiting in the therapy room is indeed familiar to this patient, it is nevertheless an ambiguous sign. I was not aware of this possible meaning during the session. I was only vaguely aware of some implications of waiting in the therapy room. I felt uncomfortable because I sensed that this situation was not good for my patients, yet I had done nothing to change it. At that moment in the session, however, I was blind to having been careless. I know now that it was much easier for me to believe that the patient reacted in a pathological manner to an appropriate intervention than to realize that he might have reacted realistically to my inappropriate arrangement. Even though I did not think that a five-year-old boy could read the clock on the wall of the therapy room, the patient knew that he was too early, because I tell all patients as I let them in that I will come back on time for their session.

In principle, the patient might have reacted to both implications of the waiting as is evident from his play fight with the bears. In the session the patient repeated the fight many times. It is possible that he perceived me as someone who not only provoked a fight with him by expecting him to wait for me but also that he provoked a fight with me in reaction to feeling hurt by me. His instructions to me clearly showed what his reaction to such a provocation looks like. Now I understand the story about the bears as well as the patient's instructions for fighting as a derivative portrayal of the conflict which was triggered by my intervention. I had attacked his sense of dignity. I believe that my intervention triggered in the patient symptoms which were expressed in the themes of his play: the bear became a wild beast, he suffered abuses and insults and it all led to serious injury.

When the patient took the doctor's case and asked for medical care I understood his play as a request for therapeutic help. In order to formulate an understandable and effective interpretation the following type of the patient's material is needed: (a) an indicator, (b) a derivative complex and (c) a manifest, direct mention of the adaptive context which had triggered the patient's response (Langs 1992b). An indicator tells us that there is something in the patient which is in need of cure. It can come in the form of a symptom or a resistance. In this part of his material several symptoms were observed, as described above. A derivative complex demonstrates the unconscious personal importance to the patient of what happened, how the patient unconsciously evaluates this perception and how he reacts to this evaluation. In this case, the derivative complex came in the form of a story about the repeated fighting of the two bears. Up to this point in the session the patient had not yet mentioned the adaptive context manifestly. Because he did not say it, I did not know what exactly I had done to provoke his intense reaction. While he was asking me to act therapeutically, all I understood at the time was that I was involved in a fighting situation with him and that I must have done something that he perceived as a provocation to this fight for power and victory.

In such a clinical situation the communicative theory of therapeutic technique proposes that the therapist intervenes with a type of intervention called the play-back of derivatives, which enables the patient to mention consciously the triggering event on his or her own. The patient would thus be shown a path towards his or her own identification of a link of his or her themes to the corresponding themes and symptoms in the session. In this session, the play-back of derivatives might have been formulated like this: 'You are playing a game with me. You see us as two opponents who fight a fierce battle, so strong that we both become very wild and that we hurt each other. Something must have happened here that made you feel that you need to fight this battle against me.'

This was not my actual intervention. When the patient passed me the doctor's case he seemed to be quite sure that I would be able to act therapeutically. It is possible that my being relatively passive during the whole sequence, i.e. the limitation of my activity to simply carry out his orders and to not take over the role of fighting made him believe that I would be able to act therapeutically.

I think that playing in child psychotherapy often offers a good possibility for active communication not only by the child but also by the therapist, and that certain technical recommendations can be derived from such play. For instance, while I was caring for the injured bears it seemed to me that the patient communicated a play-back of derivatives on his own by repeating the same theme. This repetition seems to have led the patient to changing his play. Suddenly he exclaimed, 'Get out of your hole, or I will get really angry!' The emergence of this image in his material made me realize that I was the one in the hole. I suddenly understood that while he was waiting for me before his session began I was sitting in my 'office-hole', and this made him angry.

According to the communicative psychoanalytic theory of technique the material in the session was now complete to form an interpretation since it contained all the necessary information and I intervened as follows.

'When you arrived today you were a little too early, and I let you wait. You might have thought I intended to fight with you about time and you felt angry like the bear who said, "Come out or I will get mad!" So you might have thought: if someone wants a fight, you, too, must fight and you have to win, just like the two bears who fought each other, and each wanted to win. So you thought I had wanted to hit you and you reacted by deciding to hit me. But when I didn't fight you might have become uncertain and tried to convince me by showing me how to fight. You found out that such a battle ends up in seriously wounded bears who then need help. You seemed to think that someone like me, who could manage not to fight, is the right person to be of help in situations like this.'

This intervention started with my mentioning the event which was obviously emotionally important to the patient and was followed by his symptomatic actions. From the very beginning of this session it was clear that the patient and I were in a fight situation, and that he was determined to fight to the end and be victorious. The fighting situation in the session is typical of his life outside, and it was to help him with this symptom that the patient was first brought to therapy.

The communicative psychoanalytic theory explains that symptoms are a reaction to an interpersonal situation. They are a communicative act which becomes understandable by identifying the real implications of a concrete intervention which is perceived correctly, albeit unconsciously, by the patient because of a specific psychic importance. This importance is the basis for the patient's specific reactions. This boy's symptomatic reaction in this situation was exactly the same symptom that had brought him to therapy. So here we have an opportunity to see a trigger activating the communication of unconscious meaning and a symptomatic reaction to this trigger, all as an unconscious attempt by the patient to master this conflict. We also observe the opportunity to offer to the patient a conscious recognition of his unconsciously communicated meaning.

The trigger which I identified was my intervention to let him wait. According to our initial time arrangement, my handling of the situation was correct. However, what was not correct was to invite him into the consultation room and to ask him to wait there. The patient reacted to my letting him in and then leaving him alone as one reacts to an insult. It is difficult to say whether he reacted to the correct or to the incorrect implication of my intervention, or to both. My actual interpretation only mentioned the correct side of the intervention as the trigger for his reaction. I did not mention the incorrect arrangement as this was not conscious to me at the time. Depending on which trigger the patient had reacted to he will either validate or invalidate this part of my interpretation.

In my interpretation I offered my understanding of him as someone who reacted by feeling hurt or degraded when he was asked to wait for me, and also as someone who regularly reacts to such offence by fighting and wanting to be victorious. I understood his attacks and insults merely as his intention to force me into fighting and as a symptomatic expression of his irritation because I did not fight. Possibly there were other underlying contents, and because of many relevant experiences in his life, the patient might expect that someone whom he attacks in this way will respond by fighting back. My interpretation did not take this issue into consideration. Therefore, I would expect the patient to express this lack of my consideration unconsciously, since this seems to be the patient's deep unconscious belief. His attempt in the session to teach me how to fight back could very well be yet another expression of this belief. Although my interpretation did mention these issues it did not consider their specific deep unconscious importance to the patient. My interpretation also mentioned his knowledge that fights like this lead to serious injury. Since I only touched on this topic accidentally, as he did in his play, it is possible that I did not consider fully the emotional importance of this knowledge to the patient and that he might react to my omission on the unconscious level.

I attach a lot of importance to the patient's repeated demands on the therapist and the source for his demands, i.e. my intervention to not take part in the fight. Doing so, I volunteered as a competent assistant not as a combatant. Not only did I not react to an offence with fighting back, I helped with healing the wounds resulting from his fighting.

Thus, I predict a validating response to my interpretation by the patient because I took his material as the basis for making the connections of meaning. Since his material portrays the theme of a clear offer to help, I am not overly concerned with his unconscious beliefs and with his knowledge about serious consequences of fighting as I was already represented as having been competent by not accepting his offer to fight. Therefore, instead of a non-validation of my intervention I expect to get further material from the patient.

In the session, while I was speaking, the patent was looking at the two bears, touching each of them kindly with one hand. He seems to be pensive, sitting in his chair. He then pushes the bandaged bears into the corner of the table, saying, 'They have to stay in hospital for some days.' He then went to the 'toy shop' and proclaimed it open by banging two glasses against each other which sounded just like fine bells. He shouted, 'The shop is now open, you have to come in and buy things!' Since nothing happened, he added, 'This is just a play, it is part of the play that you follow my orders.'

I think that something important happened when the patient stopped play fighting while I was still speaking and, instead, started to handle gently the two bears. I think that we can easily observe how the patient spontaneously gave up his symptomatic behaviour of fighting and began to manifest the beginning of a new behaviour portrayed by the image of a principally good relationship (gentle handling of the bears) as a validation of my interpretation. Stroking is an act expressing a loving, caring, mothering relationship. This attribute appears to have been inherent in my interpretation as well as in my acting as a play doctor. The patient expressed an *interpersonal validation* of my interpretation. Stroking both bears simultaneously in the same way could also be a hint by the patient to me that giving up of his symptoms could happen in his outside world if he and his brother were to be treated equally by loving, caring, motherly people, most importantly by their mother and their father. If this meaning was in fact part of the patient's play it would represent a cognitive validation of the same interpretation.

When he became pensive and restful one could see that he was occupied with thinking about something that still needed to be dealt with. The same psychic contents were expressed in his play order: the animals had to stay in hospital for several days, which meant that they needed further healing. In the session, it meant that my interpretation did not take into account all the relevant issues, perhaps his unconscious belief and his unconscious knowledge about the consequences of his everyday symptomatic behaviour.

When the patient began with a new play, with the play shop, he portrayed a different quality of a relationship. Instead of fighting, he introduced characters who accepted professional (commercial), balanced roles which benefited both sides. He took the time to arrange the shop in such a way that he gave a concrete expression to his unconscious ideas. And this is what I was doing while he was waiting for me alone in the consultation room before the beginning of the session: I was preparing myself for my task and I entered the consultation room on time. It is possible that he was saying, with his play, that my letting him wait before the session was an act of helping him in a professional manner.

At the same time, it might also have been a derivative of a hint for me to rectify something that was still wrong in his therapy. It might be that the patient was saying that psychotherapy must be done in a careful manner. When he made the 'bell ring' by striking together the glasses he gave a clear sign that he was announcing the beginning of new play. He might have been telling me that I ought to make a clear announcement of the beginning of his session by ringing a bell. This same message seems to have been even clearer when, after my passive waiting in the session, the patient said that this will be 'just a play' and that the rule will be that I follow his orders. He seemed to be saying that one must obey certain rules in order to be able to play in therapy. The theme the patient continued to work over was the same as before: preparing for and then beginning a joint venture which is psychotherapy. Although his carefulness about preparing the place could very well have been a hint for me to be as careful as he was in setting up the room, I was not aware of this issue during the session. Then, I understood his careful preparations as a confirmation of my own carefulness regarding the punctual beginning of the session. During the session, I understood his clinking of the glasses as his way of saying that a principally correct action of mine (i.e. of having been careful) was the trigger for his symptomatic reaction. I am wondering now why the sequence of the themes in the patient's play did not call to my attention a much more puzzling meaning during the session. I am now convinced that the patient reacted to both implications of my intervention: first, to my not making a clear distinction between meeting him before his session and the beginning of his session at the appointed time and, second, to my decision to let him wait before the session in the consultation room.

It is possible that he wanted to convey to me not only that my letting him wait was a proper thing to do. His play might also have carried a simultaneous derivative meaning of a call for rectification of the arrangement of my office. He might have been saying that it is necessary to be very careful when arranging the layout of a therapy office. When he clinked the two glasses, giving a clear sign for the beginning of a new play, he might have expressed his conviction that the beginning of his therapy session must be announced by the ringing of a bell. This same message seems to be even clearer when, after my passive waiting, he said that this will be just a play, and that the rule will be that I follow his orders.

It appears that the issue the patient was working over was the same as before: preparing for the beginning of a joint venture. Although his carefulness in preparing the place of his play is very likely a hint for me that I ought to be careful preparing my therapy room, I did not consider this issue during the session. Instead, I took his actions of careful preparations as a confirmation of my own carefulness regarding the punctual beginning of his session. His clinking of the glasses made me more 'certain' that a principally correct action of mine served as the trigger for his symptomatic reaction. In retrospect, it seems extraordinary that I was not even puzzled by his play during the session. I think now that he reacted to both implications of my intervention. The patient needed my help to make it clear to him on the conscious level what my rules were regarding his starting of play as psychotherapy as opposed to his play as waiting for his session to begin. When I intervened in the session I did so spontaneously, without giving proper consideration to his unconscious material.

I understood his sudden giving up of the fight and his beginning to gently stroke the teddy bears as an interpersonal validation of that, which did not require an intervention in the form of an explanation. In the session, I felt pleased and reacted by smiling, as did the patient. In principle, all of the patient's material that followed represents the basis on which to formulate an interpretation. The trigger for the patient's response was my offer to help him, which was not helpful by itself. Therefore, he further attempted to get help from me with the same issue: how can he respond clearly when he feels he is being treated arbitrarily? 'It is part of the play that you follow my orders' is a very good portrayal of his unconscious dilemma: if I never question the precondition, he is forever left at my mercy. The first is a derivative, the latter is a symptom. If I use his material to formulate an interpretation it would run as follows.

'When I offered you my help you took great care to arrange things in your shop. Perhaps you wanted to show me that in order to work properly one must first prepare everything very carefully. With your careful preparations in the store you also gave me a clear sign for the beginning of an activity. Doing so you might have pointed out to me that I did not make careful preparations and that I had treated you badly when I made you wait in the consulting room. At the same time, you might have shown me how to announce the beginning of an activity. You told me to follow your rule. But since you asked me what to do about being treated arbitrarily I will now show you that I will not let myself be pushed around by you.'

In the session, what I actually said, as if to myself, was this, 'Ah, the little boy as salesman seems to be trying to achieve what he couldn't achieve as a little boy, that is, to force me to do what he thinks people must do to one another: he wants me to force him. But he also had shown me that he expects my help with the wounds arising from such fights. So, I will show him that I do not allow myself to be pushed around by him.'

My above intervention neglects the depiction of the unconscious interpersonal and intrapsychic emotional processing of the patient. Instead, I concentrated on his symptoms and on what I assumed was his anticipation of my actions. I believed that he wanted unconsciously to provoke a new adaptive context: that he expected me to intervene in a specific way which might help him to overcome his symptomatic reactions. To find out whether my intervention was helpful to the patient depends on whether I had recognized correctly the adaptive context and on whether the patient 'knew' the missing parts of a complete interpretation. I think that the intervention was correct in principle. In his play, the patient formulates a clear demand. The situation in his therapy was one he often experiences in his everyday life, with which he needs help to handle. All of the components necessary for an interpretation have been given. I think that waiting any longer in silence would have increased the interpersonal pressure, this time due to my behaviour.

In the session, the patient was listening very attentively and spoke with his usual tone of voice, 'Today my shop is open until 8 o'clock.' He then sat down on a little chair in the shop and waited.

His interest indicates to me that the intervention was suitable. He responds by giving up the interpersonal pressure. By speaking in his usual tone of voice, he offers a relaxed atmosphere. His communication about the opening time gives a certain sense of space at one's disposal. Simultaneously, it could be a hint about termination of the therapy session which I did not see at this time. The mention of a full hour (8 o'clock) could allude to our appointments which start on the hour. He appears to be waiting for me until I am ready. It is clear that, at this moment, waiting is not experienced by the patient as something done to him with impertinence. Therefore, my intervention had a curative effect on the patient's symptom of aggression. The image and the atmosphere point to a positive introjection.

In the session, I proceed with getting a knapsack and toy money and I start walking towards the salesman. I walk the length the room talking to myself, listing what I will buy. I then enter the shop, saying 'Hello' to the salesman-patient.

Here, I accepted his offer to take part in the play. This I understand as a demonstration of my sense of an equal relationship between the two of us. My walking in the room means that I have accepted the patient's implicit offer to wait for me. His response will show whether my suppositions and my interventions were correct.

The patient then greets me, saying, 'It began to rain outside, so I built a roof above my entrance (gesturing accordingly) in order to keep you and me dry in my shop.'

I understand his welcoming me by conveying to me the wonderful imagery of a protective roof for both of us as his expression of having created an island of well being for us, being close together while round us there are still hurtful circumstances. We have 'brought our sheep into the dry' - as the German proverb says. We have created a therapeutic situation for being together in this way.

With this in mind, I decided to go on playing with him. I buy things, he advertises special offers, enters the prices into his cash register, weighs things and wraps them up. Then, suddenly, the bell rings. We jerk, both startled and irritated. I look at the watch: there are still five minutes left of his session. The patient jumps up from his seat, runs to the door and opens it, no doubt expecting his father, who usually rings the bell to inform us that he is ready to pick him up. After opening the door the patient finds two unknown children and a man standing there. The patient runs back to his seat and sits down immediately, holding on to his chair. I tell the people to wait and I close the door, leaving them in the hall.

In this segment of the session, we both enjoyed the play, which was marked by mutual respect and reciprocal usefulness, by appropriate exchange of service and payment. The bell intruded directly into this atmosphere, and we both reacted with irritation. Although the patient did not yet know how to read the clock, I knew that he had a good feeling for the passing of time. His spontaneous running and opening of the door was, I think, an automatic admission that his father was a more competent judge of time. I must add that his father deserved this attribute since he had never before rung the bell before the end of the session. Younger children are usually brought to and picked up from their sessions by adults. The task to finish the session and to say good-bye to the child patient in principle belongs to the therapist. It is also the therapist's responsibility that younger children, who cannot walk home on their own, are given back to the accompanying adult who is responsible for them. In the treatment of this patient there had not been any difficulties until this moment. I finished the session on time and the parents picked up the patient on time. Usually, he would just be putting on his jacket when the bell would ring. This would be the sign for the patient that his parents have arrived to pick him up. He would then walk the small distance from my door to the entrance of the house on his own and greet them there. I stayed close to make sure that the child was picked up by the right people. The button for the electric door opener, which was located in the consultation room, might be a disturbing modification of the therapy frame and this arrangement is my responsibility. The child patient would press this button to let the parents in when they came to pick him up. (I have since moved the button for the door opener into my office. I now tell the parents at the time of our first meeting that I will be sending their children out on time and that I will make sure that the parents have arrived before I allow their children to go out.)

In this case, the patient pressed the button and found strange people standing at the door. As he immediately went back to his seat, he conveyed to me the meaning that he was sure that this was his rightful place at this moment.

In the session, the patient goes on and asks, 'How much time is left?' I tell him that the people ringing the bell were mistaken regarding the time, that my arrangement with them was for them to come later. The bell rings again: this is now his father who has come on time. The patient jumps up from behind his desk, pulls down his coat from the wardrobe in a hurry, leaves all doors open and runs out of the building.

The patient's question about the time showed his consciously registered uncertainty, with which he addresses me. My answer was to the manifest meaning of his question. I assured him that he was right, that this was his place at that moment. This explanation was given nearly at (or perhaps just after) the true end of session which was now indeed announced by his father ringing the bell. This meant that it was not I who ended the session - very likely a further disturbing modification of the therapy frame. The patient's hasty escape from the room and past the intruders, might be understood as his symptomatic reaction to the situation which had triggered it.

Session 46

The patient arrives just in time, carrying a little glass cup for the toy shop. He goes to the toy shop straight away, puts the cup with the other things in the store and tells me he has brought raisins, especially for goblins. He says that I can come immediately and buy some and give them to the goblin.

I understand his bringing of the glass cup as a reparation for damage done. In Session 39, the patient had played in the toy shop, too, one glass broke when he struck two of them together to give me the sign of the opening of the shop. During the same session, he announced that he intended to replace the cup. Since then, he had made the same promise several times. Whenever he played in the shop he noticed that he had not yet carried out his intention. He became angry and vowed to remember. At the time, I understood this as a mild conflict, did not take it up as a serious symptom and did not interpret it. I regarded his intention as appropriate and relied on him carrying it out some time in the future. I thought that interfering in any way by commenting on it might be superfluous, perhaps even hurtful to him, as it might have interfered with his struggle for self-regulation and independence.

In this session, the patient carried the glass, swinging it in the air. Bringing it in at this moment deserves special attention. Breaking it might have been a mild symptomatic act, however, as such things happened to the patient every day. At that time he had wanted me to play in a way he prescribed just as he did in the last session, but he had anticipated that I would not do so. He had tried to force me by making special emphasis and thus had struck the glasses together too strongly so that one broke. In the session I had intervened, and afterwards he had intended to replace the glass. As the broken pieces of glass might have hurt him I had considered removing all glasses from the toy shop. But, as I saw how carefully he treated the broken glass and since I did not recognize any hints for rectification in his communications I did not change anything, and he continued to use glasses to 'ring the bell'. His honest intention to compensate for the broken glass had been evident to me. Nevertheless he had not carried it out. When he was playing in the shop he would remember, say he was sorry about it and would again vow to repair the damage. I had assumed that this was a test for me from him to see whether I would hold interpersonal boundaries, or would I perhaps act pedagogically, reproachfully, claiming compensation, devaluating him with a sense of 'There is no use expecting you to repair what you broke.' I decided to wait and see what would happen to his intrapsychic contents concerning the broken glass.

It is interesting to note that he brought in a glass now, in precisely this situation, compensating for the damage he had done some time ago, just after the people rang the bell too early and did damage to us both in the session by using the very arrangement of the ringing of the bell that I had initially set up. I understand his action of bringing the glass as an assurance that the patient needs: now he has his own 'bell', for his own use, which he can ring when he decides and thus the ringing of others will no longer bother him. I think there is also the aspect of reparation in his bringing of the glass, which also means that he took responsibility for his action and thus obtained freedom from guilt. Doing so the patient corrected the frame of his therapy as he acted according to his conscious and unconscious convictions.

His good mood in the session affects me. I was initially worried about the events at the end of our last session. Now, I become less concerned, freer. I feel obliged to him and I enjoy his play. He sets up the toy shop, mentions that he has brought along raisins for goblins - and now I see that the little glass is indeed filled with raisins.

Bringing into the session things from outside the therapy room may be a derivative hint that we are dealing with something from outside. The raisins seem to sweeten the glass, they are contained in it, and as long as they are inside the 'bell' will not sound. The raisins in the glass seem to be an image representing the fact that the patient's concerns are contained by me (the glass is now my property, a replacement for the broken one, the raisins contained in it are, however, his property). This image might be a derivative hint that the patient is trying to convey to me the relationship between precious contents and fragile frame. In our therapeutic relationship, the glass represents the interpersonal frame as it is expressed by me with the arrangement of my office. The raisins might represent his psychic issues which are valuable and which had just started to emerge at the end of the last session before the bell rang.

The session continues with the patient taking a toy goblin from another part of the therapy room into the 'shop', something he had done often in previous sessions. The goblin is a little fur animal, one of the toys in the consultation room. It consists of a pointed head and a fur tail. Its shape is such that the observer is first frightened, on second look one becomes interested, and then the creature is eventually liked. This goblin had been discovered by the patient at the beginning of his therapy and he has often used it to represent himself as a troublemaker. It is now sitting in a corner of the shop. 'Goblin' is also a nickname for the patient his mother used in order to get along with the trouble-making part of his personality. By introducing a third 'person' into the scene he again might be hinting at the disturbance by a third party at the end of the last session.

I get up and go to buy things in the shop. I ask for some of 'the raisins for the goblin' and he tells me these are very special raisins, especially for goblins who like them very much. He tells me that the raisins are very good food for them to stay healthy. I buy some of them, pay for them and offer them to the goblin. 'I will do this for you, I'll give the raisins to him', he says and feeds the goblin in such a way that all the raisins find their way into his own mouth. The patient rubs his tummy and makes contented sounds.

The cheerful start of this session, after the previous one had ended with the patient's fright and escape, demonstrates an interesting phenomenon which can be witnessed occasionally when the therapist loses her balance and is not able to do her therapeutic work adequately. On such occasions, the patients often take on the task, to act helpfully, thus taking care of their therapists to enable them to recover their professional skills. Such an event seemed to have happened in this part of the session. Suddenly, a confused relationship emerges, it is not quite clear who has what role. The patient is also the goblin, he feeds the raisins I bought and they disappear into his own belly instead of the goblin's. This play seems to be an especially contrary portrayal of our momentary situation in derivative form. In this roundabout way the patient enables me to do good things for him. He is very successful in this. His behaviour enables me to give up all my background considerations completely and to feel contented in his presence. He, too, is obviously fine. I am free of thoughts which had tormented me. I am affected by him, perhaps relieved or grateful, in any case I feel obliged.

Half an hour into the session, the patient suddenly asks, 'How much time is left? Will there be other children coming to you when I leave?'

Asking this question, which momentarily disturbs my contented mood, he carries us back into the previous session. The patient thus manifestly points out that the adaptive context which arose in the last session (i.e. the physical arrangement of my practice which does not prevent somebody from intruding into the session) is still active. He brings up this issue in a way that enables us to work it over now, something that was not possible in the last session. His sudden remark strikes me like a thunderbolt, just like the unexpected ringing of the bell in the previous session.

I do not answer at once, and he says, 'The newspaper says there is a thunderstorm and a gale coming up, and there will be snowflakes as big as snowballs. All of this is written in this newspaper here which has just been delivered to my shop. I will bring it to you.' Saying this he has scribbled dots and lines on a sheet of paper, and now he delivers this 'newspaper' to 'my house'.

My short silence is foremost an expression of my consternation. Simultaneously, it appears to give the patient the space to express to me his unconscious perceptions of the above-mentioned adaptive context derivatively. The thunderstorm and gale corresponds to my sensations of being struck as if by a thunderbolt. His words, 'There will be snowflakes, as big as snowballs', offer an image of winter with cold and frozen water, admittedly figured as pretty crystals - snowflakes - a winter scene which might make one feel reconciled with the burdens of winter. The image 'as big as a snowball' immediately makes a projectile out of this beauty, an image demonstrating the impact which I actually experienced, as it is inherent in the image of the snowball. With this story of the thunderstorm, the patient very suitably offers an appraisal of the implication of a real event and thus, also, of my initial intervention to have organized my office in that way. This story is imbedded in the story about the frame which the patient told when 'reading the newspaper'. Thus, the patient makes it clear that he is reporting about something which has suddenly and temporarily shifted. A newspaper informs about past events or announces something that is expected. This piece of information in the 'newspaper' seems to be important, as it is this which the patient produces and gives me in reality: his scribbling of the report is given to me in order that I take note. He seems to be saying: read it carefully, then read it out loud and thus make it clear to me. The patient is thus asking me emphatically for a therapeutic intervention.

To formulate an interpretation at this moment in the session let us look at what material I have at my disposal. There are some derivatives, i.e. a detailed description of the implication of an event in very plastic images produced by primary processing. Our being together in a comfortable, friendly atmosphere is suddenly disturbed by a threatening event. There is also the indicator in the form of the actual symptom: being together in a friendly, comfortable atmosphere he thinks that evil might happen and reacts to this symptomatically, interrupting this good situation. He is not sure that the good relationship we have developed will last. According to the communicative theory of technique, the third ingredient needed for an interpretation is the patient's manifest mention of the intervention context. This mention is rather weakly encoded by his asking of the question, 'How much time is left? Will there be other children coming to you when I leave?'

In the session, I make the following intervention: I take the 'newspaper' from him and read out loud that although the weather seems to be very nice at the moment one has to be aware that bad thunderstorms might come out of the blue sky, that a storm might make a sudden end to the nice weather. I add, 'It is the same with us: we have had a very nice situation together with shopping and raisins for the goblin which did him good, and suddenly you ask me how much time is left and whether other children might be already waiting behind the door like gales, thunderstorms and snowflakes as big as snowballs. You seem to be thinking of someone who might disturb our peaceful situation and threaten us in the same way as in the last session, when we had a nice situation together, and suddenly the bell rang and someone came in whom you didn't know. You think it was a child that comes to me after you leave.'

In my intervention, I make use of his play, and I say out loud how I understand his communication, what kind of psychic state he conveyed to me and which event I understand as the trigger for such a disastrous outcome. His communication seems to include no starting point for a resolution except the repetition of the situation. I hope to get more material from him, especially hints for rectification of this situation.

The patient then says, 'I will write you a letter now.' He scribbles on a sheet of paper and brings it to me, saying, 'Look, here is written "Dear Mrs Berns" (he points at the scribbles on top of the page), and here it says "Your dear patient" (he points to the scribbles on the bottom) and this (pointing to the middle) says that we shall immediately leave our houses.'

With this communication, the patient declares the frame of his play which seems to have proved itself as a good medium for communication. His message consists of three parts. It is formal, however, also very individual. The form of greeting at the beginning and at the end of his letter is common style in a German letter to a friend and they form a frame around his message in the middle. This frame contains the image of a caring relationship, and I consider this as validation of my preceding intervention. His core message, however, is an order to 'leave the houses'. It seems that with this message someone gives advice to his friend in a situation identified as threatening. The connection to the event in the previous session is evident and the message seems to be, 'this office arrangement is not good for what we do here since it does not offer protection against intruders from outside - we should leave this house'. Each demand, especially in the verbal form of 'someone should do something', in principle communicates a proposal for rectification. In principle, the patient is correct. The arrangement of my office is in need of certain corrections. I cannot exclude the possibility that someone rings the bell at the front door and the patient and I get disturbed by this. Nonetheless, it should be possible to organize my practice in such a way that no one can personally intrude into a session by walking into the consultation room. A waiting room would minimize the opportunity for the disturbance in the previous session as would another location of the electric door opener. Thus, the patient's advice to leave 'the house' is in principle a good one as it rectifies the present situation. There is also the possibility that the patient is thinking of the external background context of his family moving into a new house in order 'to live in a better one', as his parents used to say. If so, the patient might also be referring to termination of his therapy, i.e. we both have to leave each other. Considering his forced termination because of the family move, the patient might be saying that this termination is a threatening event in his therapy, and thus he proposes that I should go with him, not leave him, since I now have the same reason to move to 'a better house'.

At this point, I intervene, 'There is something evil that is approaching and it seems to be so threatening that you propose that we ought to flee from here just like you did last time, when your father came. Now, you are proposing that we both should flee together, because last time I didn't do anything to prevent the disturbance. It might be that you don't believe that I am able to correct the situation.'

In my intervention, I only consider the threatening event of the previous session. I interpret his advice to leave the house not as a correct measure to rectify the situation but as a symptomatic flight response, extended also to me after he experienced me as someone unable to prevent this interference and thus not deserving his trust. Simultaneously, I also point out that I might be able to do something. My intervention does not take into account the above-mentioned background context of moving as it is not conscious to me at the time.

The patient takes a quick glance at the door button, then at me, and I continue with my intervention, 'I think you now have the idea that it is my job to press the button to open the door when the bell rings, and that I should go and look who has come. I certainly will do this: I will open the door when it is time to do so and I will not allow anyone to enter this room during session.'

In this sequence, the patient immediately reacts to my effort to try to do something and I immediately respond to his glimpse of the door button. I explain to him that I interpret his glance as his acceptance of my effort and as a hint for correction.

The patient then takes the two teddy bears, creeps into a cloth tunnel, hides from me and says, 'When my father comes he will certainly think that I am not here.' The patient remains in his hiding place until the bell rings. I open the door, his father enters the room together with the patient's little brother, who immediately finds the patient in his hiding place. The patient emerges from the tunnel, says good-bye to me and leaves together with his father and brother.

By hiding, the patient shows that he is in need of more protection (hiding place) and more reinforcements (the two bears) which he finds for himself. By doing this, he is hidden from me, too, separated. My offer was obviously not very helpful. Perhaps he is saying that he is no longer here, that he does not exist. Perhaps he is saying that I might be thinking something about him that is not true, something shameful. On the other hand, it is possible that he feels helpless and is now resigned to letting me have my way and do what I proposed.

In the session, what I really did was allow access to his father and brother, just the opposite of what I had promised. This action of mine allowed his brother to find him immediately in his hiding place. It is important to take into account that this office arrangement generates a constantly present trigger for the patient's symptomatic reactions which thus become chronic. His brother was the child who followed him and whom the patient sees as an intruder. He wants to defend himself against or to flee from his brother. Nevertheless, he leaves the session in a calm mood, with no observable symptomatic reaction. I expect that the patient will process these implications in the sessions that follow.

Session 47

In the next session, the situation seems to be repeated. Again, the patient creates a comfortable, friendly atmosphere for the two of us, and again he asks, in the middle of the session, about the time and about the children who come after his session. Then, he mentions Christmas, and at last I understand that there is a connection between the ringing of the bell and the time for the forced termination of his therapy. I also think that the patient has, perhaps, assumed that one of the children ringing the bell was to become his successor in therapy with me.

Conclusion

In the reported section of this patient's psychotherapy, every detail of the patient's material can be seen as a response to the actual relationship between the patient and the therapist. I think the material shows clearly that the patient selected the very components that he needed for communication. I would like to emphasize that the physical components of the arrangement of my rooms, i.e. the lack of a waiting room, the fact that anyone can disturb the session by ringing the bell and the fact that the electric button for opening the entrance door is located in the therapy room are 'lifeless' components of the therapeutic frame. Nevertheless, they are not so physical and lifeless when one considers the fact that the therapist is the one responsible for the arrangement. As the patient responds to these modifications of the 'ideal' frame, his material attests that they are contexts relevant for him against the background of the events of his life and acquired attitudes.

In the two sessions presented here in detail, the patient shows no response to some other facets of the arrangement of my practice, e.g. the sharing of the entrance with my professional colleague and the poor soundproofing of the walls. I do not remember whether there were any actual disturbances from these two sources. It is possible that my colleague was not in her office during his sessions and that he never registered any actual signs of anyone else being in the other set of rooms. If this was in fact the case, his lack of response is understandable.

Yet another important event was not manifestly mentioned by the patient in these two sessions: that I had regular meetings with his parents during the time of his therapy. In fact, his father and brother actually do get to 'participate' in these sessions, and it is I who allow their participation by way of the physical arrangement of my practice, even though there were good signs at the beginning of these two sessions of the ability of the patient to separate from his family. Instead of fostering this strength to separate, I permitted his father and his brother to intrude upon our therapeutic space.

Chapter 17
The terminator

PETINA BOWERS

This is the case of an eight-year-old girl and a trainee therapist. What follows is a detailed account of three therapy sessions with this patient. The sessions have been taken almost verbatim from the process notes that I wrote after each therapy session while in clinical training. These notes were written from memory as soon after the end of the session as was possible - generally between one and seven hours. I did not inform any of my child patients of this activity and I do not believe that they had any conscious knowledge of it. Additional details, concerning the therapy room, particular toys, explanations of particular games, etc., were included later. These details did not appear in my original notes, and are given as a means of providing, as honestly as possible, the fullest possible description of the therapeutic interaction between the patient and myself. During the reporting of these sessions I have included retrospective reflections interjected throughout the text. This is provided as a means of further elucidation of the therapeutic process or specific moments, activities or communications. The therapeutic encounter took place within the confines of a primary school in an economically and socially disadvantaged area of south London.

Therapy was provided by a private charitable society (referred to as the charity) which offers psychotherapy to children in socially deprived schools across London. My employment contract was with the charity (not with the school) for a period of one to two years. A notice was required from both sides in the event of premature departure one term before termination of employment. There are three terms to an academic year: September to December (autumn term); January to April (winter term); and April to July (spring term). The only person to whom I was required to report about the children whom I treated, was my clinical supervisor.

Treating the patient in a primary school setting inevitably compromised her therapeutic frame, particularly with respect to the impingements on privacy and confidentiality, and the involvement of third parties in her treatment. Another significant misfortune affecting her therapeutic frame was that I had other roles within the school, in addition to being a therapist. Most of the children in the school knew me by name. A number of them (whom I had previously worked more closely with in small groups doing arts and crafts) were particularly familiar with me, and I with them. The current charity had replaced another charity offering similar services, and a number of the children (including the patient) had previously been seen by other therapists. Many child patients had experienced unilateral forced termination by the therapist at the time when the previous charity withdrew from the school. The charity organization occupied several rooms within the school, two of which were reserved for psychotherapy. The consultation rooms were located on the third/mezzanine floor of the main school building. The outer door to the rooms lay off one of the three main staircases that serviced the main building. The door was kept locked and required a key to enter - all of the therapists had their own set of keys. Behind this door lay a small corridor which also served as a storage space for the children's artwork in individual boxes in full view of the patients. This shared space was accessible to everyone who entered a consultation room. From here led the doors to the two consultation rooms which were locked from the inside. The rooms were brightly painted with images of cartoon characters and small children at play. They were filled with toys - dolls, doll's house, Barbie/Sindy dolls, Action men, dressing-up clothes, toy animals, castles, cars, Lego, kitchen centre, play food, tea-sets, washing centre, reading books, colouring books, paints, pens, plaster mould kits, paper, beads, board games and the like.

It was the charity's policy that the children must be picked up from, and returned to, their classrooms after each therapy session, instead of allowing the children to make their own way. This was because of the requirement for the whereabouts of all children in therapy to be known at all times. This arrangement had the unfortunate effect of severely compromising the privacy of the psychotherapeutic situation. The whole class, and anyone else in the halls or corridors, were able to witness the patients going to and coming from sessions. This arrangement also created other problems, such as curiosity, jealousy and resentment in the children who did not 'qualify' to receive this 'special' individual attention (as therapy in the school was generally perceived).

The patient was eight years old at the time. Her parents are black, from Ghana, and she was born in London. She described herself as Ghanaian. She has an older brother, who at the time was about nine years old. He also attended the same school. Her baby sister was under the age of one. The patient was referred to me through my superior at the charity. Her classroom teacher had voiced grave concerns about the patient's disruptive behaviour and her violence towards both the teacher and her classmates. The patient portrayed a lonely figure, often isolated and left on the side by her classmates as they in their turn tried to establish order in the face of the patient's seeming desire to cause disruption and chaos. She was often excluded from school. I, her therapist, was born and brought up in England, although my mother is of West European origin and my father from the West Indies.

Confidentiality of her treatment was breached regularly due to the therapist's unavoidable interaction with classroom teachers. In particular, teachers often tried to engage therapists in discussion about the recent misdemeanours of the children receiving therapy. I tried to keep these interactions, and particularly my responses, to a minimum, while at the same time I was trying not to alienate the teachers, who were also trying, in their way, to do the best for the children in their care. The patient was also under the watch of social services because of suspicions of physical, sexual and emotional abuse.

I began working with the patient in January. Therapy was unilaterally terminated by me the following December. The sessions that I shall describe took place in November. I received weekly supervision for the entire year.

Unilateral termination of therapy, on the part of the therapist, is perhaps the single most disrupting and disturbing frame deviation that any child patient can be exposed to. Working as a communicative psychotherapist, I was fully aware of this theoretical supposition. I believe it relevant to point out that the forced termination had a profound effect on me. I experienced a great deal of ambivalence and guilt about my pending departure, the evidence of which was clearly manifested during the therapeutic encounter with the patient.

Session 1

During our first session in January, I explained to the patient the boundaries and rules of working together. Briefly, these were that I would see her three times a week (Tuesdays, Wednesdays and Thursdays), at the same time, nine o'clock in the morning, for 50 minutes. The issue of confidentiality was conveyed to her by telling her that I would not chat with other children, teachers or her parents about what happened or was said in the room. The exception to this promise was that if I thought that someone was hurting her, we would have to tell some other adults. In this event, we would talk about it first to see if it was necessary. I did not tell her then that there was a time limit for her therapy. I explained that therapy was 'special time' for her to play, or not, talk, or not - that it was her time to do what she wanted. I told her that in therapy, there were no rules like the ones in school or at home. The only rules that we had were: (a) she was not allowed to hurt herself or me; (b) she was not allowed to deliberately break any toys; (c) she was not allowed to take anything from the room, except at the end of term when she could take the things she had made herself; and (d) that she could have her own box to keep special toys in or things that she made.

During the initial contract I had not discussed with the patient the period of time that I would be working with her. In June (during the spring term), I made the silent decision that I would leave and I gave notice to the charity one term before. I left in mid-December, at the end of the autumn term. During the first week of the autumn term I had planned to tell all the children I worked with that I was leaving. Unfortunately, as there was no way I could tell all the children at the same time, I ran the risk that some of the children might acquire this knowledge from their classmates before I had the chance to tell them directly in the session. This patient, regrettably, found out about my leaving from another pupil at the school.

The three sessions which I shall recount did not follow one immediately after the other; instead, I shall report three successive Tuesday sessions. In addition, the week in which the first session falls, was also the final week before the mid-term holiday, which lasted for a period of one week. The second session was the first session after the mid-term break and the third (and final) session recounted here took place one week later. There had been two sessions in between. Thus, there were four scheduled sessions for which I had not written any comprehensive notes within the time period of the three sessions detailed below. Thus, the three reported consecutive sessions were numbered 75, 78 and 81 and they fell between the reported first and second sessions, and the second and third sessions, respectively. No sessions were actually missed during that time. During the year that I saw the patient, there were 92 sessions in total.

Session 75

The patient seemed quite jolly and full of spirit as I picked her up from her classroom. She skipped off straight down to the shared area. After I had unlocked the outside door, she marched directly into our therapy room. (I do not recall if we encountered anyone on the way). She was smiling, and seemed to be pondering what to do, when she left the therapy room to get her box from the corridor just outside. She was examining its contents for a while. She then looked round the room and at the shelf that contained all the art material and books. She spotted some adhesive stickers which she liked very much. She picked them up and hid them under her jumper, making no attempt to conceal this act from me. She seemed pleased with herself.

The patient: 'Let's make some moulds. Let's make the Hercules ones.'

There were a number of different character moulds available in the room, such as a cat and dog, wild animals, a vase with 101 Dalmatians puppies, characters from the Hercules animated film, jewellery, etc. We spent the next 35-40 minutes making these moulds. During this time the patient was more verbally communicative than ever before. She seemed very relaxed, and repeatedly completed entire sentences, which was rare. As we worked on producing these plaster mounds she would invite me to take part. We took turns in the various tasks and stages of their production.

No interventions were made at this stage because the patient had not displayed any signs of distress. She seemed fully engaged in her play. While we were waiting for the moulds to harden, she placed herself on my lap, facing me and hugged and kissed me.

Therapist: 'I wonder what all these big hugs and kisses are about?'
The patient: 'I don't know.'
Therapist: "Perhaps you're feeling good about me today and you'd like to show me that.'

Later, I realized that I had been feeling quite uncomfortable with so much affection from the patient. I therefore made an intervention that would distance her from me. With a mixed feeling of both relief and guilt, I achieved my aim.

The patient then turned away from me, noticing some coloured felt-tipped pens on the shelf to the side of us and pointed to them.

The patient: 'They're like mine!'

(The patient had the same pens in her pencil case that she used for school.) She reached over, remaining in physical contact with me, and took the plastic container of coloured pens from the shelf and seemed to be examining them. She counted out three black pens, three green and three red, placing them in the lap space between us. The sequence of 'threes' brought to mind the issue of three people, that is a third party in her therapy, but I decided not to remark on this at that point.

The patient wanted me to hold the pens. As I had my hands full with the drying moulds and her, I suggested that she tuck the pens under my chin. She did this, and then took the green pens out again and tucked them under her chin. She wanted to give me more pens from the container to add under my chin. It was becoming increasingly difficult to hold all the pens, the two drying moulds and the patient on my lap at the same time. The patient then tried to add more pens under her chin, but a few of the pens repeatedly fell out as she tried to get them all to stay there again and again.

The therapist: 'It seems like we've got a lot to hold, with all these pens. I wonder if you're wondering whether I can hold all of you.'

Later, I felt that it was not surprising that this interpretation did not receive derivative validation. It was too vague, failing to highlight and connect the significant frame deviation, that is, the impending forced termination of her treatment, with her narratives and with her indicator.

While it was occurring, the situation seemed unclear, incoherent and uncomfortable to me.

The following is how I might have responded to the patient given the perspective I have today.

Intervention: 'Perhaps you feel I'm like the pens. I'm slipping away from you by leaving the school, but you're trying to get me to stay. Perhaps you feel that lots of hugs and kisses might be one way to persuade me to stay' (referring to the indicator).

In the session, the patient continued to play with the pens, asking me if I could see certain coloured pens, which she had now turned upside down, with the ends instead of the nibs of the pens pointing upwards.

The patient: 'I wonder if you can see the green pen.'
The therapist: 'Yes!'

This kind of interchange continued for a while. Each time she used the same phrase but a different coloured pen. I was silently asking myself what this was all about. Did she think that I was not seeing something? I was not sure, so I said nothing. Here, as on other occasions in the past, I observed with tentative amusement the patient's mimicry of the common phrase-ology to the opening of my interventions, such as 'I wonder...'. There was an almost burlesque quality to her use of this idiom. It is possible that the patient was trying to convey to me, unconsciously, that something was obvious, clearly visible, right under my nose, something I knew (e.g. the green pens in her narrative) which symbolized what was ailing her - my leaving. The fact that I was 'blind' to (or unconsciously denying) the obvious carried with it a sense of irony which she conveyed through the vaguely sardonic tone of her statement.

The plaster moulds were nearly dry and I told her so. She became very excited and was eager to get them out of their rubber casings. Because she was sitting on my lap (facing me) and because removing the plaster moulds was quite a messy business, I said to her, 'Perhaps you could do that over the table so that all the bits don't go all over us and on the floor.'

She got off my lap, went around to the other side of the small table, sat down and started to remove one, while I did the other. By this time the session had almost ended. Once both moulds were removed the patient said: 'Can I paint them?'

The therapist: 'Yes, you can, but it's very nearly time to go back to the classroom, so perhaps you will paint them tomorrow if you still want to. Now, you can help me clean up the room a bit.'

She sat there examining the moulds, while I was putting toys away. When I finished, I said: 'Will you please put back the stickers that you've been keeping under your jumper?'

Suddenly, she marched out of the room, up the stairs and headed for her classroom, one floor up. I followed.

This patient experienced great difficulty with separation. During the year in therapy, she had all but stopped taking toys out of the room with her. However, the 'threat' of separation was now imminent with my approaching departure. My leaving became very real for her, again.

As we entered the large hall from the staircase, the patient's teacher was giving the rest of her class a physical education lesson. Outside of her classroom, I crouched down.

> The therapist: 'Can I have the stickers, please? You know the rules, that you're not allowed to take things from the room.'

The patient stood in front of me clutching the hidden stickers under her jumper with one hand, her head hung down. I was looking up at her, holding and gently shaking her other free hand from side to side. Suddenly the patient spun round and marched off, through the doors on the opposite side of hall. I followed. The whole class, including the teacher, were watching us. The patient barged through the doors leading down the other main staircase of the school. I ran and caught up with her just as she was entering the girls' toilets, just off the staircase. The patient went straight into a toilet cubicle and bolted the door. After a few seconds, I heard the toilet being flushed. The patient then emerged, saying: 'I've flushed them.'

I looked into the toilet bowl. Since the stickers were inside a sealed plastic cover, I expected to see them floating in the water. They were not.

> The therapist: 'Although I can see you'd like me to believe that they've gone, I think that perhaps you've still got them hidden.'
> The patient: 'No, I haven't. I haven't. I flushed them!'

The patient was becoming increasingly agitated and cross. She then went back to the toilet cubical and threw the stickers into the bowl. I, too, was becoming agitated, time was pressing on and I was already thinking about my next session, for which I was anxious not to be late.

> The therapist: 'That's not a good thing to do. I think that perhaps you're really angry with me, but I think we should try and find another way for you to let me know your anger without destroying the toys.'

The patient then went to the toilet bowl, fished the stickers out again and wrapped the wet, dripping stickers in her jumper.

> The therapist: 'No, you mustn't do that. It's very dirty in the toilet and you can get very sick from doing things like that. You've got to wash your hands with lots and lots of soap. And we've got to throw the stickers away now because they're too dirty to play with.'

She was clearly very upset and angry. Eventually, after some persuasion, she washed her hands with soap, leaving the stickers on the edge of the sink. I picked them up so that I could dispose of them later. The patient then aggressively splashed water from the running tap in my direction and stormed off back to her classroom. I ran after her, leaving her only after she had walked back into her classroom. The rest of her classmates were now all back inside.

This clear demonstration of emotional distress and the potential interpretation of the unconscious messages held within it lost all conscious significance for me in terms of frame deviations, while I struggled to contain the situation at hand. I was no longer interpreting the patient's derivative communications, but responding more or less automatically to the manifest content of her actions and words. My 'schoolteacher-like', punitive tone was my out-of-control response and an indication of my own 'madness' because of the gross deviation in the interpersonal boundaries which I, as her therapist, was responsible for creating. Unable to contain such a chaotic situation, I was not able to maintain a secure frame. I totally lost sight of my therapist role as I took dubious 'sanctuary' from turmoil in the imitated guise of parent/teacher. In the process, I also violated the rule of therapist neutrality. On many occasions, I felt, almost tangibly, the conflict within me as my role of her therapist was threatened with taking on other roles and duties. I struggled with myself as I battled to maintain neutrality in circumstances that perhaps warranted a complete shift - given the chaotic therapeutical setting within the primary school and given my clinical inexperience at the time.

Session 78

This session was our first after the half-term break. The patient seemed slightly 'off' when I picked her up. She seemed to be avoiding my eyes. We walked together to the room. On the way, several people were saying 'hello', for some reason more enthusiastically than usual, which I understood as relief about my being back after the half-term break. Before we even reached the top of the staircase, one of the children whom I also treated, and who was in the patient's class, ran up to me and very eagerly sought confirmation and reassurance that I was going to see him the following day, as usual. I felt the unmistakable air of annoyance from the patient. We continued our way to the consultation room.

Encounters, such as the one just mentioned, were extremely commonplace at that school - whether I was walking with a patient or not. However, in the course of the year, a perceptible difference began gradually to emerge. The children behaved differently when I was alone than when I accompanied a patient on the way to a therapy session. As I made an effort to minimize both verbal and non-verbal contact with other children when in the presence of a patient, there developed an unspoken code, if you will, between me and the pupils at the school, even those who were not in therapy with me. This shows how the therapist can influence the behaviour of others when she herself attempts to keep the boundaries. The other children responded to my distancing stance by actively reducing the level of their enthusiasm, which they enjoyed more fully at other times, when we happened to meet without a patient being present. This was also evidence of their sensitivity to the perilous nature of such conditions. The situation was still far from ideal in terms of a secure frame. There were many instances of third-party involvement which were reflected in the profusion of third-party themes in the derivative communications by all of the children with whom I worked at the school.

When we arrived at the small corridor of the therapy rooms, the patient looked at a painting drying on the shelf and said: 'Is this mine?'

> The therapist: 'No.'
> The patient: 'Where's mine?'
> The therapist: 'In your folder.'
> The patient: 'Where's mine? (Pause.) Where's mine?'
> I remained silent.

In retrospect, I understand that the patient's manifest inquiry was possibly a disguise for her concerns for privacy and a need for protection against intrusion of third parties. Unconsciously she was also drawing my attention to, and reminding me of, her exclusive right to my time during the next 50 minutes. This is understandable, given the intrusion she had just recently encountered in transit (i.e. the triggering event), and her annoyance with it (i.e. her indicator) had not escaped my attention.

The patient then turned to her box, which was on the shelf in the small corridor along with all the other children's boxes. She rummaged through her box and took out a picture that I had drawn of her, at her request, before the half-term break. She took this and went into our therapy room. Closing the door behind me I sat down in the chair closest to the door (I always sit in this chair because it gives me the best view of the rest of the room, unless the patient specifically asks me to sit in the only other chair in the room). I was observing her movements and her general demeanour. She appeared to be sulking, she was clearly withdrawn and looked annoyed. She did not sit down. She stood next to, half leaning on, a large cabinet. There were several different types of dolls. She picked up one of the 'baby' dolls, briefly looked at it with an air of nonchalance, before dumping it back down again. I remained silent.

At this point, there was not enough clarity in her communication to make an interpretation. Although, with hindsight, it is possible to offer a speculative hypothesis, connecting her removal of the drawing of herself from her box, in her depressed mood, and the discarding of the baby doll. The tentative understanding is one of the patient who tries again and again to communicate her desire to enter the room 'alone' with me - hence the drawing. My silence was telling her that I had still not 'got' the message, so she picks up and then discards a baby doll. This is a possible symbolic communication of how she felt she was being treated by me - especially in the light of the forced termination that I was subjecting her to. I did not respond to her unconscious concerns, so she felt discarded, abandoned by me.

She then went over to the shelves where all the toy animals were. She picked up a fairly large crocodile and a small lioness and rammed the lioness into the open mouth of the crocodile. She repeated this action several times. She then did the same with other, smaller animals (smaller in terms of the comparative size of the toys). At one point she picked up a larger lion and placed the crocodile's open mouth round its leg. Then she introduced a horse - first a small one, but she discarded this for a larger one. She put the big lion on the horse's back, then violently threw the horse on the floor.

The patient then turned her attention to the adjacent shelves where there were several small cars of all varieties, including a toy garage and a car park. All the toy cars were lined up neatly on the shelf. The patient went over to them and mixed them up into a heap. With her back to me, I could still see that she was playing with the cars and the garage, and mumbling to herself. What she was doing more precisely was hidden from my view. This continued for about three to five minutes. When she decided to do something else and walked away from the shelf, I managed to catch a glimpse of the last toy car that she had been playing with - it was an ambulance. She then walked across the room towards me, briefly glancing in my direction, and looked up at the shelf behind me - the art material and book shelf.

It was time to offer an interpretation. The images contained within her 'narrative' play were strong and quite clear. In addition to that, she had unconsciously allowed me to notice the ambulance. This was very likely a request for help: for an interpretation. An ambulance is a very common appearance in child's play 'saying' that someone is in need of urgent medical attention. In this case, the patient (and perhaps the therapist, too) needed help.

At this point, I intervened: 'I wonder if you are trying to let me know that you don't feel so good today. I was wondering if maybe I was like the horse, and that you feel angry with me. (Pause.) I was also wondering if that had something to do with the fact that I didn't see you last week because of the half-term holiday. And, as we were coming to the room today lots of people were talking to me. Maybe you felt attacked or eaten up like the animals in your play. Maybe you feel that your time is being eaten up, as I did not see you at half-term, and the fact that I am leaving at the end of term.

The patient was standing still in front of me, just silently listening.

As confusing as it can be in the midst of a session with a distressed child, finally enough derivative material was beginning to emerge to make things clearer. This is perhaps evidence of the generous spirit of human nature, even in small children, when such an imprecise and clumsy interpretation as I had given, nevertheless hits the mark. My intervention received positive derivative validation by the patient. My experience has shown the following: as long as the therapist offers an interpretation that highlights the major frame deviations, identifies a symptom and then draws out the links between that and the derivative images, a positive validation will follow, no matter in what clumsy manner it may have been delivered.

As soon as I finished the interpretation she reached up for the colouring books from the shelf beside her. She chose a book that we had used in previous sessions. She was briefly flicking through this book when she came across some of the pictures that we had coloured in together last term (i.e. the spring term). She paused at one picture (a train engine).

The patient: 'We did that together.' (Pause.) 'Pencils!'

(The patient was indicating, as she often did, what she wanted me to get her by pointing to the particular item and saying its name.)

The therapist: 'Pencils, you want the pencils?'

The patient nods her head, takes the book and sits down on 'her' chair. I reach over to the shelf and pick up a selection of pencils.

The patient: 'You sit here!'

(She says this in a very bossy tone, and at the same time pats at a space she has made for me to sit beside her on her chair. I take up my 'position' on her chair. She briefly searches for something in the book to colour in until she comes across a picture of two friendly gnomes standing side by side with their arms around each other's shoulders.

This picture of the two gnomes was a clear, positively toned image and as such, represented an unconsciously given *interpersonal validation* to my preceding interpretation. One of the gnomes had a smile on its face, the other wore an expression of surprise or, maybe, shock.

Having made the decision to colour in the gnomes, the patient settles down.

The patient: 'You help me!'

Again, this was said more as a demand than a request. I picked up a pencil and began to colour in.

Although the previous interpretation was validated to some extent, there was still a remnant of unconscious dissatisfaction in the patient's communications. This, I believe, was being articulated through the manifest orders, or demands, contained in her further requests for my participation in her play.

After a few moments I said, 'I wonder if you're also asking me to help you in other ways, and I wonder if there's a way that you can help me understand how I can help you. Because now we only have six more weeks left to work together before I leave.

For a while the patient continued to colour on her own and seemed much calmer.

Here, it is difficult to judge whether the immediate 'calm' that befell the patient following the above interpretation was a sign of validation or just of her need to think. The intervention very likely did not go far enough in addressing the patient's unconscious concerns with regard to the violations of the frame. Her subsequent unconscious appeal was for me to also do something that would change this intolerable situation – 'You help me!' Probably, my perceived resistance to rectify the deviation represented the barrier to a clear and satisfactory validating communication from her. It was as though the patient were saying 'OK, fine, you've identified the problem of the unilateral termination, so, now fix it!'

What followed was the patient going through an elaborate, confused discourse on when I was leaving. She also referred to a senior member of the teaching staff leaving just before half-term. I answered her questions to give her information and clarity. At one point she said, 'So you'll be leaving in December. What comes after December?'

> The therapist: 'January.'
> The patient: 'And then February, which is my birthday. It'll soon be my birthday. I'm nine already.' (In fact, the patient was eight, not nine.)
> The therapist: 'I wonder if you're telling me you're nine because your birthday is something you can look forward to in the future, unlike me leaving in December which is not something nice to look forward to.'
> The patient: 'You saw me when I was seven didn't you?'
> The therapist: 'Yes, that's right, and then you had your eighth birthday.'

In retrospect, here is a clear example of my own unconscious, defensive communications. Instead of interpreting the patient's first statement and subsequent question – 'So you'll be leaving in December. What comes after December?' – I responded to the manifest content of her derivatives by answering, 'January'. It was highly probable that the patient was asking me unconsciously, 'What happens to me after December, when you've gone?'

Several minutes had passed and then the patient said, 'Is it time to go?' On a conscious level I took this to mean 'was the session over'.

> The therapist: 'I wonder if you're feeling worried about the amount of time we have left until the end of term, since I always let you know when it's time to go back to the class after session.'

The patient continued to colour in the two gnomes, encouraging me to work with her on the picture.

The patient's 'encouragement' for me to continue working with her on the picture could be understood as a validation of the intervention that preceded it. However, it was perhaps yet another unconscious communication, offered as guidance to the way I might have rectified the deviation of termination, meaning, 'Stay and work together with me. Don't go!'

After a while I said, 'I've noticed that these two people we are colouring in look like good friends with their arms around each other. (Pause.) I wonder who they are.'

> The patient: 'You and me. This is you (she points with a pencil to the smiling gnome). And this is me (pointing to the surprised or shocked looking gnome).'
> The therapist: 'It looks like I'm the one with the smile and you're the one who looks shocked. Maybe that's how you see us – that it's perhaps hard for you to be happy and be my friend, because I'm leaving and that makes you sad and angry at me, too.'

We continued with the colouring. Once we had finished colouring the two gnomes, there were five minutes of the session left and the patient started to whistle.

> The patient: 'You do your whistle.'

What she was referring to as 'my' whistle, was a very loud wolf-type whistle that I had demonstrated to her sometime in the past. I whistled. She smiled and giggled. I repeated this three times at her request. When she asked me for a fourth time I said, 'No, I think that's enough now.'

> The patient: 'Please? One more?'
> The therapist: 'No.' (I said this in a very calm and gentle way.)

The patient looked at me very sternly and said simply: 'Cow.' (Pause.) 'Cow, cow.'

What was the unconscious significance of the whistle? A whistle is usually used to alert someone or to attract attention. This was what I now believe the patient was unconsciously trying to do. There was very little time left – until the end of the session and, most importantly, until the end of term and my departure. Speculating, the whistle might have symbolized something like the sounding of a siren, alerting both of us to the impending danger of my departure. The fact that I missed the opportunity for a possible interpretation along these lines, and thus missed the possibility of making her understand the situation better, is perhaps demonstrated by the subsequent rapid degeneration of communications between the two of us. Almost as a special emphasis on the non-validation, on the incorrectness of my inaction, she was becoming increasingly agitated as she started to knock pencils on the floor and then ordered me to pick them up.

The patient: 'Pick it up!'

This was repeated several times. Each time I did as she ordered. As I was doing this I said: 'I wonder if you're getting upset with me because you know it's nearly time to go back to the class. Maybe feeling cross with me and calling me names is a safe way to be cross at me.'

The patient just stood there leaning against one of the shelves with a sulky expression on her face.

A few moments later I said, 'It's time to go back to the class now.'

Suddenly, she became very difficult, grabbing at some costume jewellery which she was threatening to break by holding a necklace in both hands and pulling it apart. She was looking at me very defiantly. I looked back at her and slowly shook my head. She then threw some more pencils on the floor.

The therapist: 'This is not a safe way to be cross. Perhaps you can think of another way to be cross at me.'
The patient: 'I want to kick you.'
The therapist: 'Well, I wonder if I held the punch-bag in-front of my legs, perhaps you could pretend kick me.'

The symbolic representation here of the jewellery as something precious, and the threat of its destruction, could conceivably be the patient's unconscious perception of what she felt I was doing to her. The end of the session and of the treatment was 'threatening' the integrity of something precious, the approaching end of therapy was 'threatening' the destruction of the patient. And further, just as the patient, who held this 'precious' piece of jewellery in her hands, would be responsible for its potential destruction, in the same way I, who 'held' the patient, would be responsible for her potential destruction.

From the jewellery box the patient then removed a plastic, toy watch, hid it in her hands, and calmly went towards the door to leave the room.

The therapist: 'I guess that it might feel like it helps you to leave the room if you can take the time with you, because we're running out of time – we've come to the end of our session and also, it's not long before I leave.
The patient: 'Yes.'

I did not try and stop her removing the watch from the room. However, once in the small corridor just outside the room I said: 'Perhaps you'd like to put the watch in your box until we see each other tomorrow. She became very agitated and said: 'I don't want to leave.'

Taking the toy watch (holding on to time) momentarily alleviated the patient's anxiety enough to enable her to pass over the threshold of the door between the therapy room and the small corridor just outside. As long as she held the watch, time was temporarily suspended for her: a pretend watch, symbolizing pretend time gain. She then attempted to take other things that were around in the corridor, and tried to destroy some artwork belonging to other children which was drying on the desk in the corridor. I tried to physically prevent her from doing this, and I removed any objects I could from her hands. I could not see the watch. After a short while the patient decided to leave. She opened the door, with me following close behind. She did not want me near her and was gently pushing me away. We walked up the stairs, with the patient leading the way. Outside her classroom I crouched down, held her hands and said: 'Can I please have the watch back?'

The patient: 'I haven't got it.'

I paused for a moment as I was deciding whether or not to believe her. She seemed very calm at this point.

The therapist: 'OK. I'll see you tomorrow then.'

She turned and calmly returned to her class. Back inside the corridor of the therapy rooms I found the plastic toy watch discarded on the floor. I put it into her box.

The patient's distress at leaving the session was a possible expression of her frustration and impotence at not being able to affect a change in my stance and in my decision regarding my departure. By gently pushing me away, she was communicating her reluctant realization (or acquiescence) of the inevitability of an unacceptable, hurtful situation. The surreptitious liberation of the toy watch from her possession was perhaps an act of rebellion, symbolizing her quest for some modicum of autonomy in the face of such domineering external forces.

Session 81

The patient was late today. She did not come up from the playground with her teacher and classmates. She arrived at the classroom late, together with four of her classmates. They had all come together and had apparently been at a friend's house that morning. (This particular friend was the other child from the patient's class whom I also treated). The teacher was clearly not at all happy about the situation. The patient, however, looked quite happy and triumphant among her friends. I could not help smiling to myself as I witnessed her joy and the sense of belonging that, this 'pissing the teacher off' with one's fellow classmates generated for her. This was the very opposite picture of the patient in the past. She had always been alone and isolated on one side of the fence, the teacher, class and the rest of the world on the other. It was, in a way, a triumphant, momentous occasion for her.

She put her coat on the peg in the classroom and emerged skipping and jolly, and rushed off to the room. Once I caught up with her outside the rooms she looked relaxed.

The patient: 'Can I go to the toilet?'
The therapist: 'Yes, of course you can.'

The patient led the way down the stairs to the infant toilets on the bottom floor. She ran on ahead, and as I was approaching the toilets through the large hall where the infants were about to begin their morning assembly, she stuck her head out into the corridor.

The patient: 'Come!'
Then, inside the toilets she continued, 'Will you hold the door?
The therapist: 'Yes. I'll hold it with my foot.'

I slid my foot under the door and kept it closed with my toes. When she had finished she smiled at me, washed her hands, had a drink of water and then we headed back to the rooms. Her mood suddenly changed. She now seemed reluctant to go and was moving in such a way as to drag her feet in an exaggerated manner. We walked together quite slowly, I let her set the pace. Once outside the rooms, I unlocked the door and she sort of slid in. I went slowly in and shut the door. On the small desk in the little corridor there were some ceramic bowls that one of the other children must have made. She picked one up and examined it for a few moments. The patient slowly walked into our therapy room, I followed. We both stood for a while. Leaning on one of the shelves she picked up an odd looking 'tasselly', rubber-ball and exclaimed, 'I went swimming yesterday.' (Pause.) 'I went swimming with my mum.'

Smiling back at her I repeated, 'You went swimming with your mum?'

Seldom did the patient ever talk about people or events that occurred outside the room, and even then this was invariably restricted to things taking place within the school. So, my senses were heightened at the mention of her mother. However, I could find no unambiguous connection between our trip to the toilets, her mood change and swimming with her mother. So, I waited.

She then turned and made her way over to the large doll's house and asked me to help her lift it. As I did this, she selected a large Cindy doll from the shelf above the doll's house. After I had put the doll's house on to the small table, she asked me to get 'the little people', but she explained that she only wanted the children. (There was a box containing an assortment of miniature toy people.) The patient wanted a particular type of little person. It was a type that she had previously played with. I went over to the 'little people box' and brought it back to where the patient was now sitting on 'her' chair. I checked with her to confirm which type she wanted before removing all the different characters I could find. Crouching on the floor beside her, I was sorting through all the little people, on occasion I would come across an adult. I was about to discard it when the patient, who was keeping one eye on what I was doing, and her other on rearranging the doll's house, piped up and said, 'Yes, that one too.'

In the end, I collected a toddler boy, two small girls, a small boy, two men and two women. A lot of these little people were either naked or half-dressed. Inside the box there were a few bits of loose clothing. The patient was looking through these and asking me which clothes went with which little person. She also asked me to find particular items of clothing, which I could not find. One of the male people (with clearly defined male genitals) was naked, the patient asked, 'Is it a boy or a girl?'

> The therapist: 'I suppose this one was meant to be seen as a man because he has a penis.'

The patient wrinkled up her nose in response to that, and then wanted to know what he should wear. I suggested a few things, such as trousers, shorts, caftan. None of these suggestions seem to satisfy her. I then suggested that he could wrap some material around him like a towel. She seemed to like this idea and nodded enthusiastically. We spent the majority of the session making and replacing clothes for these little people. She would ask me to make something for a particular person, I would do this, and she would subsequently play with that character. She seemed very content and calm.

After about half and hour of this, smiling, the patient suddenly proclaimed, 'Their clothes are dirty. (Pause.) That's why we have to make new ones.'

I just looked and smiled back at her. A few moments later she continued, 'They're all changing their clothes.'

I repeated this, she smiled and said, 'Because they've just been in bed.'

She still seemed to be very calm and lucid. Most of the session had passed without an interpretation being offered. I could not make any clear sense of her play in terms of themes relating to frame deviations. She did not appear distressed in anyway. There was no symptom that I could discern. Thus, my relative silence seemed appropriate at that time. However, the trigger of the unilateral termination had not been, and would not be rectified in the future. So, the chances were that more specific derivative communications would soon emerge. I did not have to wait long.

The patient then asked me to go to her box and get 'Sally'. (This was the name she had given to a baby Cindy doll that she had kept in her box since the first week of us working together. She had claimed it when it was brand new and by now had assumed exclusive rights to it. She never forgot to return it to her box after she had finished playing with it). Playing inside the open doll's house, the patient then tried to place 'Sally' on the knee of what looked like a woman who belonged to the 'little people' whom she had propped up in a miniature toy chair. Even though 'Sally' was in effect a toddler, the actual size of her was perhaps double that of the woman 'little person'. As she was attempting to do this, she asked me to sit on the other side of the table from her – indicating with her head where she wanted me to sit. I sat down on 'my' chair. I was in effect sitting on the outside of the doll's house, while the patient played inside.

The therapist: 'Perhaps that's how you see me – on the outside looking in at you.'

The patient just lifted her eyes to meet mine. We peered at each other through the windows of the doll's house. Her expression did not alter. She lowered her eyes again and continued her play.

Was this intervention validated? No, I do not believe it was. For as such, it was incomplete, more aptly reflecting my own defensive feelings of rejection. I had been excluded from her private little game that was taking place inside the doll's house. I was relegated to the 'other side' (to the outside of the house): shut out. My intervention did not go far enough to interpret the full 'picture' of the situation. It was not so much about looking in as it was about being shut out. I had lost the privilege to be party to her inner world, to play with her inside the doll's house. Because I was leaving, she was beautifully communicating that separation.

Deep in concentration, the patient was trying to prop 'Sally' up on the woman's knee. I said, 'I wonder if that's mummy.'

The patient: 'No. They're all children. (Pause.) This is mummy.'

The patient indicated the large Cindy doll that she had earlier placed into the doll's house. The patient's frustration began to show as she failed to get 'Sally' to stay freely on the 'woman's' knee. The patient's distress was increasing by the second.

The patient: 'She keeps falling off. (Pause.) Help! Why won't she stay?'
The therapist: 'Perhaps you feel that I, too, keep letting you fall. (Pause.) Because I'm not staying either.'
The patient: 'Yes.'

She then tried again to rearrange 'Sally' on the 'woman' doll's knee. She achieved this with her first attempt and generally seemed to become calmer.

In an attempt to (re-)connect with the patient, and by way of trying to forge a link with my curiosity of her reference to 'mum' earlier in the session, I impatiently made an intervention that I hoped might reveal some contiguity of meaning – 'I wonder if that's mummy.' The patient manifestly responds to the manifest content of the intervention, and subsequently displays and communicates distress. I had strayed from her unconscious concerns to my conscious ones, the consequences of which were all too apparent. Setting me back on track, the patient obligingly guides me through her narrative to reveal her unconscious message clearly and succinctly. The evidence supporting the validation of the interpretation is in her suddenly managing to arrange Sally on the knee of the woman doll in such a way that she stayed in place.

The patient then got up off her chair and went to look at some large Cindy dolls. She selected one woman and two Action men, and incorporated them into the doll's house game. She took one of the 'little people' boys and put it in the arms of one of the Action man dolls. She was acting and speaking his 'role'. Lowering her voice she said, 'Oh what a cute baby boy, so sweet.'

She repeated this a few times, and then gradually began to add the other 'little people' dolls into the arms of the Action man doll. She manipulated his arms in such a way that he could hold and hug them all without dropping them. The patient now spoke the parts of the children, 'Daddy, Daddy. Daddy, Daddy, Daddy.'

The theme of 'holding' was still very prevalent. But, there was a difference too that the patient was trying to convey. The previous series of narratives contained in her play had centred around female figures. Now, the characters were male. However, up to that point, there was not enough information for me to discern the significance of this.

Time was up. I said this to the patient. She continued to play while I tidied up. I said, 'Perhaps you would like to put the dolls in your box.'

The patient did it. She then helped me put the doll's house away. When that was done she sort of threw herself at me. I tried to catch her, or at least prevent her from falling hard on the floor. She did this a number of times – each time wriggling enough out of my grasp so as to ensure that she was eventually sitting on the floor.

The therapist: 'Maybe you'd like me to be able to hold you, because you feel that I've been letting you fall.'

The patient continued to hurl herself at me.

The therapist: 'Perhaps if I hold on very tight I can stop you falling.'

I did this physically. That is to say I managed to support her weight, by half standing and half squatting, with the patient on my knees. We remained in that position for a few seconds. The patient was smiling but had a mischievous look about her. Then she suddenly said, 'How's your back? Is it still sore?' (I had injured my back and was unable to lift heavy things. The patient knew about this.)

The therapist: 'Yes, it's still sore.'
The patient: 'We can do pretend carry?'
The therapist: 'Yes, we can do pretend carry.'

With that, the patient got off my knees, kissed me and we 'pretend carried' her out of the room and into the small corridor. ('Pretend carry' was an expression we devised to describe me simulating actually carrying her, when I could not, in reality, do it physically. So instead we walked along face to face, the patient's arms wrapped tightly around my waist, me hugging her about her shoulders. I would be walking forwards, the patient backwards.)

The patient left the room relatively easily and held on to me all the way to the classroom, although by the second run of the staircase just holding my hand sufficed.

Unconsciously, I had tried to be like the male Action man and physically held the quite considerable weight of the patient, as he had held all the children. Given her size, this was an achievement for me and I felt pleased with myself for having managed it! I was desperate to give her something 'real' (i.e. manifest, concrete, tangible) – something she had manifestly requested on numerous occasions in the past. I was again missing her unconscious message in trying to meet my own needs of placating my tremendous feelings of guilt at leaving her. The patient, far from immune to my genuine desire and efforts to help her, 'rewards' me for trying. Unconsciously, she perceived and appreciated my difficulty in 'holding' her and offers a consolatory solution by suggesting we do 'pretend carry'.

The poignancy of 'pretend carry' has even greater significance when one considers this in light of the impending unilateral forced termination. It dramatically symbolizes the conflict and contradiction of me as the therapist trying to create a therapeutically healing environment for the patient, while simultaneously undermining, and thus violating, the fundamental premise upon which it is based, i.e. the pretence of 'holding' the patient in the sure knowledge that I will ultimately let him or her 'fall'.

Conclusion

The patient was a masterful derivative communicator. Her unconscious perceptions, not only of the violation that unilateral termination of therapy represented, but also of the violations of therapist neutrality, confidentiality and privacy, to name but a few, were clearly evident. One can only marvel at the patience and tenacity that the patient displayed in her endeavour to communicate her unconscious messages to me. With the benefit of hindsight and post-analysis of the sessions, what could have been construed as isolated, random, even chaotic expressions of child's play, all at once reveals a more cohesive, thematic meaning – when listened to from the specific premise of the theoretical perspective of communicative psychoanalysis. The thematic meaning and links that emerge, can be traced to this patient's concerns with the therapeutic frame. The patient, like some of the other children I worked with, did not communicate a great deal by way of articulation. It was through the choices or preferences she made about what to play and through the nature of her play that the majority of insight was gleaned; choices revealing narratives that were imbued with unconscious messages, and messages the thematic tie of which was interpreted as frame-related.

Nevertheless, even within her sparse articulations, clear, concrete derivatives were identified. This was especially evident when the whole 'picture' of both her verbal and non-verbal expressions was brought together and viewed from the context of frame violations. During the entire period from when the patient was first made aware of my departure right up until our last session (approximately three months), there was not a week that went by without the deviation of unilateral termination being represented in one unconscious communication or another. This was perhaps one of the most unexpected challenges I was to face. The relentless regularity with which this theme arose not only provided a constant source of fuel to fan the flames of my guilt, but also taxed my inner resources and capability for therapeutic vigilance. My inexperience was tested to capacity by my defensive need to deny its manifestation.

There exist a variety of perspectives from which to view and interpret the patient's communications, whether manifest or derivative. The communicative approach focuses its attention on the derivative context of communications, and as such certainly offered me a constructive way to work with the patient. When I began work within this primary school setting, I was at first truly overwhelmed by the chaos I found myself in. Boundaries in general appeared to be under constant attack and violation. My preference to work communicatively is perhaps a reflection of my unconscious need, especially at the time, to create some semblance of order, not only for the sake of my own sanity, but for the benefit of the children with whom I was assigned to work.

Finally, I would like to add that the title of this chapter is perhaps more aptly an expression of my feelings and judgements of myself as a therapist than it is a reflection of how the patient viewed me. I wanted to be the benevolent 'fairy godmother', capable of granting her every wish, but in reality I was 'the terminator'. I was confronted with my own desire to genuinely make things better for her, juxtaposed with the actual harm I felt I was putting her through by leaving. The struggle to find a way through this apparent paradox was evident from my own communications of 'madness' expressed during the last three months of 'our' therapy. I did not want to be the 'baddy', the mean person, 'the terminator'. Through the support of supervision I came to accept the demons that accompanied my decision to leave and the subsequent impact it had on the patient.

There was no way to avoid or deny the pain my leaving was causing, but perhaps I could offer her something less obvious: by taking responsibility for my decision and its ramifications, I was offering her a safe space to express her feelings of rejection, abandonment and persecution, without further reprisals. This was perhaps the most I could hope for at the time.

Part III
Are we created equal?

V. A. BONAČ

Chapter 18
A Faustian tale

If we were to do what most often happens when therapists discuss process notes of therapy sessions, there would be numerous explanations offered about this or that segment of the patient's material. It would be considered bad taste and poor collegiality if one tried to argue that one explanation might be better than the rest. Various schools of therapy would be reflected in the comments in about the same proportions as the training of participants. Frequently, discussants of patient material 'know' what the patient meant, what must have happened to the patient in childhood and what the 'dynamics' were on the basis of the manifest meaning of the material alone. The physical appearance of the patient might also be mentioned. Whether the patient was likeable or difficult would be important and usually taken as a characteristic of the patient. Some discussants would want to speculate why this patient brings misfortune, or fortune, upon himself or herself. Above all, psychoanalytic theories would be generously employed to explain that the patient did this or that because of the 'Oedipus complex' or, due to 'paranoid-schizoid position', the patient might be 'splitting' and was surely 'projecting'. With child patients, some discussants might point out that the child behaves the way the family wants him or her to behave or, perhaps, in reaction to what he or she wants. Kleinians may point out that unconscious phantasies drive the child's behaviour and that the child's narrative or play reflects the bizarre creations of their inner world. Such discussions are most often fragmented evaluations of those segments of the material that seem to most obviously reflect one or the other psychoanalytic theory. They rarely take the totality of the details in their sequence and hardly ever consider the unconscious meaning of the patient's material in the current context of the session. I hope that the reader has had the opportunity to observe the unique way of discussing a session by using the communicative methodology.

As the phenomena described in the vast psychoanalytic literature are portrayals of what was observed by the sensitive therapist, such theoretical knowledge is invaluable and certainly necessary in order to recognize in our own sessions the manifestation of various psychological phenomena and different courses of development. However, the hypothetical discussants above are *a priori* wrong in all they said because they took the actual phenomena in sessions in isolation, without considering the immediate environment in which the events occurred in the session. The sequence of events and the framework of therapy are rarely considered. This is the most common mistake made when trying to understand a session and a patient. From my experience in discussion groups, the most common outcome of such evaluations in isolation is that the truth about the therapist is eventually mistaken for the truth about the patient. Even when the individual situations in sessions are correctly identified (e.g. projecting), the 'blame' for the irrational behaviour is automatically put on the patient. Little effort is generally spent on verification and the sequence of events is hardly ever considered.

After reading Part II, the reader may have come to appreciate the necessity that one needs the complete data in order to enter into any discussion about the session or the patient. Even one complete single session cannot usually provide the necessary information to reach much understanding of what was going on because the essential information, i.e. about a change in the frame, is most often contained in the previous session. I hope that the detailed manner in which the sessions were discussed by the five therapists gave the reader sufficient sense about the unexpected nature of the flow of material. New meaning emerges at every turn and the therapist can take nothing for granted.

For instance, in the second clinical presentation, 'Seeing, touching, destroying' (Chapter 14), the therapist's acknowledgement of her fault of not attending to the patient in the session had the most powerful, immediate effect on the patient. Because the patient was experienced as too demanding and too controlling by the therapist, one could be justified in agreeing that the patient was just too much for anyone to take for long. This therapist felt just as uncomfortable in the patient's presence as any other, yet she was able to resolve the potential impasse by decoding the patient's communications in the light of her present intervention, that is, her non-attention. It was her interpretation of the current situation, and not of his past dynamics and of the internal conflict in the patient's life outside, which brought about the incredible relief of the child's serious symptoms. Even more startling is the patient's own insight into the source of his nightmares which followed the therapist's interpretation: the destructive power adults hold over a child when they do not acknowledge their mistakes. We would expect that the serious physical damage caused by the car accident and the repeated operations would exert a far greater influence on that boy than any attitude of the adults around him ever could. We learn, however, that it was the current attitude of his parents, the doctors, the police and in particular of the woman who had run him over which was of critical importance to the current suffering of the boy. To not pay attention to the child was experienced as deadening and persecutory. To be ignored on the road the second time by the woman proved nearly fatal to the patient in the literal sense. To not admit the wrongdoing was persecutory.

The lifting of the patient's repression (he told a previously repressed traumatic memory of the accident) and the resulting freedom from further nightmares of persecution are good examples of symptoms being 'miraculously' alleviated by cognitive insight provided by a communicative interpretation. So long as the memory of the trauma was hidden from this patient's consciousness, the theme of persecution remained ever-present and active in his dreams. To hit someone the second time, after seeing him injured, is to persecute. I think it is incredible that a child so young reveals the unconscious knowledge of such sophisticated hidden implications of a violent act. The boy knew that his persecution by the woman's second hit was aimed to hide her guilt of having done so much damage. To hide her first crime she went after him with a harder blow – no matter how preconscious and instantaneous it all was to her conscious experience.

Without witnesses, adults could do what they like with a child and commit the ultimate crime of 'pushing away the orphan who then commits suicide' – a theme so well taken by the Italian novelist Roberto Calasso (1993) of an old Greek tale. After a king pushed away a hungry orphan who had begged for food, she disappeared and was later found hanging from a tree. The land did not recover from drought and people continued to go hungry until the king learned about what he had done and introduced a change. The 'orphan' is every child without adult protection who is refused nourishment of the body or of the soul. When we are young we cannot be alone. The 'suicide' of the soul occurs whenever the child's plight, expressed by his or her communicative strivings, is repeatedly ignored in therapy, or in any other situation. The child gives up all effort, stops striving and withdraws into silence. We are all orphans when we are turned away unprotected. The child's violent persecution by 'hunger' was turned into a violent rejection. The king, not hunger and not even the rope, killed the orphan. Thus, suicide of an orphaned child is murder committed by adults. When several adults conspire to hide a crime, the persecution of a child becomes total. When we talk about the outside life of a child patient we seem to be more able to admit the truth about harm having been done to the patient by parents, accidents, strangers. When it concerns the current interventions of the therapist, our minds are more reluctant to see the connection between the symptoms in the patient and the interventions of the therapist.

Calasso is right: it is not that we should rediscover the ancient stories (e.g. Greek myths), it is the stories that are waiting to be reawakened. Ancient? As old as the human race, but always present and always the same, wherever there is tragedy. Stories are created and live in our consultation rooms. They are testimony to the present – they may be repeated from the past, or expected in the future, but either the repetition or the expectation is taking place now. Some say there are only 36 dramatic situations (stories) and only two without origins in antiquity: the multiple and confusing legends of the Middle Ages surrounding the court of King Arthur and the story of the 'restless middle-aged doctor/adventurer – Faust (Shattuck 1996, p80). The rest of the stories have all been told before in ancient Egypt, Greece, Judea and the Near East. The two 'modern' myths may not even be myths because they lack clarity. Temporally the latest of European tales, the Faustian myth, is of special significance to psychotherapy. The learned doctor is thought to have been fashioned after the historical figure of Johann Faust, a scholar and charlatan in black magic who lived around 1500. The essence of the tale is in the doctor's selling of his soul to the devil to obtain supernatural powers. What is startling and most disturbing in this tale is that 'Faust is not damned for his pact with the devil: he is saved' (Shattuck 1996, p81).

The therapist who ignores the patient's unconscious communications gains 'supernatural' powers over the patient. The patient, child or adult, will never know who is the 'perpetrator of crimes', the two of them in the consulting room will forever be talking about other people at other times while doing terrible things to each other – employing the automatic mechanism of repression by way of symbolization and the displacement of facts. Will the therapist be 'saved' the way Faust was? Well – was Faust 'saved'? Here perhaps lies the failing of the telling of this myth in any of its various forms, from Johann Spiess in 1587 to Goethe in the early nineteenth century. I agree with Shattuck that the ending of this tale is missing – there is no insight into what really happened, Faust only compiles experiences and forever moves on until natural death. This is the reason why the story of Faust is an immoral tale (Shattuck 1996). What appears to be the justification for gaining deep knowledge is not fully exposed as being fraud. In the Faustian legend, only pseudo-knowledge is gained: the full extent of the illusion that any real knowledge has been obtained, even when disregarding the tragedy of human sacrifice, is not told. Goethe's Faust dazzles with poetic brilliance and virtuosity of expression. It correctly identifies the dramatic situation which has been tormenting human beings in the modern world: 'We strive without knowing adequately what we are striving for and believe our thirst for knowledge and experience is protected in high places' (Shattuck, p90). The philosopher Faust goes from experience to experience, yet does not learn from his experience – a lack of progressive development so well described by Bion in his 'Experiences in Groups' (1961/1985). Faust's experiencing is a vicious circle of a string of experiences, a desperate hunger which only death can break. The reader of the long epic of Faust gains the knowledge that Goethe was a genius of virtuosity.

I think that, in therapy, the details of the unconscious exchange of information show ample evidence that real insight, that is new knowledge, is not possible without the unconscious validation of a correct interpretation. Where there is no cognitive validation no new knowledge has emerged. As there can be no correct interpretation without securing of the frame in reality, nothing new happens and nothing new is learned. So, by remaining unconscious of committing the crime of betrayal or of destruction by abandonment, one cannot gain any real new knowledge. Faust, and the world of knowledge, could not have gained anything. While Shattuck focuses on the question of morality as Faust is praised for his striving for knowledge, I would like to add that no real, complete knowledge can be gained without the unconscious truth being told. Faust's brutal egoism is always there, his immorality victorious, his strivings fruitless. As Shattuck believes, instead of being a proper myth/tragedy, 'Faust' remains an unfinished tale and the knowledge gained by its protagonist, and the reader, is only pseudo-knowledge. The human sacrifice brought Faust only the confirmation of his illusion and his death ended a confused life.

And so the therapist. Seemingly escaping the disturbing truth contained in the unconscious perceptions (and from a child!) by remaining unconscious or, knowing – yet not securing the frame – the therapist sacrifices not only the well being of the patient but also his or her own inner growth. No new knowledge *about the therapist* emerges if the therapist does not change the frame in the way the patient unconsciously and specifically requests. If there is no improvement in the bipersonal field of therapy (securing of the frame) for the patient, there is none also for the therapist. Each instance of the 'sacrifice' of the patient is simultaneously a 'crime' by the therapist, while to both, the full knowledge of it is never found. If the 'unconscious' therapist writes a tale, it would be a never ending Faustian legend.

I believe that this unconsciousness in writing about psychological phenomena is responsible for the extravagant revolt and opposition by the public (mainly women) to the recent exhibition of Freud's work in Washington, DC. In a way, the public was right. Something important might be missing from the displayed body of knowledge as it was obtained at the expense of the well being of Freud's patients, no matter how unconscious Freud and his patients were about where the damage was being done. I think that the compromise that was eventually reached is a telling one. By allowing that the exhibition includes also the criticism of Freud's ideas, the disturbance caused by the 'Faust' in Freud was appeased with the complaints being heard.

Chapter 19
Empirical ethics

I am saying that the question of ethics is really the same as the question of knowledge: unconscious and conscious. In a damaging situation, no new knowledge can be gained in therapy except the knowledge about yet another damage which is in principle the same as the one before. By hiding from the truth, by remaining unconscious to the immediacy of the situation, the therapist gains nothing – the gain is Faustian illusion.

The therapist in Chapter 14, 'Seeing, touching, destroying', was ultimately extraordinarily helpful to the patient. Her success with the difficult symptoms and the difficult parent would be a 'feather in the hat' of any experienced therapist. Before the therapist gained insight into her need for ignoring the patient, was she in any way 'conspiring' with everyone else to hide the truth from the patient – by remaining unconscious of her turning away from him? Was the therapist truly causing as much of a harm to the patient as the woman driver who injured him twice? Was the patient suffering as terribly? We may never know the full extent of the patient's suffering during sessions, what we hear is only *simile* of the unconscious experiences. Yet, we may not need to know the comparative meta-psychology of experiences in order to cure a patient from persistent, distressing symptoms and troublesome behaviour – the themes are the same. If we follow the string of themes to their immediate source, that is to the therapist's frame-related interventions, and if we can link these changes in the frame with the patient's themes, we can explain the symptoms. Such interpretations produce extraordinary results. When we are overwhelmed by our guilt of having hurt the patient and are hiding that from the patient, we are repeating what others had done to the patient before and thus reinforcing the patient's symptoms. Thus, unwittingly, we join the persecutors. Initially, much of this happens out of consciousness to the therapist. The relief happens to both when the therapist is able to decode the unconscious meaning.

Hearing one session alone, especially when reported in isolation, without the details of the state of the frame, it would be easy for most discussants of child cases to 'blame' the patient for his sense of persecution. Psychoanalytic theories abound which would explain paranoia as generated in the psyche with little or no outside provocation. I have heard such bizarre explanations given to traumatized children 'explaining' the patients' experiences of persecution that one cannot believe that 'transference' can be 'interpreted' so freely and so often. For instance, a fairly common Kleinian intervention seems to be that the child's fear of persecuting creatures, told as free association in the sessions, is the result of the child's own sexual phantasies about the parents. There appears to be little effort at verification that there might be someone in the child's life who is forcefully 'after' the child, perhaps including the therapist. Such interventions, as the example above, are considered explanations of transference. The direct implication is that the child only imagines that the source of persecution is on the outside as the suffering is the result of his or her own extravagant wishes.

I have found that not only is the manifestation of transference response a relatively rare phenomenon in the practice of psychotherapy, but also that transferential phenomena are, in general, even more infrequent in child patients than they are in adults. This clinical finding makes sense since, with time, the number of traumata can only increase in the course of life. Thus, there is less 'damage' to the younger person than to the older, on average. This thinking is based on the finding that real traumata, not the inner, intrapsychic illusions, are the source of mental anguish. On the other hand, if one believes that we are born with intrapsychic fantasies which distort our perceptions of the reality of our environment, then the opposite would be the case: one might believe that unconscious fantasies lose their potency with age and that adult patients will communicate fewer distorted ideas than when they were younger. The situation becomes absurd when the tables are turned and the following is proposed. How can any therapist formulate interpretations about the reality of the patient's fantastical experience, if the therapist, too, is distorting the very reality about the patient's experience that he or she is trying to elucidate? Training analysis cannot have worked miracles and the reliance on theory cannot explain that which has not yet been defined.

The lower frequency of the transferential phenomena in child therapy is, by itself, of little use to the clinician who must take each moment in a session as it comes. The therapist's never ending task, whether treating children or adults, is to constantly verify who is doing what in the session and whether the patient might be irrationally expecting the future – all through the painstaking task of uncovering the unconscious meaning of the patients' communications.

Cognitive validation of the therapist's interpretation is a remarkable phenomenon. When we look closely at what happens to the patient, we observe that his or her conscious understanding of what happened in the session, as provided by the correct interpretation, also leads the patient to gain, on his or her own, the conscious understanding of some aspect of his or her own past. We can observe that some aspect of a conscious memory was obviously unconscious to the patient until the very moment when something *in the present*, which was in some vital way similar to the event in the past, was explained to the patient. We can say that the patient has recovered a repressed, previously unconscious aspect of a memory. This is the only way I know of that makes the recovery of an unconscious memory possible – albeit it never occurs spontaneously and never under pressure from the therapist!

Ironically, what is commonly, but quite erroneously, termed 'traumatic memory recovery' is nothing more that the patient's communication of a *perception about the therapist's current* traumatic behaviour towards the patient. It is the therapist who is revealed as the propagator of a traumatic act which is similar to the very past trauma now remembered in the session. Much ink has been spilled in vain about the veracity of the 'recovered' memories. For some reason, few professionals want to hear that there exists a body of clinical knowledge that explains what is happening in sessions when a patient 'remembers' past trauma. There is a strange and pervasive ignorance of the basic principles of human unconscious communication. Countless painful disputes between patients of all ages, their therapists and sometimes even their parents would not have reached the courts (at least not in the same manner) if this fundamental knowledge about human functioning would have been known to the professionals and they would have been spared the confusion, accusations and pain. The whole quagmire of the 'memory recovery' movement and of fruitless professional activity surrounding this issue would never have happened if the *immediacy of the specific situation* in which a memory was told by the patient were considered as the critical context. In therapy, it is not the veracity of a memory that is of concern to the therapist (that quality of a memory is important elsewhere!), but the theme that the memory carries.

It is amazing and alarming how slowly new discoveries of psychological phenomena find their way into the professional life in general, considering that countless psychological trivia and unfounded tales about the human psyche are quickly adopted and eventually seep into the public domain under the guise of accepted 'scientific facts'. Poorly informed journalism is really not fully to blame for propagating such misleading content. The reports in print most often repeat what professionals in the field tell the journalists – and thus pseudo-science is propagated until it overshadows the value of true discoveries. A recent excellent discourse of this topic from another perspective was written by PR Gross and N Levitt in their book *Higher Superstition* (1994). It is the ignorance of serious literature by the professionals and their beliefs formed on unfounded reports that are truly appalling, especially when carried into practice.

For a therapist to send a patient to accuse his or her parent(s), in the courts of law, of having sexually abused the patient in the past – at the very moment when it is the therapist who is currently abusing the patient and is responsible for the traumatic actions in therapy – this bizarre situation is just too mind boggling. Yet, this is exactly what was happening in recent years all over Canada and the USA. When I say that it was the therapist who was responsible for the current traumatic actions in therapy towards the patient, I do not mean that the therapist actually forced a sexual act upon their child or adult patients (although this, too, has happened). As shown in this book with the examples of therapy sessions with children, the way human unconscious communication works is via themes and images. What is true and reliable is the theme. So, when the patient reports the memory or a story about sexual molestation or sexual violation, we know that it is the *meaning* of this story that is very likely happening in therapy.

Once, when I touched a doll with which a patient was playing in the session, the child immediately told a story about looking under the dress of a sexy girl. I have never again touched toys while in session. In child therapy, memories of sexual abuse are often told when the child is asked to sit on the therapist's lap, when the therapist takes the child's hand or when there is any physical touching initiated by (thus, needed by) the therapist. If such themes do not emerge it might be that other breaks in the therapy frame are even more pressing for the patient. In adult therapy, sexual themes are common occurrence when the patient is seen in a consultation room located in the therapist's home, when the therapist physically touches the patient, when the therapist invites a colleague to 'watch' the session, when an audio- or video-tape is made of the patient (to be viewed later, possibly by whoever takes hold of the tape in the future), and the like. Many times sexual themes give way simply to themes of intrusion, violation, invasion, unwanted contact, indecent behaviour and so on. In all cases, the veracity of memories is a moot therapeutic question, it is their *themes* that tell the story about the therapist.

The type of professional ignorance, as is the case with the phenomena of unconscious communication in psychology, is a situation which cannot even be imagined in the sciences. After the discovery of a phenomenon in science or engineering has been made public for a time, after the observation of the same phenomenon has been repeated by numerous other authors, the discovery becomes common property of the body of knowledge of a discipline. The professionals in the field simply have to know it, or else they are considered charlatans and likely to be dangerous to the public. Reports based on falsified data have happened in science, but they are rare exceptions that did not survive for very long. Even in the case of falsification of results and of holding back the publication of new discoveries out of professional envy, what was happening had to do with the manipulation of true evidence not with cultivation of professional ignorance.

Harold Searles's discovery of unconscious perceptions, and Robert Langs's discoveries of the phenomena of unconscious communication and of unconscious validation have been known for over 30 years. A good-sized body of literature exists in this field. If one disregards theoretical speculations and clumsy empirical reasoning, nobody has yet empirically refuted the existence of these psychological phenomena with solid evidence. A few theoretical disputes were published but no systematic empirical studies which would refute the validity of the findings (see also Smith 1991). On the contrary, the body of empirical evidence is growing rapidly in the communicative literature. The argument, that one can never really 'see' what happens in a 'good' session, which is necessary to provide the complete data that show proper validation of a thesis, is a true statement, but it does not apply to verification of discoveries. Such argument only avoids facing the amazing truth about the fact that every skilful and well-trained therapist can in fact reproduce the same 'experiment' by providing the same conditions to treatment at every moment in their sessions. When I say to a therapist that I can predict the content of what their patient will say (not *how* they will say it) if the therapist tells me the conditions of treatment by telling me all that happened in the previous session, I am not surprised that they are surprised.

The predictability of unconscious phenomena is truly amazing, something that few believe and even fewer are willing to spend the time and effort to find out. The human psyche just is not so simple that one could take a brief look and understand. What baffles me is not professional incredulity, because the phenomena are truly incredible. It is the wall of apathy and the lack of serious interest in these phenomena, so fundamental to psychotherapy and to human psychology in general, that are alarming. It is perhaps a telling story about the field to find that there are more people interested in the new research and the new findings who are outside the field of psychotherapy than there are those within the field. So, there are still many therapists who do not take the trouble to seriously study this body of knowledge. There are training institutes and universities where students are not taught about something so fundamental to human psychology. It is difficult to believe that the only reason for not getting serious about studying these unconscious phenomena is their alarming nature. To not know the work on unconscious communication by Robert Langs three decades after it has been published in more than 15 books and twice as many journal articles is astounding.

Robert Langs, trained in traditional psychoanalysis, has taken the same royal road to the unconscious which led Freud to the smouldering cauldron of drives and wishes – and discovered a new, royal road to the core of human meaning and wisdom. All that a therapist needs to do is listen carefully and systematically to what a patient of any age is telling him or her unconsciously and all that the therapist really needs to have is the knowledge of the methodology, not the theory. Only a theory which has been derived from numerous and diverse data, and the propositions of which have been validated, can claim to be empirically derived and can fruitfully guide the clinician from one moment in the session to another. I believe that the communicative theory of technique, although still evolving, is such a theory.

Thus, the ethics of human acts and intentions, whether in psychological therapy or in everyday life, can be found empirically. The therapeutic process is open to the investigation of which interventions are beneficial and which were harmful to the patient. There are two major venues of investigation, using the patients' perceptions and employing communicative self-analysis. The past can always be investigated, given sufficient data. It is the future which is of concern to ethics. First, what to do, and what not to do, to comply with the Hippocratic oath and do no harm to the patient? Second, are the mistakes we make unwittingly, reparable? And third, what interventions to use to be therapeutic in psychotherapy? I hope that these questions have been addressed throughout this book and that readers have found the examples and the theoretical explanations helpful in forming their own views by finding out for themselves what happens in their sessions. Ethics no longer needs to be left to the mercy of the goodwill of those who formulate contracts, agreements, procedures. The ethics of psychological therapy can be derived empirically from the detailed understanding of the unconscious processes. The perceptions, the models of rectification and the validation of interventions are all there, communicated daily with the unconscious purity of 'vision' by our patients. Even when our very human failings make us blind to it all during sessions, we can still see it in retrospect from process notes of sessions. Therapy sessions thus become data from which we derive human ethics. One could say that all ethics lies in the unconscious models of rectification. In fact, only when therapy is ethical, can it be therapeutic.

Many think that children ought to be treated differently in therapy because they are not adults. As can be seen from the clinical examples in this book, in principle, the communicative therapist treats children and adults in the same manner – with the same respect for their rights as patients and also with the same interventions. There are exceptions and modifications. Children are always brought to therapy by adults, most often their parents, and the fees are paid by other people, most often their parents. Is therapy possible with someone who has not come of their own free will, who has not consented to therapy, that is, did not make the decision to enter, remain and discontinue the therapy, and did not choose the therapist? In his classic text, *The Ethics of Psychoanalysis*, Thomas Szasz is convinced that it is the specific conditions of psychotherapy (the therapy frame) that enable the therapist to be of any help at all to the patient. He writes:

> The underlying rationale for these conditions rests on the premise that both the patient and I must retain our autonomy vis-à-vis each other as well as our responsibility for our respective behaviours. It follows that I must not have any direct influence on, or power over, the patient's life outside the consulting room, and neither must he over mine. Accordingly, many of the practices

psychoanalysts engage in – such as child analysis, training analysis, . . . , communicating with the patient's spouse – are incompatible with the minimal conditions . . . (1965/1988, p. x).

As always, Szasz focuses on the legal-political context of human relations. Psychotherapy is first and foremost a relationship between the patient and the therapist. Does communicative psychoanalysis provide the conditions in which the child is truly helped or do we simply assume that therapy happens when we do psychotherapy with children?

When we, human beings, are still young – too young to be able to do what we can do as adults – others act on our behalf. When they do not act in our interest, then they act against us. It is, in the end, all a matter of power and the issue is how power is used and misused. We should like that the use of power, possessed by some of us due to temporary circumstances, is used for our protection and to make learning available to us when we are young. Throughout our lives we always resent and protest, often only unconsciously and silently, whenever power is used to control us and to restrict our freedom. We need powerful people most when we are very young, ill, illiterate, emotionally unstable, insane, physically impaired in our capacity to learn, blind, deaf, lacking limbs, pregnant and lactating, and when we are very old. We expect the rest, the normal, the temporarily stable and temporarily healthy adults to provide for us. In this way, they would return what ought to have been given to them when they were very young, ill, illiterate, emotionally unstable, ...

In some cases control has been found to become so relentless, so overwhelming and so destructive to the young person that some people might conclude, as Thomas Szasz did, that child therapy ought to be made illegal in the way child labour is illegal in civilized societies.

Thus, communicative research of child material reveals that children require the same interventions and the same type of treatment setting – they deserve the same rights. Exceptions in technique are surprisingly few and pertain to payment. Thus, the general implications about how to deal with us, when we are young and before we grow into adults, may be alarming to those who take care of the young, especially of the troubled and the troublesome. Mental health clinics, schools, counsellors, psychologists, psychiatrists, prisons – and most importantly – families and therapists, all hold great power over the young. This book calls attention to the less obvious – to these unbidden and undeclared means of control which severely hinder growth towards independence and do damage to the path to maturity. The elaborate structure of an institution may generate cruel and repressive measures as unintentional side products of the administrative process. If this book offers individuals and institutions reasons for self-examination of ways the young are being treated by adults, then it has served its purpose.

Chapter 20
The communicative theory of psychological development*

This chapter consists of a brief outline of my theory of human psychological development and the basic methodological concepts for its empirical basis. The course of the emotional development of the growing human has been found to be, to a large extent, the function of the inborn capacity for valid unconscious perceptions by the growing infant of his or her 'mother' from birth onwards. For the purposes of communicative psychoanalytic investigation, *'mother'* was defined as the noun which represents *the totality of the conscious and unconscious interactions of the mothering person with the growing human*. It needs to be emphasized that both definitions, i.e. for 'unconscious' and for 'mother', have been operationalized by the underlying mental processes which are described within the context of known conditions determining the interaction. These known conditions are the dependent and the independent variables of the therapy 'frame' as defined by Robert Langs. The communicative theory of human development is based on the naturalistic observations of children from birth onwards as they interacted with their caretakers, mostly their mothers. Any patho-genetical data, derived from the early memory material of adult patients as communicated manifestly in sessions, is considered to be secondary evidence. Genetic information is thus taken as an indication of the possibility – and therefore the starting point for a further empirical investigation. The hypothesis that needs confirmation is the following. The effects of all emotionally significant interactions, conscious and unconscious, which take place in infancy and early childhood, may retain their dynamic force throughout our lives. The effects *can be observed in the present* as the dynamically triggered, unconsciously communicated meaning in such situations that bear *emotional similarity* to the situations experienced in the distant past, including in the earliest days of our existence. The emotional similarity lies in the

* Ideas in this chapter were first published in 1995 as 'A communicative psychoanalytic theory of human development – Part one: Introduction, methodology and theorems' in International Journal of Communicative Psychoanalysis and Psychotherapy 9: 99-105.

similarity of the conditions provided by the interpersonal frames. The following Postulate 1 of my theory is also a principal proposition that could be readily deduced from Langs's interpretations of clinical material and is a logical extension of his theories of the communicative therapeutic technique.

Postulate 1: The emotional similarity of an interpersonal situation is the equivalent of the frame similarity of any other interpersonal situation, regardless of the elapsed time. The emotional similarity is operationalized as the same configuration of active specific frame-breaking and frame-securing actions.

The great majority of my observations of infants under the age of 12 months were of breastfed infants; all were born physically healthy to healthy mothers. Observations of three of the children were continuous from birth to their adolescence and included monitoring of a total of over 1000 breastfeeding intervals. When interpreting the observational data of children, I took into consideration the wealth of empirical information compiled by child researchers from various psychoanalytic schools as well as the exciting findings of researchers from the fields of clinical psychology. On some occasions, my interpretations of their data differed from the interpretations offered by the authors. Most of the differences are a direct consequence of my particular focus on the *unconscious meaning*, as opposed to the manifest and preconscious meaning, of the same material. Such research focus adds new information from the same existing pool of data as not only the manifest but also the derivative meaning of the same data is considered. An attempt was made to formulate the essentials of an empirically derived communicative theory of human development, based on the data of my naturalistic observations of children that is informed, but not influenced, by the historical precursors. I also made an effort that my familiarity with the various developmental theories would not influence my empirical observations, my interpretations of data and the resulting theoretical conclusions. The method used in the understanding of psychological processes – as they became observable to me in the course of a child's life as well as during therapeutic sessions – was Langs's communicative methodology of decoding unconscious meaning.

My comprehension of the complexities pertaining to the empirical investigation of the experiential aspects of the interactional phenomena, an understanding that is profoundly different from the traditional psychoanalytical, was achieved also through the years of training in doing communicative self-analysis (see Langs 1992b). The appreciation of the deeply unconscious experiential aspects of the interactional phenomena was, I believe, the foundation for my new understanding of the otherwise elusive child/mother interactions and for looking at the growing human being from another perspective.

Thus, my theory of human psychological emotional development is a natural extension of the early works of Robert Langs. However, my observations and my conclusions differ from Langs's writing on the evolution of the emotion-processing mind (Langs 1996). The critical and integral part of my work, essentially different from all other methods of psychoanalytical investigations of human development, is my application of a modified communicative psychoanalytic method of investigating the process of human interactions with its fundamental principles intact. This method was applied to research data in the same manner as it is applied by the communicative therapist to the material in session. Thus, a strictly defined sequence of distinct tasks was carried out:

1 *naturalistic observation of the process* – listening to the manifest and latent meaning of the verbalizations of the 'mother and child' with each other and with the observer, within the context of the on-going realities of the observation process
2 *the formulation of a communicative* hypothesis based on the totality of conscious and unconscious meanings of the verbally communicated material as they relate to the realities of the observation process
3 *the communicative self-analysis* of the observer's experience after each observation was studied to complete both the observation data (unconscious perceptions by observer) and the validation of hypotheses
4 *searching for the unconscious validation* of the original hypotheses in later communicated material and in the behaviours of the 'mother and child', and finally
5 *a synthesis of the understanding* of the unconscious interactions *only if* the original hypothesis was indeed found to have been subsequently validated.

The communicative research method relies totally on the *verbally communicated material*: not only is the verbal material the *only* data that can be interpreted unequivocally (by skilled observers), the verbal material is also the data that are invariably produced by patients of all ages, from the time they can speak, if they are given the opportunity to express themselves in any way they can (free association) in the secure context of their therapy or of the observation process. Although the *principles* of the investigative method I used with pre-verbal infants were the same as those that form the essential methodological tasks developed by Langs, *the specific ways of achieving these tasks* were adapted to the specific, non-verbally communicated material. Such material is obviously different in an infant as well as in the mother communicating with an infant, but *not* different in the verbally reported experiences by the mother. For example, comments by the mother during an observed breastfeeding interval pertain as much to the observer as they do to the infant. The available data for researching the unconscious meaning of the mother/infant interaction are thus found in three sources: the unconscious perceptions of the observer, of the mother and of the infant.

'Verbal' is taken to mean 'pertaining to words', while 'non-verbal' communication was found to include a great variety of communicative modes, including voice-sounds in their full complexity of nuances which cannot easily be classified in a dictionary but with which we, especially the nursing mother, are genetically 'programmed' to understand well. Thus, the main modifications to the communicative research methodology which were developed with, and intended for, verbal people, were made by inclusion of additional *types of the data* considered communicatively interpretable, as well as essential, to the understanding of the child/mother interaction, i.e. the rich variety of sounds made by the infant.

The basic principles of the communicative method were therefore applied not only to the verbalizations that comprised unambiguous sentences representing thoughts, but also to other modes of human conscious and unconscious expression. Thus, crying, smiling, and the various expressions of the face and body were included in the data for analysis. Although a point can easily be made that such non-verbal data cannot be unequivocally interpreted in their total complexity and with all the nuances of meaning, a point I fully acknowledge, it is also true that certain non-verbal communications and expressions are *unambiguous enough* that meaningful conclusions can be made with much certitude and little margin of error. For example, it is true that a sudden cry from an infant can be as much the result of a sudden somatic pain (originating in the infant, e.g. colic pain) as it can represent the infant's *negative* response to the mother's input that immediately preceded the cry. However, it is also true that a sudden cry *cannot* represent the infant's *positive*, that is pleasurable, response to the mother's action. If this characterization is nevertheless considered open for methodological debate, then my above appraisal of the understanding of the infant's reaction must be taken as an *explicit assumption* of my study and as *Axiom 1* of my theory of development.

Central to my theory of emotional development presented here is Langs's discovery that humans, in situations of danger, verbally communicate veridical perceptions of interactions with others outside of their consciousness and in such a way that an unambiguous decoding of these communications is possible when the specific triggering event, which creates the danger situation, is known. This finding of the capacity for unconscious perception, and of unambiguous verbal communication of these perceptions, was extensively confirmed by my study of the therapeutic process with children aged four to 12 (Bonac 1991) as well as by the sessions presented in this book. The unconscious communications of children have been found to reflect the unconscious information processing of a sensitive, responsive and wise deeply unconscious system of the human mind (see also Langs 1988). My thinking was also greatly influenced by the writings of Harold Searles (1965, 1975, 1986). Although Searles did not formulate a comprehensive theory of human development, his keen eye and honesty about the interactive aspects of the therapeutic process greatly contributed to my learning about the historical psychogenetic aspects of current interactions.

The goal of organizing my observations of children was to develop a theory of human development that would consider the new discoveries of unconscious perception and communication and to formulate a theory that would explain, in an empirically testable and predictable manner, the healthy and the pathological interactions of children with their caretakers.

The following propositions form the outline of my theory:

- *Principal Theorem 1*: The capacity to unconsciously perceive interactions with others in a veridical manner is an inborn capacity of the human mind.
- *Theorem 2*: Unconscious perceptions of interactions with others are basic determinants of emotional development, healthy or pathological, at any level of human development.
  Lemma 1 of Theorem 2: The growth in the content, that is the growth in the amount and in the complexity, of the unconsciously perceived and processed information is not a function of, and is therefore independent of, the level of impairment in the mental health and cognitive capacities of the growing human.
  Corollary 1 to Theorem 2: The content of the unconscious veridical perceptions, and of the unconscious processing of these perceptions, greatly influences the cognitive, emotional and somatic states of the growing infant starting from the beginning of life.
  Corollary 2 to Theorem 2: The reality of the unconscious *intent* of an action, by others or by self, is the predominant determinant of human emotional development.
- *Theorem 3*: The influences of the unconscious veridical perceptions, and of the unconscious processing of these perceptions, on cognitive, emotional and somatic states of the growing human, are potentially reversible through therapeutic efforts of communicative psychoanalysis.
- *Theorem 4*: The content of the unconscious veridical perceptions, and the unconscious processing of these perceptions, are *independent of* the mental or emotional impairment of the growing human.
- *Principal Theorem 5*: The capacity to influence others via various modes of communicating with others, including conscious and unconscious sending and receiving of messages, is an inborn capacity for learning of communicative skills which originates in the powerful survival *needs* of the growing human.
- *Theorem 6*: The capacity to unconsciously process the perceived interactions with others in a manner that reflects the survival needs of the growing human is an inborn capacity of the human mind.

Lemma 1 of Theorem 6: The mode of transmitting information to others, of unconscious perceptions of interactions with others, and the mode of transmitting information of the consciously experienced emotional and somatic states, are predominantly by way of the transmitting of sound, starting at the beginning of life.

- *Theorem 7*: The inborn capacity for unconscious veridical perception is directly related to the powerful inborn survival mechanisms, both somatic and psychological.

Lemma 1 of Theorem 7: The informational content, that is, the amount and complexity of the information pertaining to the unconscious veridical perceptions, is a function of the developmental stage of the child's perceptual organs: (1) it is less than the available outside information; (2) it is limited by the perceptual capacities and (3) it is reduced to the levels of the complexity of information that the healthy child is developmentally capable of processing.

Lemma 2 of Theorem 7: The growth in the content, that is, the growth in the amount and in the complexity, of the unconsciously perceived and processed information is a function of the somatic growth in the child's sensory-motor apparatus.

- *Theorem 8*: The content of the unconscious veridical perceptions, and of the unconscious processing of these perceptions, is limited by the content of the available information, and is *a function of* the inborn survival needs of the growing human.

- *Theorem 9*: The meaning of the unconscious perception of any specific action that changes the frame of the bipersonal field is equivalent to the *ethical evaluation* of that frame-changing action.

Corollary 1 to Theorem 9: Ethical evaluation of any one specific action is then empirically defined within the bipersonal field by the data derived from the unconscious perception of that one specific frame-changing interaction. (Note: This corollary, although discovered by the author, can also theoretically be deduced from the clinical works and teachings of Robert Langs.)

Corollary 2 to Theorem 9: The ethical criteria that are an integral part of any interpersonal relationship, and that define that relationship, termed the bipersonal 'frame', are then empirically determinable from the naturalistic observation of a minimum set of frame-changing interactions from the beginning of life.

Principal Theorem 10: A communicative psychoanalytic theory of *the development of the bipersonal 'frame' from birth* onwards is built on a set of theorems which form the foundation for the 'empirical ethics' of any human relationship.

One of the most important findings one can draw from the clinical studies by researchers in the field of communicative psychoanalysis is the observable fact that patients who are permitted to talk freely in the session will communicate unconscious perceptions of the therapist's actions *regardless of their age* (the earliest age of a documented case of a child in communicative treatment, that was completely validated, was four (Bonac 1991); also the author, treated children as young as two), *regardless of the degree of impairment of their mental health* and *regardless of their cognitive abilities*. Mentally retarded children communicate unconsciously the same type of meaning as mentally normal children (Langs 1991, personal communication) which is also confirmed by my clinical experience. There are clear differences in the style of communicating that affect the quantity and clarity of data. These differences are very similar to the categories of communicative types in adults as described by Langs (e.g. 1978/79, 1982). Mendelsohn (1985) wrote on the structural foundations of unconscious perception in the earliest phases of development. An original contribution by Kumin (1993) compared the communicative types of adults, as developed by Langs, with the findings of the infant development research by Ainsworth (1885), Gaddini (1978), Greenspan (1992) and Weil (1992) as they relate to the disturbances in 'pre-object relatedness'.

Psychoanalytical theorists of human development have described the 'mother' that matters to the child in many ways, yet the views of all of them were, I think, expressed in terms that were basically phenomenological and intrapsychic. What mattered in the psychology of the child was the *manner* in which the child experienced the mother, what the child's mind 'did with' the introjections of, and identifications with, the mothering figure. A prominent influence on the emotional development was attributed to the role of the phantasy (e.g. Klein 1932, 1946) existing within the child's mind. This potent intrapsychic element, although in theory considered to be *related* to the reality of the environment, was viewed as the agent that distorted the reality of the 'mother's' actions and emotions in the mind of the child.

It seems to me that such views may take into account the reality of the specific vulnerabilities of a child as well as the reality of some aspect of the action by the mother. What other theories do not consider is what I have found to be the *dominant force* affecting the emotional functioning of any human being: the reality of the *unconscious intent* and the reality of the unconscious aspects of any human action, regardless of age – as well as the *valid perception* of such reality by the child. A similar view was occasionally recognized, and sometimes implied, by psychoanalytic writers of different schools of thought. The *impact on the child of a reality action* by the mother was acknowledged in their observations of the mother/child interactions, or else was recognized as their *understanding of the genetic material* from adult patients in therapy. Nevertheless, these rarely expressed views were not made an essential part of the psychoanalytic theories of development.

With my theory, I would like to present another, communicative view which acknowledges: (a) the *reality of the unconscious aspect of the intent* – or function – of an action; (b) *the reality of the unconscious aspect of an accomplished action*; and (c) the capacity of the human of *any age to veridically unconsciously perceive* the truth about both the unconsciously intended and the effected actions by the mother, all within the scope of the reality that *can be perceived* with the currently available capacities of the sensory-motor apparatus. For instance, the lack of information, due to the child's inability to walk out of the crib in order to see that the mother is unseen from the crib but nevertheless still there in the next room, is only insufficient information, not a distortion. And, this incompleteness of data that the child always 'suffers from', is not at all that important, clinically and in research, when we realize that *the mother knows* what it is that the child cannot know. Thus, when the mother is in another room, she knows that she is hidden from her child and cannot treat the cry of a lonely child as 'nonsense' and 'meaning nothing' since she is at home and not away. When the mother behaves as if her child ought to know of her presence, she is pretending and thus acting out her own sadism. When the child cries louder and appears angry, the child is responding to having been hurt by intentional absence. Thus, the 'lack of complete data' in the child is providing additional data about the mother. To accuse the child of distorting the reality would be like accusing the blind adult of distortion when they cannot see you.

The *unconscious perception* by the growing human of an action, or of the intent of an action, by others is thus from birth on *veridical, not distorted, and is limited* only by the various cognitive and sensory-motor developmental factors which diminish with time.

My findings from infant research do not support the thesis that we are born with faulty perception and with unconscious fantasies. On the contrary, I have gathered evidence that we are born with the most exquisite *faculty for validly perceiving the reality* of our environment and that any unconscious 'fantasies' are the consequences of the introjection of real harm done to us.

Proposition (13): We perceive unconsciously the harm done to us (a) when we are powerless to change the dangerous interpersonal frame and (b) when direct communication of our perceptions to the perpetrator of the harm would provoke retaliation, and thus further harm, to us. Thus, the inborn capacity to perceive on the unconscious level and to communicate such perceptions unconsciously are powerful mechanisms in the service of our survival, particularly essential when we are young.

When we are children the frame is most fiercely and consistently enforced by adults, most of the time by our parents, as it is driven by their unconscious needs. I have also found that unconscious perception and unconscious communication is thus as much a survival mechanism as it is the most efficient way to influence our parents when they are causing us harm. When we are children, we do not have the clinical skill to offer psychoanalytic interpretations to our parents and thus cure them. More importantly, we do not have the power to change the child/parent frame which is the key to changing the reality of the situation. Instead, we try to influence our parents in a way that is unconscious to both – the price paid is the distortion of a part of our mind. Since time began, only those humans survived infancy who were able to keep their parents parenting – unconscious perceptions and unconscious communication of perceptions kept bodies alive along enough to physically outgrow total helplessness. 'Soul murder' is better than the death of the body as long as there is a chance for healing our mind later. Thus, the capacity for selective unconsciousness in a growing child has been the adaptive mechanism that saved their lives, and thus the human race, from self-elimination. Contrary to some Neo-Darwinians and evolutionary psychologists, I believe that the overt silence about some current dangers and the unconscious knowledge of them, while retaining some power to influence the dangerous person through unconscious communication, has allowed humans to adapt to, and thus survive, the potentially fatal environment – their own families during childhood. Abandoned newborns have survived in the wild when they were taken care of by wolves – while many newborns do not survive angry outbursts or sadistic acts by their own parents. Contrary to the views of Langs (1996), I do not find that the make-up of our emotion processing minds is the result of a 'poor outcome of evolutionary testing and selecting' or that 'homo sapiens sapiens is left relatively vulnerable and inept – and self defeating – in the motional realm' (Langs 1996, p146). On the contrary, I have found that the human mind has been exquisitely 'designed' by the millennia of adaptation to our human environment to function in favour of survival and that its functioning is as life-saving now as it might have been in the distant past. We must remember that it is the human infant who requires that the immediate environment be adult human environment, rather than the rest of 'nature', for the longest time of their growing up. Actually, to speak of the 'design' of the mind is quite deceiving and certainly absurd in light of Darwin's fundamental finding: that only those species survived whose basic needs for living (long enough to reproduce) were met by their environment. Others were eliminated. The Darwinian 'selection process' is thus by elimination, due to the lack of fulfillment of the basic needs, not by selection due to superior 'design'. The essence of the process is thus the interplay of the compatibility of the environment to the needs of the species. In human terms, unhappiness and suffering alone do not destroy organisms and thus could not have been a decisive factor in evolution. The distant path of the actual evolution of the organization ('design') of the human mind as an organ for thinking can only be wildly speculated on, not derived from, our therapy sessions.

Thus, Proposition (12) of my theory of development is very different from the views of Langs (1996). Speculating on the evolutionary scenarios on 'how natural selection opted to solve' the problems of 'dealing with the excess of input' of information, he says:

> Unconscious perception spares the conscious system much of its emotional input load, so the design makes sense adaptively' and '...the mind could be arranged so that the conscious system preferentially received information and meaning that were most vital to survival – physical dangers, significant psychological dangers, and the like. The remainder – unimportant noise and strong emotional inputs of the disruptive variety – could be directed to a second system of the mind via unconscious perceptions and processed therein' (Langs 1996, pp140-1).

My research shows a picture that is almost diametrically opposite to Langs's latest views. Patients of all ages reveal that (a) the most critical of dangers, physical or psychological, are perceived on the unconscious level, and thus it is not the 'unimportant noise' which is experienced unconsciously, but that which is crucial to survival, and (b) the reason for unconscious (that is, hidden from the view of others) perception is not to spare the conscious system of the perceiver 'much of its emotional input load'. Its function is not to protect one from oneself, but from the powerful others who threaten with real destruction. The design of the mind and its purpose, as proposed by Langs (1996) would, in my view, function contrary to survival needs and make little adaptive sense. Actually, the body of Langs's early writings on unconscious functioning and on the model of the mind is much closer to my findings – it seems that Langs only recently changed his views.

Chapter 21
Human equality in unconscious experience

This book is intended to be used as a textbook by psychotherapists. In Part II, the emphasis was on the evidence of the harmful effects of some generally accepted compromises to the psychoanalytic frame, especially in institutions. The impossibility of interpreting transference convincingly under such conditions was also discussed. The clinical cases and their discussions served as examples of empirical evidence that communicative psychoanalysis is able to provide. The opportunity to improve and make corrections of erroneous interventions is thus offered to anyone who is willing to learn the skill of understanding unconscious meaning and to apply it in their own work – the patients will provide the data.

The second aim of the book is to explain the evidence underlying my conclusion that everyone ought to be given equal treatment because we all experience actions of others the same way. Both aims are intertwined and serve to focus on the ethical aspect of human relations based on empirically derived criteria. Since the meaning of the unconscious perceptions of the same type of the actions of others have been found equal in all of us, since the unconscious evaluation of these perceptions also are equal in all of us – the unconscious experience is thus equal for all human beings regardless of how this unconscious experience might manifest itself overtly in symptoms, resistances and speculations. Thus, we are all equal in our most fundamental psychological make-up – and thus require equal treatment regardless of our diagnostic profile (symptoms), 'suitability' for psychological treatment (resistances), or our own consciously considered desires and requests. As we find that the same changes in the environmental conditions (e.g., the interpersonal frame of therapy) result in the same kind of psychological changes in our deepest unconscious core we acknowledge the horror of the truth of the famous exclamation on seeing criminals led to execution in the sixteenth century, 'But for the grace of God, there goes – I'. When speaking about unbearable problems in living, Thomas Szasz put it another way: in his 1997 presentation in Vancouver, Canada, he said that, 'when you do not have madness then you have Shakespeare'.

'Are we created equal?' poses the question in its traditional usage – before the 'creationists' and the 'evolutionists' made it heavy with meaning. The answer is, Yes. My conclusions have been drawn for many years from diverse material of sessions with adults and children. The reader is invited to seek, in the therapy material, that which is fundamentally human. Even the small sample of data in this book might be sufficiently compelling for the commonly used criteria for determining what are the essential elements of human nature to be re-examined. The book proposes that our unconscious psychological functioning is the primeval shared component of what makes us human. Ironically, this same capacity also makes us uniquely different as it influences much of what we are and what we do. We all perceive unconsciously in a truthful, undistorted manner. We are all driven by reality. We only fail in correctly expecting the future when we have been damaged in our past within the same type of interpersonal frame in which the prediction is being made. Contrary to the theories of Sigmund Freud and Melanie Klein, the effect of sex on human functioning is found to be minor compared with the impact of the common-to-all unconscious experiencing of the world.

My clinical findings support the thesis that the ethics of the therapeutic relationship can be found empirically and that we all request equal basic conditions for treatment when we communicate unconsciously.

Child material provides supportive evidence for Langs's thesis that there exists an 'ideal' set of therapeutic arrangements and moment-to-moment conditions. They are the same for children as he had found in adults. The consequence of this finding is that children in therapy ought to be given the same respect and allowed the same independence as we think adults deserve. The 'charter of therapeutic rights and freedoms' would look almost the same for children as for adults.

Since 'mentally ill' patients – children and adults – have been found to maintain their capacity for unconscious perception and communications intact when the therapeutic frame is not too insane, there is no reason (certainly not on the grounds of their 'illness') to treat them differently from the way a psychoanalyst would treat a neurotic patient in private treatment. Thus, we all, at all times, need the same conditions of treatment. For instance, I have treated privately schizophrenic patients, people who have committed a crime, children with very low intelligence and very small children – all in exactly the same way. Such evidence is yet further grounds for the argument that the 'mentally ill' – children and adults – have no place being locked up in institutions as they tell us all we need to know, if we know how to listen to unconsciously communicated meaning, for the therapist to conduct therapy. The same is true for the cognitively deficient: they require better therapists and better teachers rather than to be held in warehouse conditions.

Children of all ages perceive unconsciously in a veridical manner and thus 'know', and tell us, specifically what is harmful and what is beneficial to them. This finding is new and startling considering the child's limited experience. This capacity to perceive gives young people the right to such conditions of treatment as they unconsciously 'request' rather than such as are being decided for them by even the most well meaning of adults.

Thus, behaviour is not necessarily ethical when we agree to be 'nice' to patients or when we follow a 'good' theory of technique. Ethics is in the very nature of human beings. Therapy, to be therapeutic rather than harmful, must be conducted according to what the patients themselves communicate unconsciously to their therapists at any moment of the session. Ethics in psychotherapy is not a 'gentleman's agreement' used by good people, compromised by the availability of means. Ethics is a natural state of things, existing independently of our will or conscious knowledge, available to be known empirically and used in practice at every action we take. It is accessible by the application of decoding unconscious communication during sessions. The meaning and consequences for every specific action or intent of action is available to us, at least in retrospect.

The adjective 'psychotherapeutic' means something which is good for the soul. In communicative psychoanalysis, only validated interventions are considered therapeutic. There are as many 'psychotherapeutic frames' as there are theories and many more than there are caprices of the therapists. There is always a 'natural' frame which exists at any moment in reality and defines the roles and boundaries of a relationship. Also in child therapy, this frame is created by both participants, usually spontaneously and quite unconsciously. The 'ideal' frame is the one the patient is attempting to obtain by communicating unconscious meaning to the therapist – all the while perhaps sabotaging his own unconscious efforts with actions and conscious intentions. The 'ideal' frame hardly ever exists in pure culture even when the 'best' therapist works in private practice. Since it is in the nature of our unconscious transferential pressures that we cannot tolerate certain aspects of the 'ideal' frame which the patient might be offering to us, we 'break' the frame without conscious intention.

Since we all function unconsciously in the same manner and our unconsciously expressed needs are the same, we are all 'created' equal in a most fundamental way – regardless of our age, gender, the colour of our skin and cultural background. This finding also confirms that there exists an 'ideal' set of therapeutic arrangements and moment-to-moment conditions, which are fundamentally the same for all of us. Thus, the universal quality of the therapeutic frame, hypothesized by Robert Langs on the basis of his research of adult material, is now confirmed for to children.

Glossary of communicative terms

U BERNS

(Note: Some of the communicative terms in this Glossary define complex psychological processes and are explained throughout the book and in more detail in Parts I and III'.)

Adaptational-interactional viewpoint

This is both a meta-psychological hypothesis and a clinical approach. The meta-psychological hypothesis maintains that the most compelling motivation is to adapt to the reality of the environment and especially to the interpersonal reality on both levels: conscious and unconscious. This remains true for one's whole life, from birth to death. The adaptive processes take into account the historical adaptive processes and their outcome, that is, the psychic structures built up to that point. Thus, such a view implies a developmental perspective. In the clinical situation the most compelling adaptive motivation is for the patient to adapt to the therapist. Becauses the adaptational-interactional theory, together with a developmental perspective, takes into account both intrapsychic and interactional processes, this theory is at variance with other psychoanalytic theories of motivation.

Adaptive context/intervention context

According to the adaptational-interactional viewpoint, the adaptive context is the specific real event which evokes an intrapsychic response. Thus, the adaptive context and the psychic structure co-define each other. The intrapsychic and the communicative responses of a patient show whether an adaptive context has any specific neurotic or non-neurotic meaning for the patient. In the first case the response can become conscious for the whole range of meanings implied. In this case, the response itself is direct and linear. In other cases the responses are indirect, convoluted, complex and unconscious. These intrapsychic responses are expressed also with narratives and images as well as by symptoms which are the consequence of the unconscious process of analysing and ascribing meaning. We distinguish between primary and secondary adaptive contexts. *Primary adaptive contexts* are contained in the manifest interventions of the therapist as implications of the interventions. *Secondary adaptive contexts* are those events in the patient's everyday life which are of emotional importance for the patient. Generally, in the therapeutic session the primary adaptive contexts are much more important to the patient. It is exactly these adaptive contexts that activate unconscious introjects and memories. Thus, they have the power to produce symptoms and resistances in the patient.

Break in the frame

A break means that one or several components of the frame were changed from their secure, 'ideal', state. Clinically, these changes are unconsciously evaluated by the patient in comparison with an ideally effective state of the frame of therapy. In the course of therapy the patient often manifestly proposes that certain components of the frame be kept broken. This form of interpersonal pressure on the therapist is usually introduced by the patient in order to get much-needed healing responses from the therapist. From the communicative point of view, the unconscious meaning and the reasons for the patient's frame modifications ultimately aim at enabling the patient to establish the ideal frame condition himself or herself. This part of working-through is the essential part of healing in psychotherapy.

Communicative interpretation

Generally speaking, a communicative interpretation means such verbal communication from the psychoanalyst/psychotherapist to the patient which renders conscious the unconscious meanings of the patient's verbal communication and of behaviour. In the communicative approach to expressed the psychoanalysis derivatives the term is defined more precisely. A communicative interpretation illuminates the connections between three components of any interpretation: *the adaptive contexts, the network of derivatives* and the intent to secure *the frame*. The communicative therapist aims at explaining the symptoms and resistances to the patient by making use of the patient's narratives (free associations). The symptoms and resistances are described derivatively and can be such neurotic or non-neurotic responses to the implications of the therapist's interventions (i.e. the primary adaptive contexts) which were processed unconsciously by the patient. Among the interventions of the therapist the frame interpretations are of utmost importance. If the patient has communicated meaningful extra-analytic events (i.e. the secondary adaptive contexts) these ought to be first considered as the primary adaptive contexts for the session, that is, as relevant events in therapy. Such free associations as are identified as psychogenetic (historical) narratives are understood as memories and past introjects, activated by both adaptive contexts. They have to be introduced into the interpretation to help the patient understand his or her history. For the therapist, the ultimate aim of a communicative interpretation is always to achieve the explicit therapeutic aim. This means that the therapist interprets in order to render the patient's symptoms and resistances unnecessary. The aim is achieved by using the patient's own insight into his or her actual relational experience with the therapist (see Part I).

Derivatives

A term coined by Freud used for those manifest verbal and non-verbal communications which carry a hidden, latent meaning. Derivatives are formed unconsciously as a result of the unconscious processing of the meaning of unconscious perceptions, memories, beliefs and introjects, and may be expressed as free associations. They are narratives, images or creative play just like Freud's prototype of a derivative, the dream. The formation and transformation of the latent into the manifest content in the shape of images, narratives and play comes about through the activity of the primary process. Considered from the perspective of the secondary process thinking, derivatives are the outcome of unconscious displacement, symbolization and condensation. Derivatives and symptoms are the hallmark of neurosis and psychosis.

Derivative complex/network of derivatives

A term which signifies a multitude of *derivatives* communicated freely by the patient in session, as they reveal a variety of different latent meanings of one or more *adaptive contexts* (primary or secondary).

Derivatives - close, distant

Derivatives are built in the deep unconscious of our minds from *unconscious perceptions*, beliefs, activated memories and introjects by using the 'language' of the primary process. The less they are pre-consciously defended against, the more readily they are detectable and understandable by the therapist - called *close derivatives*. The more they are pre-consciously defended against, the harder it is to understand them and to use them for interpretations. Such derivatives are called *distant*.

Frame

A metaphor for the basic conditions and the implicitly and explicitly agreed upon ground rules and boundaries of psychotherapy. Just as the frame of a picture marks it off from its surroundings so the basic conditions and ground rules distinguish the therapeutic interactions from other social interactions. The canon of the frame elements, which is under clinical conditions unconsciously evaluated as 'ideal' by the patient, provides the most basic hold for both the patient and the therapist. At the same time, certain components of this 'ideal' frame may be anxiety-provoking for the patients and the therapists as a consequence of their traumata, which drive them to break the ideal frame (see Part I).

Image

The language of images and *themes*, contained in narratives, is a primary language to every human being in addition to the secondary process language(s). Freud first described it in *The Interpretation of Dreams* (Freud 1900). Most images are *derivatives* of deep unconscious processing of information. Thus, they are the essential key to the understanding of the patient for the communicatively oriented psychoanalyst. It is imperative that the therapist tells apart positive images from the negative ones in order that they can be used in the process of any clinical *validation* of hypotheses.

Indicator

The indictors of the patient's distress communicate to the therapist that the patient needs help in the understanding and the resolution by way of an intervention by the therapist. Indicators are either symptoms of all kinds, or *resistances*, which include breaks in the *frame*. It is often difficult to differentiate sharply between them. The term is synonymous with the therapeutic context which is an important organizer of the patient's material for the therapist. Given the *adaptive context* (the triggering event) as a first organizer, and the complex of *derivatives*, the therapist can organize the patient's material a second time when the patient communicates one or more therapeutic contexts or breaks the frame.

Model of rectification

When the therapy frame is broken the associations of the patient may contain derivative hints about how the *frame* should be corrected in order to be brought to the 'ideal' condition. Such a model of rectification is the result of the patient's unconscious analysis of meaning. The patient's unconscious aim is to obtain a frame within which he or she will feel safely held and thus provide the conditions necessary for therapeutic work (see Part I and Part II).

Non-transference

This term is needed to differentiate the unconscious responses which are not transferential from the patient's *transference*. The term makes clear that not all of the patient's unconscious responses belong to transference. In communicative psychoanalysis, great emphasis is given to the therapist's task to distinguish between transference and non-transference in order to protect the patient from being driven crazy.

Resistances

To the classical concept of resistance, communicative psychoanalysis has added the concept of *communicative resistance*. Communicative resistance is discovered by an analysis of the patient's communicative network. A fully developed communicative network consists of the following: (1) the adaptive contexts with a link to the therapist, (2) the complex of derivatives and (3) indicators. The patient's failure to fully develop one or more of the constituents of this network is regarded as a communicative resistance. It is possible to be more certain that the patient is displaying communicative resistance, when the therapist is able to identify such implications of his or her recent interventions which have served, at least partially, as the triggers for communicative resistance. Conversely, if the therapist is not able to detect any contributions from a recent intervention the assessment of resistance was perhaps not warranted.

Themes

A theme is the derivative thematic content that can be condensed from the freely associated narratives, images or creative play. The process of the identification of individual themes out of the *derivative complex* is an indispensable skill for communicative psychotherapy. It is part of the translation process from the language of the primary process derivatives into the language of the secondary process thinking. It has some similarity to the understanding of symbols and metaphors. If the identification process results in themes which can be recognized as the implications of the therapist's interventions, the therapist may assume to have found important *unconscious perceptions* and perhaps responses to these perceptions. Positively tinged images may be signs of *validation* of the therapist's interventions whereas negatively tinged images may be signs of falsification of the interventions.

Transference

In communicative psychoanalysis, transference is the unconscious pathological component of the patient's response to the therapist's intervention. It is of great theoretical and practical importance to identify the amount of pathological input of the therapist in order to be able to identify the patient's response as a transference response. The traditional psycho-analytical definition of transference is not only vague and inconsistent, most of the psychoanalytic literature uses the term to describe the total relationship between the therapist and the patient. Communicative research has shown that much of what has been described as 'transference' in clinical cases was in fact found to be *non-transference* and included valid *unconscious perceptions* by the patient. The communicative process of transference is manifested only under very specific conditions and within a definite sequence of events (see Chapter 5, Transference response, in Part I).

For Freud, the patient under the influence of transference misunderstands the present in terms of the past. Instead of remembering his infantile wishes the patient strives unconsciously to relive the past with the analyst and to relive it more satisfactorily than in his childhood. This impulse to relive the past comes from within the patient, and is always inappropriate, a *resistance* and a repetition of the past.

The communicative definition of transference proper (Bonac 1998) says that it is an intrapsychic phenomenon which becomes observable in the bipersonal field of therapy as a response to the patient's own intent to secure the analytic *frame* in the absence of the pathological contributions from interpersonal sources, all this within the context of the therapist's constant offer of an ideal analytic frame. According to this definition, transference includes both of Freud's discoveries, the trauma and the seduction theories of pathogenesis when they are placed in a strictly temporal sequence of the changes in the interpersonal frame.

Unconscious communication

Communicative psychotherapists focus on the patient's unconscious communications, i.e. on the primary process communications, in order to grasp the unconscious meaning of symptoms and *resistances*. In primary process communication, i.e. communication via derivatives, the patient tells the therapist meanings of which the patient is not initially aware. The primary process language can be called the primary language of human beings.

Unconscious perception

Freud believed that all perceptions at first are conscious and only later become unconscious by the automatic process of repression. Contrary to Freud's belief, it has been shown empirically that the important perceptions of the communications from others, as well as the many implications of their manifest communications, are validly perceived on the unconscious level. Most importantly for the therapist, the derivative communications about identified *adaptive contexts* (triggering events) demonstrate valid unconscious perceptions of the event by the patient.

Validation

The possibility of having psychoanalytic hypotheses confirmed in the course of the session by the patient is of utmost importance to psychotherapy. Validation is an unconscious response by the patient to a correct intervention by the therapist and represents a means to reach the truth about a specific intervention and, ultimately, the truth about a specific psychoanalytic theory. Clinically, it has been shown that patients confirm indirectly, i.e. unconsciously, only correct interpretations, adequate silences and certain acts of rectification of the frame by the therapist. A valid interpretation always includes two components. On the one hand, it restructures the patient's material so that it is understood in a new way. On the other hand, the patient gains the experience that the therapist has done the work in a consistent way and has put his or her person at the patient's disposal in a specific manner. When the therapist's intervention is correct, the two components are reflected in the patient's response: the helpful restructuring of the material is expressed by the patient in new material extending the therapist's interpretation. This is called *cognitive validation* or validation via a selected fact. The successful digestion of the material on the part of the therapist is expressed by the patient derivatively in images and feelings of comfort and security, joy, freedom from symptoms or a reduction of symptoms etc. Langs calls this '*interpersonal validation*' or 'validation by an evoked positive introject'. (See also Part I and Part III.)

Validation process

The validation process is a crucial element of the therapist's listening process and the hallmark of communicative psychoanalysis. Complete validation consists of the *interpersonal* and the *cognitive validation*. It is a deciphering process, for which the therapist uses the theoretical knowledge, the patient's validating (or falsifying) response in the following free associations, as well as the therapist's own emotional and cognitive responses - and subjects all of this to the deciphering process. Only such interventions which have been validated by the patient unconsciously are considered correct interpretations (see Part I).

References and Citation
Index

Ainsworth M D S (1885) I. Patterns of infant-mother attachment: antecedents and effects on development. II. Attachments across the life span. Bulletin of the New York Academy of Medicine 6: 771–812. **167**.

Balint A, Balint M (1939) On transference and counter-transference. International Journal of Psychoanalysis 20: 223–230. **17**.

Berns U (1994) Die übereinstimmungsdeutung: Ein Ergebnis der Evaluationsanalyse. (German) The Tally Interpretation: an outcome of evaluation analysis. Forum der Psychoanalyse 10 (3): 226–244. Reprinted in Electronic Journal of Communicative Psychoanalysis (1998) 1. **88**.

Berns U (1996) Thirty years of psychotherapy within national health insurance system: Is sound communicative psychotherapy possible in such conditions? (Paper presented at the Annual Meeting of the International Society of Communicative Psychoanalysis and Psychotherapy , October 1996, New York) Is sound communicative psychotherapy possible given the conditions of the German national health insurance system? International Journal of Communicative Psychoanalysis and Psychotherapy 11, 3–10. **99**.

Bion W R (1961/1985). Experiences in Groups and Other papers. London: Tavistock. **86, 152**.

Bird B (1972) Notes on transference: universal phenomenon and hardest part of analysis. Journal of the American Psychoanalytic Association 20: 267–301. **18**.

Bonač V A (1991) Unconscious perceptions of children in psychotherapy. Thesis, University of British Columbia, Vancouver. Library Special Collections. **13, 164, 167**.

Bonač VA (1993a) Clinical issues in communicative psycho-analysis: Interactional aspects of requests for premature termination as reflections of secured-frame anxiety in adult and child psychotherapy. International Journal of Communicative Psychoanalysis and Psychotherapy 8: 67–78. **15, 19**.

Bonač V A (1993b) Clinical issues in communicative psychoanalysis: Premature securing of the frame as expression of therapist's countertransference difficulty with containing patient's projective identifications. International Journal of Communicative Psychoanalysis and Psychotherapy 8(4): 115–121. **15, 19, 20**.

Bonač V A (1994) A communicative psycho-analytic theory of human development: Part one - Introduction, methodology and theorems. International Journal of Communicative Psychoanalysis and Psychotherapy 9: 99–105. **13, 29, 83**.

Bonač V A (1995) The bountiful mother and the fate of transference in managed care. Presentation. International Society for Communicative Psychoanalysis and Psychotherapy October, New York. **20**.

Bonač V A (1996a) The color of money in consultation room: a communicative interpretation of transference response. Paper presented at the Conference on Mental Health Insurance, International Society for Communicative Psycho-analysis and Psychotherapy, 5 October, New York. 20.

Bonač V A (1996b) The bountiful mother and the fate of transference in times of managed care. International Journal of Communicative Psychoanalysis and Psychotherapy 10(3): 59–72. 20.

Bonač V A (1998) Perception or transference? A new clinical theory of transference. Electronic Journal of Communicative Psychoanalysis 1. Reprinted in International Journal of Communicative Psycho-analysis and Psychotherapy 11: 45–59. 18, 19, 20, 21, 22, 24, 35.

Bonač V A (1999) Moments of mystery and confusion: transference interpretation of acting-out. In Sullivan EM (Ed) Unconscious Perceptions in Clinical Practice. London: Open University Press. 19, 20, 21, 22, 24, 35.

Brenner C (1982) The Mind in Conflict. New York: International Universities Press. 84.

Calasso R (1993) The Marriage of Cadmus and Harmony. Toronto: Alfred A Knopf. 41, 151.

Dornes M (1993) Der kompetente Säugling (German) The Competent Infant. Frankfurt: Fischer. 83.

Dornes M (1994) Kînnen SÑuglinge phantasieren? (German) Do infants have fantasies? Psyche 12(48): 1154–1175. 83.

Dornes M (1995) Gedanken zur frühen Entwicklung und ihre Bedeutung zur Neurosenpsychologie. (German) Thoughts about early development and its meaning for the psychology of neurosis. Forum der Psychoanalyse 1(11): 27–49. Berlin: Springer. 83.

Dorpat T (1993) The Type C mode of communication – an interactional perspective. International Journal of Communicative Psychoanalysis and Psychotherapy 8(2-3): 47–54. 86.

Freud S (1895a) Studien Über Hysterie. GW Band 1. Frankfurt: Fischer.4.

Freud S (1895b). Studies on Hysteria. Standard Edition 2. 84.

Freud S (1900) The Interpretation of Dreams. Standard Edition 5, p532.4, 177.

Freud S (1912a) The dynamics of transference. Standard Edition 12, pp97–108.17.

Freud S (1912b) Recommendations to Physicians Practicing Psychoanalysis. Standard Edition 12, pp111–120. 17.

Freud S (1913) On Beginning of the Treatment (Further Recommendation on the Technique of Psychoanalysis I). Standard Edition 12, pp121–144. 17.

Freud S (1915) Observations on transference-love. (Further Recommendation on the Technique of Psychoanalysis III) Standard Edition 12, pp157–171. 17.

Freud S (1920) Beyond the Pleasure Principle. Standard Edition 18, pp3–64. 17.

Freud S (1925a) Selbstdarstellung. Standard Edition 10, p113. 4.

Freud S (1925b)/(1989) An autobiographical study. In Gay P (Ed.) The Freud Reader. New York: WW Norton.

Freud S (1926) The Question of Lay Analysis. Standard Edition 20, p187. 3.

Freud S (1940) An Outline of Psycho-Analysis. Standard Edition 1, p147. 3.

Freud S (1944). Vorlesungen zur Einführung in die Psychoanalyse. GW Band 11. Frankfurt: Fischer. 87.

Gaddini R (1978) Transitional objects origins and the psychosomatic symptom. In Grolnick SA, Barkin L, with Muensterberger W (Eds) Between Reality and Fantasy: Transitional Objects and Phenomena. New York: Aronson. 167.

Greenson R (1978) Explorations in Psychoanalysis. New York: International Universities Press. 18.

Greenspan S (1992) Infancy and Early childhood. Madison, CT: International

Universities Press. **167**.

Gross P R, Levitt N (1994) Higher Superstition. Baltimore: Johns Hopkins University Press. **156**.

Kahl-Popp J (1994) 'Ich bin Dr Deutschland': Rechtsradikale Phantasien als verschlüsselte Kommunikation in der analytischen Psychotherapie eines Jugendlichen. (German) 'I am Dr Germany': right-wing extremist fantasies as encoded communications in the analytic psychotherapy of an adolescent. Praxis der Kinderpsychologie und Kinderpsychiatrie 43: 266–272. **42**.

Kahl-Popp J (1996) Intrusive psychoanalytische Interventionen und ihre Verarbeitung (German) Intrusive psychoanalytic interventions and their processing. In Bell K, Höhfeld K (Eds) Aggression und seelische Krankheit. Gießen: Psychosozial Verlag. Reprinted (1998) Traumatic moments in the psychoanalytic discourse. Electronic Journal of Communicative Psychoanalysis 1. **42**.

Kahl-Popp J (1998) Bildnerisches Gestalten als unbewußte Bedeutungsanalyse. (German) Children's paintings as unconcious meaning analysis. Analytische Kinder- und Jugendlichen-Psychotherapie (Frankfurt), 29(2): 211–244. **42**.

Klein M (1932) The Psycho-Analysis of Children. London: Hogarth. **167**.

Klein M (1946) Notes on some schizoid mechanisms. International Journal of Psychoanalysis 27: 99–100. **167**.

Kumin, I (1993) Disturbances in primary relatedness. International Journal of Communicative Psychoanalysis and Psychotherapy 8(1): 17–26. **167**.

Langs R (1975) The therapeutic relationship and deviations in technique. International Journal of Psychoanalytic Psychotherapy 4: 106–141. **18**.

Langs R (1976a) The Therapeutic Interaction, vols I and II. New York: Aronson. **18, 32, 57, 85**.

Langs R (1976b) The Bipersonal Field. New York: Aronson. **6, 12, 18, 32, 35, 57, 85**.

Langs R (1976c) On becoming a psychiatrist: discussion of 'Empathy and intuition in becoming a psychiatrist', by RJ Blank. International Journal of Psychoanalytic Psychotherapy 5: 255–279. **8, 18**.

Langs R (1978a) The Listening Process. New York: Aronson. **6, 12, 18, 32, 35**.

Langs R (1978b) Validation and the framework of the therapeutic situation. Contemporary Psychoanalysis 14: 99–124. **12, 18, 35, 85**.

Langs R (1978c) Technique in Transition. New York: Aronson. **6, 35, 85**.

Langs R (1978/79). Some communicative properties of the bipersonal field. International Journal of Psychoanalytic Psychotherapy 7: 78–135. **167**.

Langs R (1979) The Therapeutic Environment. New York: Aronson. **6, 12, 18, 35**.

Langs R (1980) Interactions: The Realm of Transference and Countertransference. New York: Aronson. **6, 12, 15, 28, 35**.

Langs R (1981) Resistances and Interventions, The Nature of Therapeutic Work. New York: Aronson.

Langs R (1982) Psychotherapy, A Basic Text. New York: Ironstone. **8, 17, 20, 29, 35, 68, 69, 88, 167**.

Langs R (1984) The contributions of the adaptational-interactional approach to classical psychoanalysis. Analytic Psychotherapy and Psychopathology 1(1): 21–47. **32**.

Langs R (1984/85) Making interpretations and securing the frame. International Journal of Psychoanalytic Psychotherapy 10: 3–23. **17**.

Langs R (1988) A Primer of Psychotherapy. New York: Gardner Press. **85, 164**.

Langs R (1989) Rating Your Psychotherapist. New York: Henry Holt. **28**.

Langs R (1990) Die Sprache der Träume (German) Decoding your Dreams. München: Heyne. **31**.

Langs, R (1991) Der beste Therapeut für mich (German) Rating your Psychotherapist. Reinbek: Rowohlt. **28**.

Langs R (1992a) Teaching self-processing. Contemporary Psychoanalysis 28(10): 97–117.

Langs R (1992b) A Clinical Workbook for Psychotherapists. London & New York: Karnak. **85, 87, 89, 90, 162.**

Langs R (1992c) Science, Systems and Psychoanalysis. New York: Karnac.

Langs R (1993) Empowered Psycho-therapy. Teaching Self-Processing – A New Approach to the Human Psyche and its Reintegration. London: Karnac. **31.**

Langs R (1995) Clinical Practice and the Architecture of the Mind. New York: Karnac. **85, 88.**

Langs R (1996) The Evolution of the Emotion-Processing Mind. London: Karnac. **19, 163, 169, 170.**

Lemche E (1995). Kleinkindforschung und der Wandel der Praxis der Psychoanalyse (German) Infant research and the changes in practising psychoanalysis. Forum der Psychoanalyse 11(2). **83.**

Lichtenberg JD (1991) Psychoanalyse und Säuglingsforschung (German) Psychoanalysis and Infant Research. Berlin: Springer. **83.**

Mendelsohn RM (1985) The onset of unconscious perception. In Langs R (Ed) The Yearbook Of Psychoanalysis and Psychotherapy, vol. I. New Jersey: Newconcept. **167.**

Petersen M-L (1996) Der sichere Rahmen. Bestandteile, Handhabung und Wirkungen (German) The secure frame: components, management and effects. Forum der Psychoanalyse 12(2): 110–127. **86.**

Schafer R (1968) Aspects of Internalisation. New York: International University Press. **6.**

Searles H (1965) Collected Papers on Schizophrenia and Related Subjects. Madison: IUP. **8, 18, 35, 57, 164.**

Searles H (1975). The patient as therapist to his analyst. In Giovacchini PL (Ed) Tactics and Techniques in Psychoanalytic Therapy, vol II. New York: Ironstone. **8, 164.**

Searles H (1978/79). Concerning transference and counter-transference. International Journal of Psychoanalytic Psychotherapy 7: 165–188. **29, 42.**

Searles H (1986) My Work With Borderline Patients. New York: Aronson. **164.**

Shattuck R (1996) Forbidden Knowledge. New York: St Martin's Press. **152.**

Smith DL (1991) Hidden Conversations – An Introduction to Communicative Psycho-analysis. Tavistock/Routledge: London. **158.**

Stern D (1985) The Interpersonal World of the Infant. New York: Basic Books. **83.**

Stern D (1995). The Motherhood Constellation. New York: Basic Books. **83.**

Strachey J (1934) The fate of the ego in the analytic therapy. International Journal of Psychoanalysis 50: 275–292. **17.**

Szasz TS (1963) The concept of transference. International Journal of Psycho-analysis 44: 4432–43. **17.**

Szasz TS (1965/1988) The Ethics of Psychoanalysis. Macmillan: New York.**7, 159–60.**

Szasz TS (1970) The Manufacture of Madness. Harper & Row: New York. **7.**

Ticho E (1972) The effects of the analyst's personality on psychoanalytic treatment. Psychoanalytic Forum 4: 137–151. **18.**

Weil JL (1992) Early Deprivation of Empathic Care. Madison, CT: International Universities Press. **167.**

Wurmser L (1995). Trauma, Konflikt und Weiderholungszwang. (German) (Trauma, conflict, and the need for repetition.) Vortrag am 20.ii. Kiel. **84.**

Appendix 1
Institutions and
Publications

International Society for Communicative Psychoanalysis and Psychotherapy (est. 1981)

European Society for Communicative Psychotherapy (est. 1991)

International Journal of Communicative Psychoanalysis and Psychotherapy (New York, NY, USA)

Electronic Journal of Communicative Psychoanalysis (http://www.mortimer.com/psychoanalysiscom/)

Index